Small Craft Advisories

Small Craft Advisories

CRITICAL ARTICLES 1984–1988

Art · Ballet · Music · Literature · Film

BY

ROBERT CRAFT

T&H

THAMES AND HUDSON

To my son Robert Alexander

None of us can help the things life has done to us. They're done before you realize it, and once they're done they make you do other things until at last everything comes between you and what you'd like to be . . .

A Long Day's Journey into Night

Acknowledgments

Thirty of the forty-nine pieces collected in this volume were originally printed in *The New York Review of Books*. Others appeared in *The Times Literary Supplement, The Musical Times, The New Criterion, The New Republic, The New York Times Book Review* and *The Washington Post*. I thank the editors of these publications, above all Barbara Epstein of *The New York Review*, for improvements and for permission to reprint. I am especially grateful as well to Stanley Baron and Phyllis Crawford for valuable suggestions and disembarrassing corrections.

R.C.

First published in the United States in 1989 by
Thames and Hudson Inc., 500 Fifth Avenue,
New York, New York 10110

Library of Congress Catalog Card Number 88-51349

Printed and bound in Great Britain

Contents

LIVES OF THE COMPOSERS

LIVES OF THE POETS

PAINTERS

BALLETS

MUSICIANS

BOOKS

CODA

LIVES OF THE COMPOSERS

Mozart and "Amadeus"

In 1984 on the White House lawn, Ronald Reagan accepted Austria's gift (whether or not looking it in the mouth) of a Lippizaner called "Amadeus". The United States soon reciprocated with a film of the same name,[1] in which the impersonator in the title role presents himself to an Austrian head of state. At this point the symmetries break down, the Emperor Joseph II, having been a patron and protector of the arts. Yet one parallel remains: the excruciating resemblance of the compulsive giggles of the film-human Amadeus to the neighs and snorts of a horse.

This is not the only holdover from Peter Shaffer's earlier *Equus*, with its dramatic formula of two adversaries – psychiatrist and psychotic boy – locked in a rhetorical bout, and already familiar in the confrontation of Pizarro and the Inca king in *The Royal Hunt of the Sun*. In all three plays, an apparent hatred unsuccessfully masks a deep homoerotic fervor. Salieri's jealousy of Mozart ill conceals a desire to possess him, and in scene after scene the well-groomed, satanically dark and intense Italian reveals himself as the would-be seducer of the tousled, frivolous, fair-innocent: gentlemen prefer blonde fright-wigs. Observing Mozart's intimate manner in conversation with a prima donna, Salieri concludes "he's had her" but is really saying, enviously, that "she's had him." In the death scene, when finally the two men are alone together with Mozart securely in Salieri's web, Mrs Mozart returns suddenly and orders the stealthy murderer to leave. He refuses to go; only Mozart can rule him now.

Part of what is wrong with the film is exposed in the first encounter between Amadeus and Joseph II. Whereas the Emperor's clothes have been faithfully copied from Pompeo Batoni's portrait, the man wearing

---

[1] *Amadeus*, a film directed by Milos Forman.

them bears little relation to the real-life monarch who, for one thing, could play difficult concertos at sight without struggling over each note of a simple piece, as he is made to do on the screen. In Mozart's case, even the clothing is wrong. He "dressed elegantly," Clementi tells us, which would hardly mean glittering like a punk rock star. So, too, the description attributed to Tieck, but not written by him, of a "small, quick," but "unimpressive figure," with "weak eyes" (*not* crossed ones, as in the newly discovered and, so I believe, spurious Hagenauer-Barducci portrait), is contradicted by the cavortings of the film's hero. Mozart's playfulness was life-long, in and out of music where its manifestations are unpredictable, as in the composition of *A Musical Joke*. A recently surfaced Mozart manuscript (at Sotheby's in November 1984) provides another example: this sketch for the C minor Mass (Mozart's wedding mass in *Amadeus*, despite the minor key and the inconvenient earlier date of his marriage) also contains notations inscribed: "Von Pimberl [Mozart's father's dog] and von Stanzerl [Mozart's wife]." But to focus, as the film does, on one or two extrovert aspects of a personality of Mozart's dimensions is to reduce it to absurdity.

At the same time, any attempt to make a "factually accurate" film about "the real Mozart" could only result in an even worse movie than this one. The main obstacle is that the face of the man who wrote *The Magic Flute* cannot be "portrayed" by an actor. (Michael Kelly, though writing long after he sang in the first *Figaro*, said that Mozart's "little animated countenance . . . is as impossible to describe as it would be to paint sunbeams.") To give Milos Forman and Peter Shaffer every benefit of the doubt, we might assume that the presentation of Mozart as a fool is an intended irony, and congratulate the director for having chosen the best way to fail with an insoluble problem. Another obstacle is that to accord Mozart's father anything like his due, differentiating his practical, pedagogical, scientifically progressive mind from his son's creatively transforming one, would require several reels and considerable skill. Moreover, to have the Requiem dictated to Süssmayr, instead of to Salieri, would be to introduce a new character at the very end, and one whose possibly adulterous relationship with Mozart's wife could hardly be ignored. Finally, the unsubstantiated Mozart-Salieri theme would disappear altogether unless significance can be extracted from Salieri's opera *Scuola di' Gelosia*, or read into his reference to himself as "*piccolissima creatura.*"

Shaffer's decisions to identify Mozart's father with the Commendatore, and to have Salieri commission (and take down bits of) the

Requiem are the playwright's prerogatives and reasonable dramatic solutions, hardly contestable by people who read psychohistory and novelized biography. *Amadeus* grossly misleads not here but in the inference that Mozart's music sprang effortlessly from him, a notion that is easily contradicted by reference to the evidence of human trial and error, the rewriting, the composition of new arias to improve his operas, the many abandoned fugues (including the much corrected K.401), and Mozart's own description of his quartets for Haydn as "the fruit of [two years of] labor." Innumerable constructions in Mozart's music in "clean" manuscripts testify to efforts sustained at a scarcely imaginable level.

Since Mozart cannot be shown composing, the film tries to make the most of him performing. But this is also doomed, since no one can execute rhythms and embellishments, let alone improvise, as he would have done. Forman's worst mistake, however, is not in letting us hear "Mozart" at the keyboard but in letting us see "him" conduct, which in his time would have meant supervising the performance, setting tempos, beating time, but without the histrionics of today's TV concert spectacles. Though poor Tom Hulce (Amadeus) must have spent hours gesticulating with the help of mirrors and video cassettes, he succeeds only in looking like the Scarecrow in *The Wizard of Oz*.

That the camera trains so much on Amadeus in the pit is the more regrettable in that Twyla Tharp's stagings are not without interest. To judge from exiguous snatches of *Seraglio*, *Magic Flute*, and a parody of *Don Giovanni* featuring experiments—that would have amused Mozart—with the extremes of the digestive tract of a mock horse, Tharp should be encouraged to stage opera. Unfortunately, the question of whether or not to ban the ballet in *Figaro*, a major episode in the film, involves so much discussion that the dance itself is passed over.

But the unkindest cuts of all are inflicted on the music. It bleeds at every splice, welling up, fading out, left suspended in mid-phrase. Even the tonic-dominant *Don Giovanni* chords at the beginning of the film are unresolved, and from somewhere in the Adagio of the Serenade K.361, the listener is brutally lurched to somewhere in the Allegro finale, as if an infant had lifted the needle arm from the third band and dropped it in the seventh further along. Mozart's variety cannot be adequately represented, of course, yet the insensitive and even cacophonous juxtapositions of passages from symphony and concerto movements might have been "sacrificed" for one very short complete piece, the *Figaro* overture, for instance.

Would the language of the British soaps on Channel 13 have been preferable to American slang? "What was God up to?" Salieri asks, and, of the not-yet-written *Magic Flute*, Mozart says, "It's all right here in my noodle." Perhaps the comic-strip domestic dialogue of "Wolfie" and "Stanzie" is no cruder than some Viennese dialects in the 1780s. Yet some of the anachronisms, and effronteries, should have been excised, as when Mozart blurts to the Emperor: "I hate politics," as if this activity, in the American sense of the word, was particularly rife in Joseph's absolute monarchy.

To turn to the premise of the film, would a man of considerable intelligence but insignificant talents envy, to the extent of committing murder, the "sacred gift" of "immortal genius . . . sent to the head of . . . an idle rake"? This conceit Pushkin sustains in his brief play. But the thesis that Peter Shaffer derives from it becomes less and less convincing as the film develops. First of all, the audience never believes Salieri's argument that he is the victim of an injustice. And second, since his perception of Mozart's powers continues to grow with each new manifestation of them, to imagine Salieri wilfully extinguishing their source becomes increasingly difficult. A mediocre student might envy the head of his class, especially if he or she seems not to work very hard. But can one be jealous of, rather than marvel at, a mind that is light-years beyond one's own?

It remains to be said that a great deal of comment has appeared on the significance of the film vis-à-vis Mozart as the world's highest cultural peak. H.C. Robbins Landon, the Haydn authority, recently observed that

> Mozart is on the way to becoming the Shakespeare of music—the one whom no one can do without . . .
> For all the overwhelming greatness of the *Matthew Passion*, perhaps the forgiveness scene at the end of *Figaro* touches us in a way that Bach's abstract humanity and greatness do not . . .
> It's not perhaps a time for the Heroic Man, such as Beethoven's art represents . . .
> I believe . . . Mozart's genius will in the long run eradicate Haydn almost entirely from the consciousness of the average music lover . . .
>
> (*The Sunday Times* [London], January 20, 1985)

Robbins Landon, gentleman-scholar, knows as well as anyone that to compare masterpieces is an impertinence, and that talk about continental drift can be foolish. But these remarks indicate the radically different understanding of Mozart since mid-century.

The *Amadeus* craze has already begun to affect the manuscript market. According to the *Frankfurter Allgemeine Zeitung*, February 23, 1985, the Marburg dealer Stargardt would soon auction the holograph of no. 3 of the "Six Menuets written in Salzburg, Carnaval 1769." The estimated price of this "damaged and water-spotted manuscript" of a very minor work by the thirteen-year-old composer is ten times that of a handwritten page of counterpoint by Beethoven; higher still in relation to important Goethe and Wagner letters; and fifty times the value of correspondence by heads of state from Austria's emperors to Lenin.

The present writer, resisting more than one impulse to bolt, saw *Amadeus* through in a small, upstate New York college town. In the last twenty minutes or so, the cinema audience seemed to be feeling that music itself was the film's protagonist, which could at least explain why at the end no one left, sitting as if spellbound during the long "credits" and leaving only after the houselights had been raised, and then in complete silence.

Mozart and Magdalena

"Mozart and Magdalena" would have been a more pertinent title than *Mozart and Constanze*[1] since Francis Carr adds nothing either to fact or to conjecture about the composer and his wife, but makes Magdalena Hofdemel the central figure of what, if true, would be the most sensational episode in all musical biography, the lives of Stradella and the other Italian uxoricides not excepted. Carr does not support his hypothesis with any hard evidence, but the soft kind, of smoke indicating fire, is plausible and persuasive.

In 1789, Mozart wrote to his Masonic brother Franz Hofdemel, chancery clerk, amateur violinist, and husband of the beautiful Magdalena, Mozart's piano pupil, requesting a loan, which was granted for four months. In 1790, Mozart gave Magdalena's father a watch as collateral for a loan, a transaction that first came to light in 1956, after the death of its then owner. Mozart died on December 5, 1791, and was buried the next day. After the funeral, Hofdemel attempted to kill his pregnant wife with a razor and succeeded in killing himself with it. His death was not reported in the Viennese papers, and, in the provincial ones, the date was changed to December 10. On December 21 the *Pressburger Zeitung* reported that the suicide was the result of dejection, not of jealousy (who said anything about jealousy?) and that the widow, and the widow of the late Kapellmeister Mozart, would be provided for, by, respectively, the Empress and Emperor. This is the entire documentation linking Mozart and the Hofdemels.

In Carr's reconstruction, Magdalena was Mozart's mistress, Hofdemel his murderer. In June 1791, Mozart told his wife that he believed he had been poisoned by aqua toffana and would die as a result of it. Thinking that Hofdemel was driven to suicide by feelings of guilt for his alleged crime, Carr does not consider that Magdalena, grieved by Mozart's

---

[1] New York, 1983.

death, might have threatened her husband with exposure, for which reason he might well have chosen silence for both of them and the unborn child whose paternity would have been in doubt.

But Magdalena survived, and, from her father's home in Brno, where she had retired, occasionally visited Vienna, at which times she stayed with the Czernys, whose son, Karl, was one of Beethoven's piano students. Once Magdalena asked Czerny if he could arrange for her to hear Beethoven play some of his music. When Czerny conveyed her request, Beethoven inquired: "Isn't that the woman who had the affair with Mozart?" In 1852, Karl Czerny repeated this story to Otto Jahn, Mozart's first comprehensive biographer. Ludwig von Köchel, cataloger of Mozart's works, provided Jahn with more handed-down material about Mozart and Magdalena that Jahn believed to be true but did not use, presumably because Mozart had already become a spotless divinity.

The reader should have been given Beethoven's German word for "affair." But Carr's presentation is slipshod, scamping on questions of sources, ignoring the most elementary requirements of critical and historical method, and repeating as established facts such patent myths as a meeting between Mozart and Beethoven. Carr is also painfully unaware that masterpieces are beyond praise ("superb string quintets," indeed), and that a Mozart piano concerto is not "an ideal form of personal portrait," or a portrait at all (which is not to deny that music can have supervenient pictorial and literary ends). Nor are all of Carr's conclusions, as he thinks, foregone. "Not surprisingly," he writes, Magdalena "refused to divulge what happened the day after Mozart died." But it would be a surprise if she had *not* talked about those events later in life, though we do not know whether she did or didn't, or anything else about her after the Beethoven story—he *did* play for her, according to Czerny—and the early death (in 1804) of Hofdemel's, or Mozart's, son.

Other biographers have considered the likelihood that Mozart had a mistress, or mistresses, in 1790–91. His naturally amorous disposition had been constrained in adolescence and early manhood by a father vigilantly wary of the perils to the development of his son's musical gifts from attachments with the opposite sex. Mozart was strongly attracted to many of the women for whom he composed opera and concert arias, but, since his feelings were not reciprocated, and since he was famous, clever, high-spirited, and had good career prospects, his biographers have been forced to accept the explanation that he must have been physically unattractive.

For certainties, Mozart was short, pock-marked, and had a large nose. He had a reputation for philandering. Constanze said that he admitted to having been unfaithful to her (tumbling housemaids), and Zelter, Mendelssohn's teacher, wrote to Goethe moralizing about the success of Mozart's creations affording him too much time for womanizing. (Mozart wrote little in 1790, part of the period in question, but in 1791, the other part, he was as prolific as ever.) Beneath these appearances, Mozart must be identified in some degree, if only in imagination and the choice of subject matter, with *Don Giovanni*, *Figaro*, and *Così fan tutte*.

One of Carr's arguments for a liaison between Mozart and Magdalena depends on the circumstances of the period in which it would have taken place. Constanze was in Baden taking a cure. Mozart's pupil Süssmayr was also there, probably to look after her, though Carr thinks the relationship went beyond that, on grounds that Mozart did not urge her to return and did not visit her frequently, a journey of only 17 miles. The facts are that Constanze was in Baden for six weeks from June 4 (1791), during which Mozart was with her three times, each for three days. In mid-July he brought her back to Vienna where, on the 26th, their sixth child was born.

Mozart's letters to Constanze in Baden are sexually teasing, professing jealousy and reminding her of the dangers inherent in her overtly compliant nature. The letters are direct, but the life may have moved in bricoles—Mozart was a billiards addict—for if he could invent emotions, and masks for emotions, to fit the people in his operas, surely he could do the same for himself. He may well have tired of Constanze, a woman with few redeeming qualities, intellectual or otherwise, and he had been quick, perhaps vindictively quick, to perceive that her prettier and more gifted sister, Aloysius, his first choice for a wife, was "a false, malicious person and a coquette." Unlike the Weber sisters, Magdalena might have had an inkling of Mozart's genius.

But while the case for marital disaffection is credible, the one for the adulterous relationship with Magdalena presents obstacles of a practical kind. Mozart was well known in Vienna. The Emperor stopped his carriage to talk to him, and called "Bravo Mozart" to him in the theater. And Mozart was admired and respected by music-lovers of all classes, who would doubtless have recognized him: he could not have kept company with Magdalena incognito. Furthermore, how would she have concealed what was happening from her husband? Carr's question of whether or not her piano lessons took place in Mozart's home (where he had a valet), or hers (where she would certainly have had a maid), is of little consequence since the two residences were only a five-minute walk apart. In order to show that without a mistress Mozart would have been odd man out, Carr cites prominent Viennese of the time who flaunted mistresses. But what if Mozart's was a married woman, married, moreover, to a member of the same Masonic lodge?

Mozart's finances bear on the plot. In 1789 he began to borrow substantial sums of money. The reasons for this are not apparent, and they seem not to be related to fluctuations in his income or changes in his never extravagant personal habits. Constanze's cure at Baden may have been costly, but he was not troubled by this, as one of his letters indicates. The accepted explanation for the sudden and continual borrowing, that he had gambling debts, begs the question of why he had suddenly become a consistent loser. Mozart's close friend Michael Puchberg, who made fifteen loans to the composer in 1790–91, knew the answer—"our personal secret," as Mozart calls it in a letter to him. One thing is certain: Mozart could not have lavished money on Magdalena without her husband's knowledge. Perhaps another, more footloose, female should be put forward to account for Mozart's mysterious deficits, unless he and Magdalena had become the victims of a blackmailer.

Carr's most absorbing chapters discuss the "cover up" ostensibly necessitated by assumptions of a causal connection between Hofdemel's death and Mozart's. The hint of a scandal implicating Europe's, and Vienna's, most celebrated composer had to be stifled, for though his true stature was unknown, more than one member of the artistic-minded aristocracy understood that Mozart was the most gifted musician of the age. The obituary in the *Wiener Zeitung* (December 7) places him at the "pinnacle of the greatest Masters." That he might be revealed as an adulterer would not have been deeply damaging, but the suicide, immediately after his death, of the husband of a young and beautiful pupil, could not have been dismissed.

The crux of Carr's conclusion that a concealment took place lies in the circumstances of Mozart's burial: Mozart was not a pauper—he lived in a seven-room apartment at the time of his death—yet he was buried in a pauper's grave. Baron Gottfried van Swieten, the most cultivated musician among Mozart's patrons and the obvious choice to carry out the Austrian Government's interests, arranged for the funeral service at St Stephen's and the interment in an inexpensive grave at St Mark's. Mozart was not buried there, but in a *no*-expense, communal grave, one where the corpse would be difficult to find and exhume. Since the weather on December 6 was good, the unannounced change of site seems to be the only explanation for the absence of all of Mozart's friends. According to one biographer, the gravedigger who asked Constanze to place a cross on the place of burial, and who alone knew it, was immediately replaced. (Constanze did not attend the funeral and was only induced to visit St Mark's by her second husband seventeen years after the death of the first.)

Carr attributes the obfuscations to a determination to avoid the possibility of an autopsy that might reveal poison. And poisoning *was* suspected: it was mentioned in a newspaper report, written only a week after the funeral, in far-away Berlin. Miliary fever, given as the cause of death on the death certificate—and still accepted by *The New Grove*—actually results in death only when accompanied by complications that Mozart did not suffer.

The story of Mozart and Magdalena did not die. It was the greatly embroidered subject of an 1841 novella by Leopold Shefer. *Mozart and Constanze*, a play with music by Von Suppé, published in 1874, contains the question: "Is it not known that Mozart had an affair with a woman whose husband cut his own throat?" Magdalena is identified as Mozart's *Geliebte* (lover) in the index of a 1922 biography of Constanze Mozart. In 1932, Wolfgang Goetz published an elaboration under the title *Franz Hofdemel*. Did Magdalena Hofdemel confide in anyone? Did Michael Puchberg? Did Mozart? A letter or diary entry from parties known or unknown could still turn up.

Schumann on the Couch

Robert Schumann's life seems to be a greater focus of attention at present than his music, which is currently represented on concert programs only by his most popular songs, piano and chamber-ensemble pieces, and a handful of orchestral works. At least part of the explanation for this lies in our deficient appreciation of Schumann's poetry-in-music, whose immediate appeal hides an art of remarkable subtlety. Three recent Schumann-related books will no doubt add to our understanding of the composer's life; whether they will lead to a deeper understanding of his music is another question.

Schumann: Music and Madness,[1] by Dr Peter F. Ostwald, is the first full-length case history in English of the greatest of the German Romantic composers. The book is thoroughly researched and documented, but its shortcomings, the most serious of them stemming from the psychiatric speculations threatened by the title, almost sink it. What keeps the whole afloat—just—is Dr Ostwald's contribution to Schumann's medical history in the context of nineteenth-century knowledge and practice, and the generally commonsensical biography within the psychobiography.

It can be said at the outset that Dr Ostwald's comments on Schumann's music ought to be ignored, although it may be merely inane, and not deeply harmful, to be told that the A minor quartet has a "light-hearted scherzo," or that *Träumerei* exposes a "melody of exquisite tenderness." In the absence of a study of Schumann's innovations—in thematic metamorphosis, suspended cadences, and open-ended phrases, for example—and in the presence of Dr Ostwald's addiction to colloquialisms, the reader cannot tell whether the labeling of a section of a trio as "offbeat" means that the rhythm is syncopated or that the music is in some sense "way out."

---

[1] New York, 1985.

Mercifully, Dr Ostwald does not labor the familiar parallels between the growth of Schumann's mental illness and the changing formal aspects of his music, which is to say the abandonment of brevity, fantasy, and biographical and literary allusions in favor of classical structures and academic correctness. After all, the developments of many more or less sane composers follow a similar pattern. Nor does Dr Ostwald attempt to associate Schumann's encroaching psychoses with the thickening of his orchestral textures and the narrowing of the upper pitch range. The latter too easily invites comparison with acrophobia, from which Schumann suffered all his life. Dr Ostwald does maintain that the creation of Florestan and Eusebius is symptomatic of a schizoid tendency (could it not simply have come from a belief that three heads are better than one?); but then, Schumann's later rejection of these alter egos must logically be seen as an improvement in his mental health, which is not the case.

Dr Ostwald cautions the reader that "Psychotherapy as practiced today was almost unheard of in Schumann's time." Almost? Elsewhere Dr Ostwald tells us that Schumann "feigned" an "almost masochistic pose" toward his father-in-law. Feigned an *almost* pose? Today's psychotherapist, in any event, gives Schumann low marks in "interpersonal relationships" and "reality contact"; diagnoses "inner confusion" (as part of an "identity crisis") and a condition "close to paranoia"; contrasts Liszt's flamboyant "life-style" with Schumann's pursuit of an insular one (because of his "fear of rejection"); and traces the decline from the young verbal matador (who had taken part in "endless bull sessions") to the "inarticulate conversationalist" of later years. (Wagner reported after one of their meetings that Schumann had "remained mute for almost an hour"; but would the composer of *Tannhäuser* and *Lohengrin* have permitted an edgewise word?) The same jargon is applied to Schumann's music: the Opus 24 *Liederkreis* "deals obliquely with the problem of sexual frustration" (how?), while the interludes in *Carnaval* "probably allude to interactions between [the] main characters and may even have sexual implications" (what doesn't?).

Dr Ostwald concludes that Schumann was homosexual. "It seems clear," he writes, that the composer "had one and possibly several homosexual encounters," and that he "tried to be . . . overtly homosexual." The evidence consists of two entries in Schumann's diary, one of them the isolated word "pederasty," the other a reference to a "homosexual who thrust himself on me, and my sudden departure." If confidence in Dr Ostwald's scientific procedures survives this far, the mortal blow is struck a few pages later with his announcement of

Schumann's kinship with Schubert, who "was probably exclusively homosexual." The basis this time is the *non sequitur* that Schubert belonged to a "coterie" of both "homosexual and bisexual Viennese artists" (an unusual combination?). Luckily, Schubert "solved [the] problem [of marriage] by remaining single," Dr Ostwald adds, as if no more than a simple decision was involved.

Another argument in Dr Ostwald's homosexuality thesis is that Schumann had a "compulsive tendency to disguise [his] hostility toward women in general and [his wife] in particular." Perhaps. But his misogyny, masked or otherwise, does not seem to have constituted a serious obstacle during "several years" of sexual intercourse with the unidentified girl Christel (so vigorous at one time that his sore frenulum had to be dipped in a distillate of daffodil bulbs), not to mention his seductions of other women, his fathering of eleven children, and his ongoing (thrice weekly, according to the diaries) conjugal life with Clara.

Even so, relations between Robert and Clara on other levels must have been severely strained in the later years of their marriage, and Dr Ostwald is surely correct in adducing a resentment in Schumann toward his wife. Franz Richarz, Schumann's doctor during the two years of confinement (1854–56) in the asylum at Endenich, testified that the patient never mentioned her. Nor did she visit him, in all that time, until hours before his death. Richarz, presumably interpreting Schumann's wishes, discouraged her from coming; but she *could* have seen him—others did—especially since she was paying for his hospitalization. Richarz withheld her letters to her husband, presumably in the belief that they would have an injurious effect. But she must have suspected this, both because of the absence of any response, even through an intermediary, and because she had employed the same stratagem herself: a letter to her from Brahms reveals that he had kept back information from the doctor at her request.

Why did Richarz destroy his files on Schumann? Dr Ostwald suggests that the motive might have been to protect Clara's reputation rather than, since she eventually saw the autopsy report, to spare her some gruesome medical truth. The files could have included damaging references to her, as well as upsetting accounts of her husband's behavior and treatment. Was Schumann ever physically restrained? Sedation would have been routine, and it is unlikely that he escaped the bleedings, cuppings, blisterings, cold baths, and other contemporary methods used in treating mental patients.

Nancy Reich's *Clara Schumann* is comprehensive, clearly written, musically well-grounded, and fair in its judgments. Although less than half of the book[1] bears directly on Robert Schumann, Reich's account of the Endenich years adds details not vouchsafed by Dr Ostwald; and simply by tracing the development of Clara's career as a pianist during the Endenich period, Reich provides a new perspective. Whereas Clara participated in only ten concerts a year, on average, during the fourteen years of her married life before Robert's confinement, she performed once every three days in the last month of 1854 alone, and in only two and a half months in 1855 gave twenty-six concerts in England, travelling from there to cities as far away as Danzig. Concert-touring again in 1856, she was in England when a telegram called her to her husband's deathbed.

The radical increase in the number of engagements cannot be attributed in any great measure to Clara's new freedom from the almost continuous child-bearing of the previous decade. Her pregnancies interrupted her concertizing only very briefly; she appeared onstage close to her confinement, in one instance only a week before, which must have raised the eyebrows as well as the apprehensions of the audience. Another factor must have been that she was fleeing the thought of the asylum, while salving her conscience by earning money to support her husband and family. Above all, in exploiting her independence she was returning to the path she had abandoned, not without a sense of sacrifice, for marriage. Clara was a virtuoso pianist and public figure first, a wife and daughter second and third (or third and second), and a mother somewhere lower on the scale.

Her artistic ambitions could be fulfilled, however, only with invitations to perform. The conclusion is inescapable that more of these came, as they would today, in the splash of publicity following Schumann's suicidally-intended leap into the Rhine in February 1854. Thereafter, throughout her long life as a pianist and forty years of widowhood, the name of the great composer she bore would help sustain her fame.

Reich sides with those who feel that Clara should have demanded to see her husband in Endenich, and acknowledges that strong-willed, domineering Clara inspires dislike in many people. One relatively minor cause of this reaction comes from the Bettina von Arnim episode. Clara was flattered when the famous writer asked to visit Schumann in the asylum, but disconcerted, after the meeting took place, by the recommendation that he be returned to his family. Yet the principal source of

[1] *Clara Schumann: The Artist and the Woman.* Ithaca, N. Y., 1985.

antipathy toward Clara is her neglect of—in Reich's phrase, her "emotional insulation" from—her children. The reader still wonders how Clara could receive the news of the death of her daughter Julie, tell no one, and play a concert the same day, confiding in a letter to a friend that to have changed the date would have created difficulties.

Clara's failure to visit her son Ludwig during his first four years in a mental institution opens more room for controversy. Some see her inaction as a natural turning away from memories of Endenich. Others believe that precisely because of Endenich she might have been expected to give her son attention, sympathy, and care. In partial extenuation, it must be said that in much of her parental behavior she was following the example of her father in the home of her youth. To which one must add that Clara Wieck was too much her father's daughter to have enjoyed a smooth marriage with the great composer who was Friedrich Wieck's opposite in every way.

Reich's brief biographies of the Schumann children are so well presented that one regrets she did not go on to the next generation: two of the four daughters married, and their descendants are alive today, in Germany and Italy. It is odd, too, that Reich wrote the preface to her book in Hastings-on-Hudson, yet does not mention that Robert Sommerhoff, son of the Schumanns' daughter Elise, lived not far from there, near Poughkeepsie, where his estate, which included a Schumann family photo album, was auctioned in July 1973.

After having deplored the encroachment of Schumann biography on Schumann music, I am now obliged to admit that the still unpublished sources, including more than 3,000 of Clara's letters, are vast. The first volume of the Schumann *Tagebücher* (to 1837) appeared only in 1971, the third volume and the *Haushaltbücher* (1837–1856) in 1982; the second volume has been announced for late 1986. Though these documents cannot be expected to appear in English for some time, they have already provoked world-wide discussion. For example, in reviews of the diaries and of the Reich book (both of them in *The Times Literary Supplement*), Judith Chernaik accepts as fact the diagnosis that Schumann had tertiary syphilis, "probably contracted in early youth." Dr Ostwald, less peremptory, maintains that syphilis, congenital or contracted, is one among other possible diagnoses, and he demolishes an argument based on the use of mercury as proof of treatment for it, since the same toxic metal was prescribed for headaches, colds, sciatica, and diarrhea.

We may believe that Dr Ostwald's account of this and other aspects of the medical background is as thorough as facts permit. He examines what is known of the methods, attitudes, and careers of Schumann's doctors, even summarizing medical publications that *might* have influenced them. But not much of this can be positively traced to Schumann's treatment. Surprisingly, on Schumann's well-documented and comparatively late-in-life tinnitus, Dr Ostwald adds little, attributing it to labyrinthitis and "stress." If any area is open to investigation, it would seem to be the genetic: Schumann's sister Emilie was mentally ill and committed suicide, his father and a brother died of "nervous disorders" or "brain fever," and of his sons who survived infancy, one became a morphine addict and one died insane.

Other reviewers will complain about the insufficiency of some of Dr Ostwald's general history, noting, for instance, that the *Sturm und Drang* era "aimed at" a lot more than "reducing the impact of French Classicism and the enlightenment [sic] upon European culture." No revolution in sensibility? No change in the role of Nature? No view of genius as inevitably alienated and probably pathological? And what of the exploitation of parody, so essential to Schumann's music? And of dreams?

Most readers will notice that Dr Ostwald tends to look on the dark side of quite open questions. He tells us that after the fiasco of the Piano Concerto in Vienna, in January 1847, Schumann uttered "a tragic prophecy: 'Calm yourself, Clara, ten years from now all this will be different.'" The tragedy, presumably, is Schumann's death before that time, but the remark might very well have been intended to mean that the piece would be received differently in the future. So, too, Dr Ostwald hears a tone of foreboding in Clara's 1850 diary entry on her husband's "heaven-sent" genius: "May you, my beloved Robert, always perceive this as such and always be as happy within yourself as you deserve." Dr Ostwald comments: "In trying to free herself from the pangs of guilt for having disobeyed [her father], Clara may have had to delude herself into a belief that her husband was doing far better than he really was."

A welcome contrast to modern psychobiography are the *Memoirs* of Eugenie Schumann (1851–1938), now reprinted after almost sixty years.[1] The composer's youngest, best educated, and most musically gifted daughter writes with much charm (she knew English), ably conveying the period of her childhood and bringing people to life. She did not know her father, and before adulthood seldom saw her mother, having been brought up by her sisters and a governess and then sent to boarding

---

[1] Edited by Marie Busch. London, 1985.

school. Though Eugenie did not get along with her mother, the *Memoirs* are worshipful of her. The rumor that Johannes Brahms was the father of Clara's last child had to be suppressed—but never has been, partly because it was circulated in a pamphlet by Eugenie's nephew, Alfred Schumann. Ironically, Eugenie's story should be read primarily for her portrait of Brahms, whom she knew well and loved. Here she recalls him at "our breakfast table":

> We would often sit talking for a long time, but Marie [her sister] reminded him sometimes, Herr Brahms, you really must practice now or you will not play properly at the concert. Then he always got up obediently, went into the music room with his beloved cigar, and presently we heard the vigorous attack of his two fifth fingers, one at each extreme end of the keyboard, and arpeggios in counter movement through endless modulations followed.

Schoenberg and Kandinsky

The correspondence of the two artists comprises about a third of *Arnold Schoenberg-Wassily Kandinsky,*[1] and about a third of the forty-five or so letters from Kandinsky's side were written by his pupil and partner Gabriele Munter. The seventeen Schoenberg letters are apparently all that survive, though Kandinsky's replies indicate that more were received. The book is filled out with related writings by both men; with photographs, including color reproductions of Schoenberg's paintings, as well as Kandinsky's; and with essays by the editor and translator, some of which compound verbal and interpretative problems in the letters. But the best of the exchanges are indispensable for anyone concerned with the arts in the years immediately preceding World War I.

Kandinsky heard Schoenberg's Second String Quartet and Three Pieces for Piano in a Munich concert in January 1911, and felt such artistic "empathy," that he was moved to communicate with the composer. Schoenberg did not concur with the notions, set forth in Kandinsky's initial letter, that in both painting and music "today's dissonances are tomorrow's consonances," and that "*construction* is what has been so woefully lacking in the painting of recent times." In reply, the composer said that since 1909 he had been seeking "complete freedom from all forms," quoting the now classic definition from his *Harmonielehre*: "dissonances are only different from consonances in degree; they are nothing more than remoter consonances." He also challenged "construction" as "a word of yours with which I do not agree." No reason is given for the objection, but Schoenberg must have had beliefs similar to Chesterton's: "A thing constructed can only be loved after it is constructed, while a thing created is loved before it exists."

---

[1] *Arnold Schoenberg-Wassily Kandinsky:* Letters, Pictures and Documents. Edited by Jelena Hahl-Koch, translated by John C. Crawford. London, 1984.

By the end of the year, Schoenberg is categorically denying the usefulness of theory:

> I do not agree when you write . . . that you would have preferred to present an exact theory . . . We search on and on (as you yourself say) with our feelings. Let us endeavour *never* to lose these feelings to a theory [December 14, 1911].

A month earlier he had told Kandinsky: "In a few days I will have begun a series of 8–10 lectures on 'Aesthetics and the Theory of Composition' . . . as you can well imagine, the object is to overturn both" (November 11, 1911).

On "points of contact" between the arts, Schoenberg accepted Kandinsky's observations concerning "color in comparison to musical timbre," but, probably deciding that his correspondent would not be able to grasp the implications of atonality, avoided the subject and turned to generalities. On style, for instance, Schoenberg wrote:

> Although I have certainly developed very much . . . I have not *improved*, but my style has simply got better, so that I can penetrate more profoundly into what I had already had to say earlier and am nevertheless capable of saying it more concisely and more fully.

His elaborations on this distinction regrettably weaken it by introducing the false opposition of "not what I say but how I say it," as if a poem could be "said" in some other way (prose).

Kandinsky invited Schoenberg to contribute music, graphic work, and critical articles to *Der blaue Reiter*, and the two men were soon exchanging photographs of their paintings. Compliments followed, Schoenberg expressing his appreciation of the work of Emil Nolde and pleasure in the "salutary simplicity" of Munter's paintings, in which "goodness and love are hidden." Kandinsky contributed an article on Schoenberg's pictures for a 1912 *Festschrift* about the composer, which was acknowledged with a memorable remark: "You are such a full man that the least vibration always causes you to overflow."[1]

---

[1] The imagery in Schoenberg's letters of the same period to Ferruccio Busoni is on the same high level of imagination. In his concert arrangement of the second of Schoenberg's 1909 piano pieces, Busoni begins with an octave effect that in the

Kandinsky resumed the correspondence after World War I, explaining that he had been living in Russia for seven years, totally isolated from the West. Schoenberg answered that during the same period of a hand-to-mouth existence in Vienna, religion was his "one and only support." The name "Schoenberg," he added, may now be less well known because of his music than because of the feats of his football-playing son Georg. Now, too, Schoenberg complains about his disciples: "These atonalists! Damn it all, I did my composing without any 'ism' in mind."

In 1923 Kandinsky invited Schoenberg to become director of a reorganized Bauhaus music school. The response could hardly have been more surprising: Schoenberg would like to teach, but cannot accept, having learned the lesson that "I am a Jew." He charges Kandinsky with anti-Semitism, of having been aware "of what really happened" during Schoenberg's summer stay in Mattsee, where Germans had made him feel unwelcome, an experience that deprived him of "peace of mind to work at all." (Alban Berg wrote to his wife that anti-Semitic restrictions imposed by the town council had forced Schoenberg to leave Mattsee.) Though the underlying provocation seems not to have been the Mattsee incident, and though Schoenberg seems to have been mistaken about Kandinsky's role in the persecution of Jews in Russia, Kandinsky's answer is not satisfactory. Neither he nor Schoenberg can have anything to do with "lumping together," even though "particular characteristics, negative and positive," are found in individuals and in nations. Among his friends, moreover, Kandinsky counts more Jews than Russians or Germans. (This old, irrelevant story was the basis of the 1984 Bayreuth exhibition, "Wagner and the Jews.") A "Jewish problem" exists, Kandinsky goes on, and he regrets not having had the benefit of Schoenberg's views about it, since it must be examined by human beings "who are free."

Schoenberg's reply is both psychologically revealing and profoundly moving:

---

original had been subtly anticipated. Schoenberg observed to him that "A hero who will shoot himself in the third act must be portrayed in the first act in such a way that an intuitive person can have a presentiment of his fate." In the same arrangement, Schoenberg says that where the entry of a chord is for him "as if someone has pressed away a tear," in Busoni's version, "the person blows his nose as well."

> When I walk along the street, and each person looks at me to see whether I'm a Jew or a Christian, I can't very well tell each of them that I'm the one that Kandinsky and some others make an exception of, although of course that man Hitler [*this was written in 1923!*] is not of their opinion.

Happily the two men became trusted friends again later in the 1920s. In 1936 they resumed their correspondence. By this time both of them were refugees, Schoenberg in Los Angeles, Kandinsky in Paris.

The Emperor of China

The history of early twentieth-century music has yet to be written, and where it has been writ large must be rewritten, the editors of *The Berg-Schoenberg Correspondence*[1] declare. This chronicle of the relationship between two of the period's greatest composers, and of the interaction between them and Central European musical life in the years 1911–35, immediately establishes itself as part of the rewriting. As fragments of autobiography, the letters fascinate far beyond the confines of music history.

Fewer than half of the eight hundred items in the not yet completely collected correspondence have been included, but the selection seems trustworthy, and, in any case, not many readers will be left feeling hungry for more. Nor are they likely to object very strongly to the cuts and substituted summaries in several of Berg's letters, which outnumber Schoenberg's more than three to one and are at least six times longer. Berg's side of the correspondence is a trove of information, but it is so lacking in candor, after he has learned what will and will not go down, that the reader can hardly wait for Schoenberg's ripostes. And Schoenberg, the same man to everybody, never diplomatic or political, has the more original mind.

Berg's thralldom to Schoenberg and the contrast between their antithetical personalities provide the main interest of the letters. The two rarely discussed music at the level of discovery and innovation in composition. Schoenberg, in his introrse creativity did not confide in Berg on such matters, did not, on the evidence of this book, so much as mention the existence of *Pierrot Lunaire* to him until a few days before the premiere. For exchanges about music, apart from questions pertaining to the publication of Schoenberg's works and comments on concerts and

---

[1] *The Berg-Schoenberg Correspondence*. Selected letters. Translated by Juliane Brand and Christopher Hailey and edited by them and Donald Harris. London, 1987.

their preparation, we can look forward to Schoenberg's and Berg's letters to Webern, with whom, the editors tell us, both composers were "much readier to share . . . artistic motivation."

The first communications, during the summer of 1911, are from Berg, who, at the age of twenty-six, has completed seven years of study with Schoenberg but cannot break the teacher-pupil dependency. Schoenberg, at thirty-seven, has written epoch-making music (not yet performed), is known by reputation throughout Europe, and a year later, with *Pierrot Lunaire*, will be recognized as the most influential composer and teacher of the time. As a musical radical without precedent, an esoteric, an intellectual cult figure—his pupils became his disciples—he was more harshly attacked all his life than any other composer in music history. In consequence, he became rebarbative, prickly, spiteful—and not only to his greatest pupil, Alban Berg. After more than a decade of abortive attempts to be heard without ructions in Vienna, he organized a society for private performances that excluded critics and non-member audiences. In contrast to the small, quick, dynamic Schoenberg, Berg was tall, ponderous, effete, a hyper-Romantic who as yet had made no mark as a composer. Schoenberg remained his polestar through thick and thin.

Schoenberg's letters are epigrammatic ("the modern-minded cling to the abstruse and enjoy it only if it remains unclear to them"); ironical ("the people seemed to despise me as much as if they knew my music"); tactless (he acknowledges Berg's gift of a book with "I never . . . would have considered acquiring [it] myself. . . The ones I want are missing"); and bullying ("I am extremely annoyed, for I realize how irresponsibly you treated the matter . . . Now I know I cannot depend on you"). But Schoenberg's humor balances his testiness ("Enter rehearsal numbers as follows—a number every 10th measure; . . . at the 20th measure—2; at the 30th measure—3; . . . at the 82,756,930th measure—8,275,693"). Schoenberg the teacher dominates the book, and some of its best lines are his instructions, musical and moral: Do not "skirmish with journalists," he writes. "It intensifies hate but lessens contempt." Urging Berg to "get involved in practical music making," Schoenberg gives matchless advice on how to conduct a rehearsal: "Talk as little as possible. Never try to be witty . . . There are only the following kinds of mistakes. . . ." At least one remark belongs in Bartlett's: "Of course he seems to have quite 'a mind of his own' and that is probably where he is weakest."

Berg, at the opposite extreme, is effusive and expletive-prone (countless sentences begin with "Oh," and underscoring is compulsive); hyperbolic ("How right you are in this, as in everything," "My debt to you

. . . has long since exceeded infinity"); obsequious and self-abasing ("I must *thank you* for your *censure*"); religiose (on a photo of Mahler's birthplace: "Doesn't this resemble the shelter in which Christ was born?"); and weepy ("Of the inner joy I felt when I read your words, I cannot speak—for that there are only tears").

Berg's epistolary style provokes what he refers to as Schoenberg's "affectionate admonitions," though the affection is hard to find:

> Dear Berg. . . . Please number your questions so I can find them more easily when I answer you. [There are] so many excuses, parenthetical asides, "developments," "extensions" and stylizations that it takes a long time to figure out what you are driving at . . . your formalities . . . Break that habit!!

And later: "One sentence on each point, *clear* and *concise*. . . . Surely by now you have learned from my letters." Schoenberg even complains about the length of Berg's address, whereupon self-addressed envelopes are sent, adding to the irritation. But Berg's style does not change, even though he drafts his letters.

When the correspondence begins, Berg is in Vienna, Schoenberg in Starnbergersee, where he has fled because a neighbor in his Vienna apartment house has alleged that his nine-year-old daughter was corrupting the neighbor's five- and eleven-year-old sons. In the beginning, and as it will be thereafter, most of the letters center on a real or imagined slight. The initial misunderstanding, for which Berg sends a treacly apology, is the possibility that he has "overrated" Schoenberg, something Schoenberg "fears." This leads to a new career for Berg as Schoenberg's factotum, and he is soon mediating with a lawyer in the affair with Schoenberg's neighbor; arranging to sublet Schoenberg's apartment, dispose of the contents, find a mover, oversee the shipment of furniture to Berlin; making panhandling calls on well-known music and art patrons in a campaign to raise money for Schoenberg's support. Rather more in Berg's line, Schoenberg puts him to work correcting the proofs and compiling the indexes for his book on harmony, although, as he writes, "It probably won't appear any time this century." Needless to say, these onerous and time-consuming tasks are unremunerated, except for the "honor" and "privilege."

What the reader should bear in mind from the outset is that Berg did not know the revolutionary creations of Schoenberg's greatest year, 1909, the Five Pieces for Orchestra and *Erwartung*, that breakthrough to atonality which is still the central event of twentieth-century music, and that the music he knows of the composer he quite literally worships ("dear idolized Herr Schoenberg," "your holy person") dates from an earlier period. Berg was never able to keep pace with Schoenberg, and as late as 1928 remarked on his wish to become "as familiar with your later works as I believe I am with the first half."

The correspondence concerning Berg's labors in connection with Schoenberg's mammoth *Gurrelieder*—transcribing the piano score and correcting its proofs, checking the orchestra parts for mistakes, writing the concert guide—sets the tone of the book. Not altogether unpredictably, Schoenberg rejects Berg's first and second efforts with the piano reduction as "too difficult," and raises for him the awful prospect of having to do it over yet again: "You'll make a simpler one next time." Berg's corrected proofs are also returned to him, because of "an [sic] incredibly many errors. . . . I think you frequently misread transposing instruments and various other things," and even Schoenberg's compliment on the subsequent vetting is tied to a remark about remaining errors. When the piece is finally scheduled for performance and Schoenberg wants to have the orchestra parts compared to the score, Berg, back up for once and showing an instinct for self-preservation, estimates that this would take "at least five hours a day for five weeks."

As Berg starts on the *Gurrelieder* guide, Schoenberg warns him against "poetry" and "flowery adjectives." When it is finished, Schoenberg tells him to apply an editorial bistoury and "cut 15–30 pages," which amounts to half of it! "Don't let me influence your decision," he adds, as if Berg's reactions were unforeseeable ("the least criticism from you . . . robs me of almost *all* hope"). Years later, Schoenberg returned to the subject of Berg's guides with "[if you do any more] you shouldn't design them so that they are practically unintelligible without the score . . . In . . . the *Gurrelieder* guide . . . there is a bit too much 'scientific' text with x^2 X y^3 + ab. 2[3q5 ± (f X 1^2---/ + X I^{bpa}?!---4fffsf]: 26^a A."

The pattern of humble offerings from Berg and crushing responses from Schoenberg does not change until *Wozzeck* (1925), after which Berg is accorded, but cannot fully accept, equal footing. Earlier in the correspondence Schoenberg has admitted that "the minute I see something, I immediately feel an urge to contradict." One letter from him begins: "Dear Berg, I am sorry to have to tell you that you are wrong, although you used almost two pages trying to prove you were right." When Berg talks about the "fun" he is having with his "radio set," Schoenberg says that "turning it off remains the greatest pleasure."

When Berg sends some windy observations about kite-flying, Schoenberg pounces on him with, "Your conclusion about the flight of kites is wrong," followed by the correct explanation in a few sentences, one of them containing the thought that "only the immaterial possesses stability," on which, of course, Berg battens.

After Berg claims a "tempo-machine" as his brain-child, Schoenberg says that he described "exactly the same device" to a friend two years earlier. In response to Berg's gift of a book about the Jesuits, Schoenberg tells him that it "only confirms a number of things I had already thought myself." Yet Schoenberg is no less annoyed when Berg's letters do not come: "Why haven't I heard from you? Have you lost all interest in me?" In the second year of the First World War, Schoenberg remarks that it might be "easier to bring about world peace than clear the air between us." But the belligerence seems to be all on his side.

Was Schoenberg paranoid? According to his widow, as the present reviewer can testify from correspondence as well as conversation, Schoenberg believed that he was jinxed, that an encroaching malignant force foredoomed him and his work to misadventure. His references in these letters to a "persecution complex" and to his periods of "self-delusion" are probably not of much significance, since he is constantly analyzing himself (as well as Berg, whose asthma he dismisses as "autosuggestion"). But such statements as "I must always be prepared for the nightly ambush of conspirators" and "I detect a hint of defection in the slightest negligence" certainly sound like danger signals, as does his "accusation" that Berg was "cultivating" his friendship "only with an eye to posterity."

Yet the correspondence is more surprising in testimony of the opposite kind, in the many proofs that, so far from being a "misfit," Schoenberg was an eminently sane, well-integrated, and socially responsible citizen, fully able to "function" and to "cope." At the beginning of the 1914–18 war, this "decadent" and "neurasthenic," as he was abused throughout the Establishment world, became a feisty patriot, rallying to the Austrian cause and criticizing pacifists such as Karl Kraus. He prods poor Berg, much less sanguine about the draft, into buying war bonds ("an amount commensurate with your circumstances"), and reminds him that "more than ever it is important to be a man. . . . In a few months you may have to wield a bayonet."

Berg, too, is forever analyzing himself, and in music as well as letters, identifying with Wozzeck at some level, portraying his temperament in the Chamber Concerto, impersonating himself in *Lulu* in the character

Alwa, in the asthmatic breathing of Schigolch, and, on his deathbed, in Lulu herself ("*Madame Bovary c'est moi*"). Berg knew Freud personally, and was an early advocate of psychoanalysis—in which he signally failed to interest Schoenberg. He wrote to Schoenberg that Webern's account of psychoanalytic therapy, after three months as a patient of Alfred Adler's, "seems very plausible and reasonable." But Schoenberg did not react. Nor does he comment on Otto Weininger's crackpot theories about the sexes as repeated by Berg—"How can a woman's illogic stand up to a man's logic?"—or on Berg's references to such manifestations of the psychopathia sexualis as his sister's lesbianism ("a most unpleasant family matter") and Adolf Loos's child molesting, or on Berg's repeated speculations about the deepest origins of illness being mental. Schoenberg's ceaselessly inventing mind does not have time for nonprobative hypotheses of this kind, and he does not feel the need of any help with his psyche.

What does rouse Schoenberg is Berg's conviction—which may have come from, and at any rate was confirmed by, Wilhelm Fliess's *Vom Leben und Tod*—that the number "23" had always played a crucial role in his life: "Dear Berg. . . . Everyone has a number like that . . . . You must see that you become less dependent on these lucky and unlucky numbers by doing your best to *ignore* them!"—this from twelve-tone music's triskaidekaphobe, who, sharing the superstition that governs the numbering of floors in most American high-rise buildings, wrote "12A" in his manuscripts above the measure before 14.

In December 1912, Berg mailed the score of his *Altenberg Lieder* to Schoenberg for possible inclusion in a concert. When Berg proposed to simplify Schoenberg's task by sending a piano reduction, Schoenberg took offense—"I am quite able to read the orchestral score"—and went on to criticize the music for betraying a "too obvious desire to use new means." He nevertheless liked "a number of passages" and, at "first glance," of course, thought the songs "beautifully orchestrated." True to form, Berg thanked him for his "kind words acknowledging that the score can make a pretentious impression," and proceeded with a complicated explanation that Schoenberg probably did not read. Ultimately Schoenberg programed the two songs that were not Berg's first choices, and omitted the haunting final one, whose performance the young composer most wanted, but which would not have been heard anyway, since Berg's music and the Peter Altenberg texts provoked protests that led to a brawl and stopped the concert.

The songs are masterpieces, far more striking and original than

Schoenberg's orchestral songs to that date, as well as, arguably, after. They mark a huge leap in Berg's development, the emergence of the theatrical, lyrical, and structural gifts that were to attain full expression in *Wozzeck*. All five of them, but especially the last, display a melodic character no less distinctive and much more immediately appealing than Schoenberg's. Did some conscious or unconscious intuition of this influence Schoenberg's choice?

What seems clear from the letters and other sources is that Schoenberg did not believe in Berg's promise as a composer, that he regarded Webern as the more highly endowed pupil and recommended his music, but not Berg's, to publishers. A year and a half beyond the *Altenberg Lieder* and with the score of two of Berg's new orchestra pieces as further tokens of his genius, Schoenberg could still disappoint him with: "I can't say anything about your work just yet." Writing to Berg in 1929, Theodor Adorno reminds him that he had confessed to being greatly upset when, after the *Altenberg* performance ended in a scandal, Schoenberg dissociated himself from him. But this discovery also exposes Berg's duplicity, since no hint of anything of the kind can be found in his letters to Schoenberg at the time.

Schoenberg's reaction to the *Altenberg Lieder* recurred on a larger scale with the stunning success of *Wozzeck* in Berlin in December 1925, an event that would soon be seen as the peripeteia in Berg's fortunes as well as in his relationship with Schoenberg. Two years earlier, after finishing the opera, Berg had disparaged it in comparison to *Erwartung*, that "concentration without its equal in music"—which may be true—as "3 acts of verbosity and loquaciousness"—which is false and gratuitous. This has to be said if only to help account for Schoenberg's response to *Wozzeck*. In addition, the reader must remember that when the opera was first performed, Schoenberg was in a neoclassical period and further than ever from Berg's passionate ebullitions.

Seeing *Wozzeck* a month after the premiere, and with no preparatory study of the score, Schoenberg sent Berg a brief note, unfortunately resorting to the hackneyed device of criticizing the performance first—"The orchestra stumbles, . . . the singers exaggerate, . . . [the] sets [are] irritating"—before vouchsafing an opinion of the work. "Some things I don't find good," he writes, singling out the topographical feature of Berg's vaulting style: "Every scene builds to a great orchestral FFF." But on the whole "it is very impressive and there is no doubt I *can* be proud of such a student."

Berg's craven reply is exasperating: "That you really didn't need to feel ashamed of me as a student makes me very happy." Virtually overnight *Wozzeck* catapulted him to a preeminent position among the handful of great living composers, and to a popularity that Schoenberg would never know. In the last year of Berg's life Schoenberg acknowledged: "You . . . alone in our cause managed to win general recognition." The infrequent letters of the decade from *Wozzeck* to Berg's death reflect on both sides Berg's change of status, as well as his ability to balance the two claims of artistic success and loyalty to Schoenberg. But the servility remains, an undiscardable habit.

Unlike Schoenberg, who concentrated almost exclusively on himself as a source of creativity in music, painting and literature, Berg had an ear and a mind for other voices. We are not surprised to learn from the letters that the composer who recognizes the greatness of Georg Büchner also sent Kafka's *Country Doctor* collection, Dostoevsky's *Idiot*, and Broch's *Sleepwalkers* to Schoenberg. Yet Berg could not bring himself to oppose his literary-critical perceptions to his teacher's. In one mid-1920s letter he quotes some less than immortal lines from a poem by Schoenberg and, to the reader's mortification, calls them "surely among the most sublime in the German language."

The editors warn that Berg's musical judgments are "too often colored by his eagerness to please Schoenberg," and that they betray a "garrison mentality and snobbishness that belong to the less appetizing legacies of the Schoenberg circle." A fanaticism, rather. In effect, what Berg really thought about the music of his contemporaries is all but impossible to discover. Not that we distrust his verdict on an opera by Szymanowski as "very boring and superfluous." But such comparatively favorable judgments as those on Charpentier's *Julien* ("very fine music") and Prokofiev's *Oranges* ("very engaging, flowing music," albeit in the salon class) were too obviously put forward for the reason that the composers were beneath the competition. This much is shown by the silence about Stravinsky. Culture clashings notwithstanding, Berg, an inveterate theatergoer, might have been expected to notice Nijinsky's Petrushka if not the music, in Diaghilev's January 1913 Vienna season, whether or not he attended a performance. But then *Sacre*, performed throughout Berg's world in the 1920s, is not mentioned, and in reporting to Schoenberg on a Vienna performance of his *Pelleas*, Berg neglects to note that *Noces* was on the same program.

One other omission is still more conspicuous. We wonder, not for long, why Berg's bulletins about the fates of operas by the likes of Schillings and Klenau do not include *Der Rosenkavalier*, which was triumphing just down the street. Richard Strauss had helped Schoenberg at one time, then criticized him, thus becoming an unmentionable—which explains why the reader without other books on the subject would have no way of knowing that Strauss was a figure of some consequence in German and Viennese musical life in the quarter of a century covered by these letters. Apart from a calculated remark about revising an opinion of *Elektra* downward, and a description of Strauss's "latest operas" as an "uninterrupted stream of mush," his name scarcely appears. (A footnote states that Schoenberg and Berg heard the first version of *Ariadne* together in Berlin.) As shown in this correspondence, Berg's monotheism compelled him to stoop, as he kneeled, to conceal his true feelings about *Salome*, to which *Wozzeck* owes a very audible debt.

The correspondence is herewith published in English first, before any German edition. The editors attribute their coup to "the intense interest of American scholars in the period and in the composers," and to the persistence of the "quest." In their case this has meant searching through the files of newspapers and periodicals, comparing other correspondence, tracing obscure acquaintances, and much more. One looks forward to an edition of the Webern-Schoenberg and Webern-Berg correspondence by the same team.

* * *

According to the editors of the *The Berg-Schoenberg Correspondence*, "postwar publication on the so-called Second Viennese School was . . . more reliant upon fond recollection . . . than historical scholarship." Part of this criticism can be levelled at Joan Allen Smith's book of interviews[1] with survivors—and their next of kin—of Arnold Schoenberg's Vienna circle, all of whom refer to him with a reverence appropriate to the canonization process. But the other part does not apply: Smith's scholarship is sound, and her book adds substantially to existing character studies of Schoenberg, as for example those published in recent years in *The Journal of the Arnold Schoenberg Institute*, as well as of Berg and Webern (*ibid.*), "the two sentinels watching outside Schoenberg's house [to make sure] that nobody [comes] near it."

The author tells us that her presentation of oral history is based on a technique of juxtaposition employed by Karl Kraus and Walter Benjamin.

---

[1] *Schoenberg and His Circle: A Viennese Portrait*. New York, 1986.

However that may be, the side-by-side testimony of different witnesses to events of more than half a century ago yields many remarkable similarities and no significant disagreements. The only reservations about the book that the reader may have are that the twenty-five interviewees—pupils, performing musicians, and friends (including Oskar Kokoschka)—were induced to speak American ("Mahler wasn't a soft guy") rather than their native tongues, that their false starts, anacoluthons, and verbal fumbles are all faithfully retained (the *ipsissima verba*), and the exegetical and background matter with which their recollections are introduced and interlarded is helpful only for those seeking first acquaintance with Schoenberg's world.

One of the most valuable chapters contains the complete programs, December 1918–December 1921, of the "Society for Private Musical Performances in Vienna," in which Schoenberg and Webern participated as conductors and Ravel as piano accompanist (for his Mallarmé songs). This most important concert series of the modernist period turned limited resources to advantage by replacing large orchestra works with specially prepared chamber-music arrangements, and two-, four-, and six-hand piano reductions, some of which, by masters including Webern, are of permanent value. From Smith's listings, which identify the *Vortragsmeister*, or coach, for each piece, we learn that Schoenberg himself rehearsed the major Debussy scores, Scriabin's *Poème de l'extase*, and the Mahler symphonies. The predominance of Reger in numbers of performances (almost sixty) begs some questions—and might have generated one or two from Smith, since Reger's music is so little known in the United States, and since Schoenberg named him in the line of descent "from Wagner through Mahler, Reger, Strauss, and Debussy to the harmony of today."

Berg's function in the Society at one time, as recalled by Felix Greissle, Schoenberg's son-in-law, was

> to see whether there were enough chairs in the hall, and that they were at a certain distance. . . . I remember Schoenberg coming. . . . "The chairs are completely cockeyed. This is ridiculous. What did you do here?" Berg, silently, without saying one word, took a measure, a tape measure, out of his pocket and measured and said, "You said you wanted so and so many centimeters; it's really all right; it's a half centimeter more."

Nothing in the book conveys the presence of Schoenberg so much as two other anecdotes. The first, an account by Greissle of his attempt to live with Schoenberg in 1923:

> After his first wife died, and when he felt very lonely, my wife and I offered to live with him, which we did, for a couple of months, you see; it was very, very difficult. We used to have fights almost every day about really minor matters, you see, and so one day, it was impossible to live further with him. We packed and moved out into our apartment. . . . The same day, at night . . . somebody threw pebbles on my window. I opened the window and down there was Schoenberg. He said very meekly, "May I come up?" So I said, "Oh, please do come up by all means." And he came up, he apologized, and he said, "I'm sorry, you are of course absolutely right, you cannot live with me, that's impossible."

The narrator of the other story is Marcel Dick, violist of the Kolisch Quartet:

> There was a graphologist in Vienna, . . . court-appointed. . . . Webern and Steuermann . . . took an envelope that had an address on it in Schoenberg's handwriting. . . . The . . . expert described completely what kind of a person he was in amazing detail and accuracy. . . . When he ended his presentation, he said, ". . . this man thinks he's the emperor of China." . . . In California, . . . Schoenberg celebrated his seventieth birthday and . . . noticed that a group of his old friends were whispering around in a corner and laughing . . . He said . . . "What are you laughing at?" . . . Finally, one of them took courage and . . . told him the story of . . . the graphologist and that he said that the man thinks he's the emperor of China. "What, what? Well, didn't you tell him that I am?"

"Of course he was!" Mr Dick concludes.

Alban and the Muses: Helene, Hanna, Lulu

The centenary of the birth and half-century of the death of Alban Berg (1885–1935) begins on a high peak of musical analysis in George Perle's *Lulu*.[1] The chapter on the opera's musical language can be understood, however, only by those who acquaint themselves with Perle's terminology and methodology, and who acquire an intimate knowledge of the score. The following comments, intended for general readers and the wider musical public, are necessarily confined to the opera's overall musico-dramatic design and the biographical portions of the book.

A study of Berg's collation of Wedekind's two Lulu plays into a three-act opera reveals that the composer reduced each of Wedekind's acts to a scene, and that Act II of the opera combines the last act of Wedekind's first play and the first act of his second. Unlike many critics of the opera, Perle does not question the viability of this sequence within Berg's three-act structure. Nor does he question the inherent limitations for musical treatment of some of Wedekind's characters, especially the Athlete, whose role, as Berg himself finally realized, was too large. Perle also refrains from discussing the social comment in *Lulu* through purely musical means, even though Berg's tonal portraits immeasurably transcend Wedekind's verbal ones. The Prince's "chorale," for example, conveys an empty gentility that words cannot evoke. And it should be said that class distinctions in the opera are as clearly delineated, and caricatured, in its complex musical idiom as they are in the simpler ones of eighteenth-century opera composers.

Subscription audiences can follow the opera's musical development in a broad way by certain traditional means of recognition—*Leitmotiven*, instrumental associations (Lulu and the saxophone)—and such memor-

---

[1] *Lulu: The Operas of Alban Berg*, Volume II. Berkeley, CA, 1985.

able thematic contours as the six successive diatonic pitches of Lulu's series. But Berg's use of series and tropes to evoke dramatic situations, to define characters and reflect their thoughts, implied as well as expressed, and to establish profound relationships and cross-connections, involves technical transmutations far above the grasp of all but a handful of listeners. For only one example, when the character identified with a certain pitch sequence cries, "It isn't true," three notes are displaced, each in a different segment of the series. But no audience is likely even to recognize the sequence, let alone the changes of order symbolizing the doubt referred to in the libretto, nor will any amount of exposure through good performances significantly increase the likelihood.

For the first time in his thirty years of nobly persistent devotion to the opera, George Perle concedes some of its weaknesses. He now tells us that when Geschwitz and Lulu switch places in the prison scene, Berg's libretto is even more confusing than Wedekind's original; and admits that the duet between Lulu and the Marquis in Act III, "Perhaps the climactic number of the work as a whole," is "disappointing." But how are we to square Perle's assertions repeated during three decades, that *Lulu* was not an unfinished opera at the time of Berg's death, with the new statement that "various tasks were required for the completion of the third act," only the melody being given in one place, and, in another, only one vocal part in a quartet?

To turn to biography, the book establishes that the late-in-life behavior of Helene Berg, the composer's wife and Perle's villainess, was dishonest as well as foolish. Still, before final judgment is passed, a deeper character study of Berg himself is needed than the one presented here. After his death, Helene demanded that all three acts of *Lulu* be published, even though it was made known that the final one had not been completely orchestrated. Later she accepted the decision that in the state in which Berg had left Act III, her request was impractical. In the first performance (Zurich, 1937), as well as in all subsequent ones for more than forty years, the opera was given in truncated form, with the third act represented by only ten minutes or so of music from the final scene.

At some unknown date, Helene changed her mind about Act III and attempted to suppress it. In the late 1940s, when interest in the opera began to revive, she had become adamant about this, to the extent of preventing scholars from examining the manuscript. Perle does not offer any reason for her attitude, not even the obvious one of the subject matter. Adulteries, the declaration of lesbian love, and murder occur in the first two acts, but the prostitution scene and Jack-the-Rippering in Act

III are more "shocking," and in the 1940s and 1950s, Helene Berg's belief that she was protecting her husband's reputation was probably justified.

Apparently trying to bury the secret of Alban's love for Hanna Fuchs-Robettin, to whom he had given the manuscript of the *Lyric Suite*, Helene fibbed about its ownership. This is indefensible, of course, even though the society of the time stigmatized abandoned and divorced women and did not sympathize with the wives of straying husbands. Helene discussed the romance in letters to Alma Mahler-Werfel, Frau Fuchs-Robbetin's sister-in-law—unwisely, since Frau Alma was a renowned gossip whose prominent social and cultural position virtually guaranteed that the story would be made public. In one of these letters, Frau Berg says that her husband

> didn't want too close an association with this woman, as he imagined her in the unheard-of florescence of his artist's fantasy, for fear of disappointment. He avoided her . . . It all comes to *a flight from reality*. In *this* way and *only* this way could the *Lyric Suite* have come to be . . . Someday I will stand with her before God.

Since Alban seems not to have pursued "the right true end of love," no "affair" apparently having developed between him and Hanna, and since he was evidently one of those "who goes to sea for nothing but to make him sick," his wife's interpretation of his fantasy life is perfectly credible.

Alban, on his side, seems to have had no difficulty in keeping up the flow of endearments to Helene, whom he describes to his "one and only eternal love," as a "person who constitutes only a completely exterior layer of myself." Perle does not comment on the duplicity, either here or in the case of Berg's silence concerning his illegitimate daughter. At age seventeen, the future composer of *Wozzeck*, an opera that ends tragically with the abandonment of a bastard child, had conceived a child with the family housemaid, who was sent away for her confinement. Berg corresponded with his daughter in later years but never otherwise acknowledged her. Perle blames his secretiveness on Helene, not Alban, yet Helene must have suffered from her own illegitimacy, even though *her* father was the Emperor Franz Josef.

LIVES OF THE POETS

Death in the Family

Has too much importance been given to the tomb-in-words that Mallarmé might at one time have intended to erect for his son, Anatole, dead at eight, too little to the poetry in which the father actually did immortalize his child? Paul Auster tells us that the 202 fragments, recently republished with his translations,[1] are not poems but "notes for a possible work, a long poem." Two of them are titled "Notes," while others contain reminders such as "idea there," "general effect," and "etc.," as well as blank spaces for words in blocked-out lines. Yet by any criteria, fragments of these fragments are poetry.

The evidence that Mallarmé projected an epic work is more solidly supported in the fragments themselves than in any testimony about it, least of all the memoir by Mallarmé's daughter published in 1926 from which Auster quotes two not-altogether-relevant sentences: "In 1879, we had the immense sorrow of losing my little brother . . . I was quite young then, but the deep and silent pain I felt in my father made an unforgettable impression on me: 'Hugo,' he said, 'was happy to have been able to speak [about the death of his daughter]; for me, it's impossible.'" Fragment 129, however, reveals something of Mallarmé's conception:

non mort—tu ne le	no death—you will not
tromperas pas—	deceive him—
je profite de	I take advantage of the fact
ce que tu le trompes	that you deceive him
—pour son heureuse	—for his happy
ignorance à lui	ignorance
—mais d'autre part	—but on the other hand

---

[1] *A Tomb for Anatole* by Stéphane Mallarmé, translated with an introduction by Paul Auster, San Francisco, 1983. The fragments were first published in Paris in 1961 under the title *Pour un tombeau d'Anatole*, Jean-Pierre Richard, editor.

je te le reprends	I take it back from you
pour le tombeau idéal	for the ideal tomb

That the dead, including Anatole, do not know they are dead ("*—pour son heureuse/ignorance à lui*") is one of the recurrent themes of the fragments. Another is the merging of identities, of the son continuing to live in the father. Reading these fragments, one thinks constantly of Stephen Daedalus on Shakespeare playing the ghost in *Hamlet*: "To a son he speaks, the son of his soul, the prince, young Hamlet and to the son of his body, Hamnet Shakespeare, who had died in Stratford that his namesake may live for ever."

Another of Mallarmé's themes is that of his guilt for failing to endow his son with a stronger body, of wanting to form him to continue his own task ("the man you would have been"), of wanting too much from him ("*hésitant de cette merveilleuse intelligence filiale*," which reminds us of Rodin's comment after Stéphane Mallarmé's funeral: "*Combien de temps faudra-t-il à la nature pour refaire un cerveau pareil?*"). Still another theme is that of the boy's clothes:

trouver absence	to find only
seule—	absence
—en presénce	—in presence
de petits vêtements	of little clothes

and

petit marin—	little sailor—
costume marin	sailor suit
quoi!	what!
—pour grande	—for enormous
traversée	crossing
une vague t'emportera	a wave will carry you

The explanation for the interest in the Anatole fragments can only be that despite much that is "obscure," "elliptical," and "unintelligible," some lines are more direct and immediate than any to be found in Mallarmé's certified poetry, where, of course, he would never have published such raw expressions of emotion as:

je le veux, lui—et	I want him—and
—non moi	—not myself

and

malade à la-	sickness one
quelle on se	clings
rattache, désir-	to, want-
ant qu'elle	ing it
dure, pour l'avoir	to last, to have
lui plus longtemps	him longer

and

moment où il faut	moment when we must
rompre avec le	break with the
souvenir vivant	living memory,
pour l'ensevelir	to bring it
—le mettre en bière	—put it in the coffin,
le cacher—avec	hide it—with
les brutalités de	the brutalities of
la mise en bière	putting it in the coffin

Auster's introduction translates the passages from Mallarmé's and his wife's letters referring to Anatole and his illness (childhood rheumatic fever complicated by an enlarged heart), the false convalescence, and the fainting fits that began shortly before the death (presaging the poet's own death, following an attack of suffocation). Writing to a friend who had sent Anatole a parrot, Mallarmé complains of being unable "to do anything literary," yet he bedizens his description of the bird, Sémiramas, whose "auroral belly seems to catch fire with a whole orient of spices."

The Introduction might have said something about the characteristic forms of the fragments, their short—never more than six-syllable—lines, the frequency of sequential pairs as well as the occurrence of the larger sets (3, 4, and 5), and the use of some of the same indicia as in the manuscripts for the so-called *Livre de Mallarmé*. A satisfactory translation of Mallarmé is inconceivable, and this attempt clearly/dearly injects the wrong tone:

. . . 1)	. . . 1)
vous qui verrez	you who will see
bien, ô ma—bien	clearly, O my—dearly
2)	2)
aimé . . .	beloved . . .

Furthermore, "knees" and "need" are knock-need:

genoux, enfant	knees, child
genoux—besoin	knees—need
d'y avoir l'enfant	to have the child here

The fragments expose the poet's imagination engendering possibilities, if not of overcoming Anatole's death in art,

—je ne veux pas	—I do not want
fermer les yeux—	to close his eyes—
—qui me regar-	—that will look
deront toujours	at me always

then of creating his survival through poetry, the reality in the image. Leo Bersani[1] has suggested that Mallarmé could not write the poem because "of a reluctance to reduce life to the trivializing nobility of a redemption through art." But the word "reluctance" in this indictment of the aesthetic of art elevated to religion implies a voluntary act of decision. Mallarmé, as these *cris du coeur* show, was stricken beyond the power of his art to help him:

tu peux, avec tes	you can, with your
petites mains, m'entraîner	little hands, drag me
dans ta tombe—tu	into your grave—you
en le droit—	have the right—
—moi-même	—I
qui te suis moi, je	who follow you, I
me laisse aller—	let myself go—

[1] *New York Times*, January 15, 1984.

Let My Cry Come unto Thee

Recent books on Eliot continue to concentrate on the life rather than on the work, with the difference that "censorship" appears to have been relaxed, the *Tom and Viv* scandal to have died down. Excerpts from unpublished letters and lectures are freely quoted here,[1] and dissenting views, including those of Harold Bloom's psychoanalytics, are more than tokenly represented.

Among the thirty-odd contributions are substantial pieces of criticism, the most valuable of them Eliot's own unpublished Dublin lecture of 1936, "Tradition and the Practice of Poetry," with its focus on rhythm: "The great revolutions in poetry are revolutions in the sense of rhythm . . . Wordsworth and Coleridge initiated a new age—not because their ideas were original, but because their rhythms were a departure from tradition." In the writings of Eliot's interpreters, an increase in references to Mallarmé is conspicuous, along with an anachronistic tendency to connect him to the poems of the *Prufrock* period, when Eliot was protesting "the labored opacity of Mallarmé" as compared to "the prose of Rimbaud." (Mallarmé would not have agreed that Rimbaud wrote prose: "*Toutes les fois qu'il y a effort au style, il y a versification.*")

In the first detailed account of Eliot's unpublished thirty-eight-line dramatic monologue "The Love Song of Saint Sebastian" (1914), now in the Huntington Library's Conrad Aiken Collection, Harvey Gross finds the poem revealing of Eliot's sexuality. The monologue consists of two stanzas, one a masochistic (self-flagellating) episode, the other a complementary sadistic (strangling) one. Though the voice of the poem is Sebastian's, the fantasies of violence are those of the poet and, so Gross argues, they qualify more as case history than as art. The Sebastian that had most impressed Eliot was Mantegna's in the Ca' d'Oro, with, in Gross's words, its "mixture of cruelty and erotic feeling" and "ecstasy of

---

[1] *T.S. Eliot. The Southern Review*, Autumn 1985.

pain." Both phrases provoke comment. First, the ecstasy is the experience of the susceptible voyeur rather than of Sebastian himself. Second, though eroticism is palpable in Mantegna's depiction of flesh and loin drapery, the cruelty is negated by overkill—Sebastian as pincushion—and by the distractingly perfect aesthetic placement of the arrows.

Another essay, by Jewel Spears Brooker, refers to Eliot's struggle "with the problem of celibacy" in the mid-1920s, but fails to note that he actually took the Church vow (letter to Stead, Osborne Collection, Yale). That Eliot was only thirty-nine might suggest that he was making a virtue of necessity. However that may be, the vow would have constituted a diriment impediment, but his marriage to Vivienne continued for five more years.

The one disappointment of the book is that the "King Bolo" stanzas described by Aiken[1] are not mentioned in any of the essays, though the healthy sexuality of these "rippling rimes," as Eliot called them, would have provided the right contrast to the Saint Sebastian story. They should be copyrighted and collected with Eliot's other verse, and not only for their rhythmic skill and inventive orthography, but also because Bolo's spouse had positive virtues. She, his

> Kween (That prac
> tickle Bacchante) Was always tidy
> fore and aft
> Although her clo'es were scanty And
> when the
> monarch & his men Went out to
> throw
> the discus the Kween sat by to rince
> her
> Kwunt and Comb her Bellywhiskus

The most interesting of the reminiscences is Brand Blanshard's account of his 1914 Christmas holiday with Eliot and a third Oxford companion, Karl Culpin. But Blanshard does not say that later, after Culpin was killed in the war, Eliot transferred his friendship to the deceased's younger brother, John, an official in the Royal Treasury. In 1932, John's wife, Regina ("Rexi"), submitted a novel, *The Dead Image*, to Faber, that Eliot turned down, and was still turning down in June 1959.

---

[1] "King Bolo and Others," in *T.S. Eliot*, London, 1948.

Regina was close to him and to Vivienne Eliot, and their correspondence puts Eliot in a more favorable light concerning his termination of the marriage. Before going to America in September 1932, he apparently did not tell Vivienne of his decision to leave her permanently, but had his solicitors deliver a letter to her while he was in the United States. She seems not to have received it until almost a year later, during which time she constantly expected his return. On October 14, 1932, Eliot wrote to Rexi from Cambridge, Massachusetts, expressing the wish "that you may see Vivienne sometimes." Obviously Vivienne was seldom out of his thoughts, and she was certainly in them exactly a year later, October 14, 1933, when he corrected the proofs for a new edition of the great poem ending

> Sister, mother
> And spirit of the river, spirit of the
>   sea
> Suffer me not to be separated
> And let my cry come unto Thee.

At that time, the poem still bore the dedication "To my wife."

Jean of All Trades

The editor's acknowledgments to his *Jean Cocteau and the French Scene*,[1] commemorating the twentieth anniversary of Cocteau's death, describe him as "the first true multi-media artist." The emphasis, therefore, continues to be on the diversity of Cocteau's talents, rather than on his poetry.

The book includes handy, though overlapping, reference articles on Cocteau's films, theater, and relationship to music by, respectively, Stephen Harvey, Neal Oxenhandler, and Ned Rorem. Dore Ashton's more ambitious essay, "Intellectual Backdrop," unintentionally reduces Cocteau to a peripheral figure simply by giving pride of priority to Artaud's theater, to Surrealist painters, and to the Buñuel-Dali films *Le Chien andalou* and *L'Age d'or*.

But one contribution deserves attention, Kenneth Silver's "Jean Cocteau and the *Image d'Epinal*," a study of the visual origins and references in *Parade*, the Satie-Cocteau-Picasso ballet, particularly since the work is receiving more exposure at present than ever before—including performances by the Joffrey Ballet and the Metropolitan Opera.

Silver sees *Parade* as a "parable of the travails of the avant-garde" vis-à-vis a disinterested public. His discussion of the piece is concerned not with its Cubist aspects, but as an exemplar of popular culture rooted in childhood memories. The 1914 war provoked a revival of the three-centuries-old Epinal (Lorraine) prints. In contrast to the "documentary images" of photography, the brightly colored folkloric ones of Epinal proclaim moral and allegorical truths, and are stereotypical—the-mother-in-law, the cook, the policeman, the young married couple—rather than specific. Probably the best known of the series is the "Cris de Paris," characterized by Silver as the street vendor's "visual lexicon."

---

[1] *Jean Cocteau and the French Scene*, edited and with a Preface by Arthur King Peters. New York, 1984.

Parade, he says, is a page from the "Cris" transformed, and he demonstrates this by tracing Picasso's costume for the "Children Conjuror" to its Epinal origin—confirming, in the process, that the conception of the work was purely Cocteau's.

A similar essay is overdue on the subject of Cocteau's Grand Mastership in the Prieuré de Sion, a secret society dedicated to the restoration of the Merovingian Dynasty and resembling the Rosicrucians in its claims to ancient Egyptian origins.[1] Cocteau's predecessor in the order was Claude Debussy, whose biographers have concealed his connection with the brotherhood as successfully as have Cocteau's. Arthur King Peters refers to Cocteau's drawings for murals in the Church of Notre Dame de France, Leicester Square, London, but says nothing about the weird presentation of Prieuré de Sion symbols that resulted: the black sun with black rays, the Horus on a Roman shield, the huge rose beneath the crucified figure's legs and feet—all that is visible of the body—and does not observe that Cocteau's self-portrait as donor is much more prominent than the Christ. "It was at Villefranche, in the chapel of St Peter dedicated to simple fishermen," Peters writes, "that Cocteau first began to decorate chapels." In fact Cocteau was embellishing churches near Lyon and in St. Mandrier more than twenty years earlier, in the summer of 1936.

Dore Ashton believes that Cocteau "came perilously close to becoming a Catholic doctrinaire." Surely not doctrinaire, even in Catholicism. All the same, what did he mean by the line in *Oedipus Rex*, "*L'autre côté de la mort*"?

---

[1] See *The Holy Blood and the Holy Grail*, by Michael Baigent, Richard Leigh, and Henry Lincoln. New York/London, 1982.

D.T.s

The sheer bulk of *The Collected Letters of Dylan Thomas*[1] comes as a surprise, so few of Thomas's letters having been published in the thirty-three years since his death, and his short life seeming to have allowed so little time for such activity. Was he wasting his talents in the long, carefully composed one-way-conversation letters with friends? Paul Ferris, Thomas's sympathetic editor, believes that the revised, corrected, and painstakingly copied-out money-grubbing letters, a principal category, eventually became a literary end in themselves, replacing the writing of poems and stories. Since drafts of other correspondence survive as well, perhaps we should simply accept Thomas's explanation (in a note denying he had a "theory of poetry"): "I like to write letters." This is evident by his straining to work in one of his puns: "genius so often being the infinite capacity for aching pains." But who said anything about genius?

Ferris groups the letters under "Provincial Poet 1931–4," "Success and Marriage 1934–9," "A Writer's Life 1939–49," and "Ways of Escape 1949–53." The first section, though dull, should not be skipped, if only because of Thomas's critical and technical analyses of the poems that Pamela Hansford Johnson had submitted to her eighteen-year-old mentor. His deprecations of her "jingling" rhymes and "adjectives that add nothing" are still instructive, and perhaps, in *his* wording, even the commonplaces can bear repeating: "Part of a poet's job [is] to take a debauched and prostituted word . . . smooth away the lines of its dissipation, and to put it on the market again, fresh and virgin." One of the book's more amusing passages is Thomas's spoof of the future Lady Snow's use of the word "testicles," titled by him "On A Testicle Made For Two."

---

1 *The Collected Letters of Dylan Thomas*, edited by Paul Ferris. New York, 1986.

The last section makes painful reading, partly because we know what the end will be and the descent to it, partly because we have already had so much begging that the repetition, no matter how varied, is monotonous. Since the letters are increasingly confined to Thomas's miseries, the world outside shrinks until it hardly exists. His horizons had always been parochial, and his participation in social and political movements was never more than nominal. But as his life drew to a close, the subject matter is reduced to reading-tour schedules and possible still untapped sources for loans (*i.e.*, handouts).

In his late teens, Thomas seems not to have faced the alcoholic's first obstacle, the admission to himself that he is one, but at age twenty he confesses that the "demon alcohol . . . has become a little too close and heavy a friend for some time now." Already then, as he says more than once, his hands shook and he was a victim of "alcoholic laziness." At twenty-one he describes a "three-weeks-accumulated hangover" and "nerves full of alcohol." One of the late letters laughs at American-university-professor "alcoholics anything but anonymous," a phrase, he had to have been aware, that applied to himself, since by this time his drunkenness had become as large a part of the legend as the poems. Yet even in the last years, and in spite of references to "drinking too much," he asks only for more money, never for help with an addiction plainly beyond his control.

The letters ramble, the sentences are long and choking with compound words, and the cleverness can be labored, especially in the Joycean jokes ("Just a song at twilight when the lights Marlowe and the Fletcher Beddoes Bailey Donne and Poe"), some of which occur more than once, or, as Thomas says about another writer: "He's always got the same cracks to grind." Over the years facetiousness becomes the tone for friends, wheedling for patrons. If the latter are socially exalted—the Princess Caetani, Edith Sitwell—Thomas is subtly and not so subtly obsequious. He is usually successful in avoiding clichés, but the failures are too often accompanied by the horrible "If I may coin a phrase." His vocabulary is astonishing, and the book would be worth reading if only for the discussions, and rejections, of words.

The letters would raise Thomas's reputation as a critic of poetry, if he had had one, both in his evaluations of other poets and as a line-by-line prescriptionist in matters of rhythm and sound. "I'm never very hot on meaning," he says. "It's the sound of meaning that I like." Sound too often signifying nothing, some will say. Hypersensitive to charges of obscurity, and to editors and readers who write to him for help, Thomas insists that his poems are meant to be understood. A correspondent who wishes to know what the poem "I make this in a warring absence" is "about" is given the plot in straightforward prose, although Thomas protests that "the 'plot' is told in images, & the images *are* what they say, not what they stand for." But his cribs are illuminating, and more of them would have been welcome.

The main surprise in Thomas's judgments on contemporaries is the extent of his reading. Yeats remained his hero ("Daybreak and a candle end"), but his public readings of Hardy ("To Lizbie Browne") were no less impressive, and around 1950 Thomas probably did more than anyone else to increase Hardy appreciation. Thomas makes fun of Eliot and those who presume an "intimate knowledge of Dante, *The Golden Bough*, and the weather reports in Sanskrit," and in his "dog among the fairies" pose, tells an editor: "I'd rather not review Auden . . . he's not sufficiently my cup of tea for me to enjoy his new poems very much . . . and I know he's far, far too good for me . . . to attempt to be destructive."

At eighteen, Thomas's virtuosity and precocity were phenomenal. From the letters written at the same time as *18 Poems*, we can now see, and marvel at, his command of his vast verbal resources, for he had been alimented by the whole library of living English poetry, as well as by some poetry in translation. Then, not suddenly, his development slows, he loses direction, and poems stop coming. But whether or not this follows the pattern of such things, *could* Thomas's career have been different? Could the poet of the *18*, published when he was nineteen, ever have worked in a bank, insurance company, English department?

The editing supplies exactly the right amount of information, as well as unobtrusive comments about Thomas's motives and truthfulness.

Sir Stephen by Himself

Stephen Spender's life as lecturer and symposiast in academic America, his quest for recognition, and his relationship with W.H. Auden are the principal subjects of the *Journals*.[1] Since the accounts of cultural conferences and of adventures on, or just off, campuses are familiar in kind, the following remarks are restricted to items two and three. It should be said that Spender's smaller, incidental subjects, his visits to the old and infirm, as well as his encounters with artists and writers, are more attractive, and though he complains of a "lack of vitally experienced observation," his portraits of people prove that he is as sensitive an observer as any of his contemporaries.

Both the reviews and the letters protesting them have shown a remarkable lack of susceptibility to the rich appeal of the *Journals* as humor. Anyone who has met Sir Stephen—and almost everyone who is anyone apparently has—will know that the favorite target of his highly developed gift for fun is himself. But even to those who are unaware of the acuteness of this faculty in him, it must be evident that his jokes at his own expense are conscious, the provocation of laughter intentional. Consider the following narrative in which he ridicules his desperate struggle to reach New York City in time for a dinner party the day after a lecture upstate:

> I went to a place called Oneonta . . . I was met by a pleasant young man . . . Next morning, he called for me . . . took me . . . to the airport . . . We were told the plane could not take off unless there was visibility of at least a mile . . . In NY I had . . . to join . . . Jacqueline Onassis . . . at a restaurant . . . I simply had to get there. I enquired about taxis and found that Oneonta had just one . . . after an hour, an octogenarian taxi driver appeared . . . After a 100 miles

---

[1] *Journals 1939–1983* by Stephen Spender. New York, 1986.

> or so . . . [he] made it clear that he did not want to drive me to NY . . . He said he would drive me to Albany . . . and there I could get an aeroplane . . . but there were no flights from Albany that would get me to NY in time . . . Finally I said the only thing was to find me another taxi.

Finally, too,

> I sat next to J.O. . . . [she] seemed to want to talk seriously . . . I asked Jacqueline what she considered her greatest achievement in life. "Oh," she said, "I think it is that after going through a rather difficult time, I consider myself comparatively sane."

Spender's failure to conceal his surprise at J.O.'s ability to rise above the level of unserious conversation is a minor lapse when measured against the proof, in revealing his maladroit question and her devastating reply, that he does not lack the courage of his candor.

In another droll story on himself, Sir Stephen dreams he is made pope:

> I sat in a large room, waiting to deliver my first sermon before about a million people . . . Numerous flunkeys, autograph hunters . . . kept on interrupting me . . . My sermon was intended to bring the full weight of starvation, preparation for nuclear war, etc., into the consciousness of the people, so they would change the world . . . Everyone would be grateful if I spoke, say, for five or ten minutes . . . delivered some brief tremendously moving exhortation.

So far from being confined to anecdotes, the Spender wit assumes a multitude of forms. One even suspects that some of the *Journals'* errors, factual as well as verbal, were committed on purpose, for the fun. This is very obviously the case with the footnote he attaches to a passage about the "South Seas" (with a reference to Tahiti and Gauguin), locating these waters in "the Caribbean." So, too, the misrendering of his line beginning "Spender's simple spondees offer this . . ." as "Spenders, simple Spenders, offer their. . . ," has a special appeal, as does the anachronism in the entry of September 4, 1939, comparing King George VI's broadcast voice to an "often interrupted tape machine"; and the confusion elsewhere about other sounds: "They played the Schubert Octet . . . Oboes, flutes, clarinets always bring to mind . . ." (There are no oboes and flutes in the Octet.)

On the verbal side, charmingly, disarmingly, the young Stephen, in one of his *Letters to Christopher*,[1] admits to "not knowing one end of a sentence from the other," and predicts: "If I go on writing badly enough, it will become one of my qualifications." The *Journals* confirm the astuteness of the forecast. A tangle such as the following has a distinctiveness that would not survive a grammatically sorted-out version:

> I have the sense of an underlying depression like a large squid lying at the bottom of a tank, which if I don't act with resolution, will come up from the depths and embrace me in its tentacles.

W.H. Auden is referred to in the *Journals* more frequently and at greater length than anyone else including the author's wife and American friend, B., about whom we are told little more than that he lives alone in a trailer. The reflections on Auden could be subsumed under the title that Spender used for another book, *Love-Hate Relations*, though "Settling Old Scores" would be more accurate. "Did I really like Wystan?" Spender asks himself, when someone puts the question to him. The answer is complicated, and never forthcoming in monosyllabic form. He reflects on Auden's contemptuousness when they were young ("I imagine he laughed at me a lot behind my back"; he certainly did when they were both older) and reviews the less accommodating features of Auden's character: the dogmatism and arbitrariness, meaning the Petrine approvals and disapprovals in accordance with one principle at the expense of all others; the hypocrisy (of feigning indifference to his publicity); and the vanity ("They loved me," "They were entranced"). Auden's blindness to painting is held against him, his vocation for religion dismissed as a subterfuge: "The effect of cultivating a bad Christian conscience has been to free him of interest in social problems." It now appears, as well, that there were two Audens, the mean and the absurd. One could respond to this by saying that a little of the former and lots of the latter were always evident, and that, in small doses, the latter could be highly entertaining. One may doubt, too, that Auden agonized from a bad

---

[1] Black Sparrow Press, Santa Barbara, 1980. The *Letters* provide background, not found in the *Journals*, for Spender's young friend Georg—he sat for "an hour or so at my desk trying to copy my signature to see if he could forge a cheque successfully"—as well as editorial curiosities: Oliver Risdale Baldwin, for example, is identified as "a biographer married to Victoria Sackville-West." (Was Harold Nicolson aware of this?)

conscience, or that he ever had any deeply felt, as distinguished from theoretical, interest in social questions.

Quite new is the emergence of certain reservations about Auden's poetry. In the early years it had an "idiosyncratic sensibility," but lacked "a center of his own personality." Still, and unlike the later work, it was inimitable, whereas a young poet who could match the technique of Auden's later periods could conceivably fill his carpet slippers in other ways as well. The speculation is unarguable, of course, and unfortunately Spender does not hide other feelings: "of our group—Auden, Day Lewis, MacNeice, myself—Auden has activated teams of scholars and research workers." In contrast, Sir Stephen lacks confidence in even the one young man writing a book about him and "trying to support my reputation."

The subject of Auden's homosexuality comes up again and again, but as camp, not as a factor of any significance in Spender's life. After Auden's death, when reading about A.E. Housman's Parisian male prostitutes, Spender exclaims: "How I longed to tell Wystan." Jokes are made: "Wystan asked Bill to go to bed with him in the nicest way possible, so that it was easy to refuse." So, too, a mock-serious discussion of Auden's aptitudes as a husband and paterfamilias—unnamed friends assert that "he was not gay"—is built toward a punch line, which, however, loses its quaintness without Auden's too high and cranky voice delivering it: "What I hate is the fucking."

Next to Auden, the most abiding concern in the *Journals* is with what Spender sees as a lack of recognition. Why does he feel "such a resistance to writing poetry"? His answer, "From the sense not so much of failure as of non-recognition," could hardly be more frank. He is delighted when people ask if he is *the* Stephen Spender: "I'm afraid I've only heard of one Spender—Stephen Spender— and he's dead I believe"; "the man at the desk asked whether I was related to the poet Stephen Spender. So I said 'That's me.' He looked pleased and said 'Gee, a near celebrity.'" During a stroll in the dark some youths overhear him breaking wind and cheer him for it, but then "a self-important thought came in my mind. Supposing they knew this old man walking along Long Acre and farting was Stephen Spender?" (What, indeed?) That the matter is no laughing one becomes apparent in a mirror scene headed "Thoughts while shaving":

> A thing I am ashamed of is that I find suggested confirmation of my identity by reading my name in the newspapers. My heart really does do something journalistic—stops a beat, gives a jump—if my eye looks on the printed word "Spender."

The recommendation for a knighthood forces the question into the open: "There comes a time when one craves for recognition—not to be always at the mercy of the spite, malice, contempt. . . of one's rivals." But the slings and arrows, certainly not aimed by "rivals," have continued, and we only wonder how, after fifty years in the arena, the newly beknighted Sir Stephen could have expected them to stop. Not his enemies but his friends flinch with each of his cruel self-exposures: "My life was in some ways ambiguous, like one of those photographs, which if you look at it from one direction has a different face from that which you see from another." And, "Being a minor poet is like being minor royalty." Regardless of whether anyone today can claim an assured place as a minor poet, Spender goes on to say that one of the last of the majors wrote "perhaps [his] greatest poem ['The Circus Animals Desertion'] when he was 74. 'I have four years then,' I thought."

For all of Spender's determination to present himself as paranoid ("I imagine the young reading nothing of me but the bad notices other young critics write"), many of his self-criticisms, anticipating ultimately less well-intentioned ones, are silver-lined. Sometimes the turnarounds and powerful upbeat endings occur in the same sentences:

> Everything I had done—or nearly everything—seemed a failure, not that of a person who does not use his talents, but worse, does not use them enough even to discover how much talent he has.
>
> * * *
>
> I also experience despair as the result of not having a disciplined mind [and of] feeling overwhelmed by the material and the uncontrollable rush of my own ideas.

Some of Spender's poems, criticism, memoirs, translations have contributed to the formation of a period, which, to some extent, they now represent. Indeed, no lines express the feeling of the 1930s more memorably than

> *We who live under the shadow of war,*
> *What can we do that matters?*

Yet Spender himself stands taller than his work. The least insular writer of his generation and the most generous, he is a kinder man – *hypocrite lecteur!*—than most of us deserve.

Wystan in and out of Love

Have the experiences of living together been assembled; for example, the experiences in the monasteries?

Nietzsche, *The Gay Science*

Charles Miller's book[1] tells us more about him than about W.H. Auden. To even the most trivial remarks of the poet, Miller gives his own reactions in full: "'Aren't the fireplaces handsome?' Wystan enthused, and yes, I thought of the previous century when those fireplaces heated the generous rooms." Noting that after a certain incident he never again heard Auden pronounce the word "ate" as "et", Miller feels it necessary to add: "Though he may have said it outside my hearing." What did Wystan "get" from him? Miller asks at one point, and he provides the answer: "My offbeat, 'amiable anarchist' wisdom, my ability (finally!) to laugh at life." Lucky Wystan.

What did Charles get from Wystan? Not much in the way of literary inspiration. Abraham Lincoln is described as "that lanky New World Napoleon of emancipation." On one page Miller recalls that "we stood in equinoctial sunlight," and, on another, he refers to an "equinoctal [*sic*] afternoon," apparently unaware that these occasions, unlike etesian days and nights, occur only twice a year. Unfortunate, too, are his attempts to spell out Auden's accent, and the failure to mention the distinctive timbre, intensity, and tessitura of the voice. To this reviewer, in any case, "deah me," "I caaahn't," "nevah," "veddy nice," "nah-sty," etc. certainly do not evoke Auden's speech.

Miller and Auden met in Ann Arbor in January 1940, during the poet's lecture-visit to the University of Michigan. In New York one day in the

---

1 *Auden: An American Friendship*. New York, 1984.

autumn of the same year, Miller attended Auden's class at the New School and was introduced to Chester Kallman. Returning to Ann Arbor as a faculty member in September 1941, Auden invited Miller to cook for him and become his housemate, an arrangement that ended with the war, when Miller left to work on a farm. A further meeting took place while Auden was at Swarthmore, and in later years Miller frequently visited the poet in New York. Thus Miller was well placed to observe Auden throughout his American period. Yet the book is stronger on the squalor of Auden's apartments than on the brilliance of their tenant, and the only comment about poetry that the author has chosen to repeat is not by Auden but by Robert Frost: "I'm often asked which tower belongs to that poem. But a poem is written about a feeling a poet has in him."

Miller quotes Auden: "Freud points out, correctly, that a homosexual may be normal in every way, except the sexual . . . I am normal in most ways." This theme, "normal in every way except the sexual," is repeated as if it were true. But surely Auden's intellect cannot be described as "normal," not to mention his cultural prejudices ("The French, my dear, are hardly white"), his absentmindedness (walking into and partly through the glass front door of his apartment building, like Charles Lamb's George Dyer who, "without a sufficient pair of spectacles," walked into the New River one Sunday noon), and other eccentricities of behavior (going to dinner, getting out of the elevator on the wrong floor, ringing the wrong doorbell, being admitted—by the Jason Epsteins, who recognized him—and asking for and imbibing a martini before departing, apparently unaware that he was the only guest). What may have been most normal about Auden was precisely his homosexuality, a principal subject of the book and one that apparently fascinated the author, who preserves remarks by Chester Kallman on the conspicuous quantity of Vaseline kept by his bed, by a homosexual friend from Ann Arbor on transvestite activities in the Auden menage there, and by Auden himself, horrifyingly, on a trip to the home of his father-in-law in California: "At the Manns', we took turns screwing a friend on Thomas's big bed when the family was away."

The portrait of Chester Kallman is accurate—he "held the coveted key to Wystan as person and poet"—except that Kallman was never self-confident. He *did* have "pale blue eyes . . . a large moist mouth . . . light yellow hair," he *was* "well-fleshed," and he smoked "compulsively." Also, to some, he exuded sex (Auden's verb). But Miller does not mention Kallman's intelligence, sense of humor, and musicality (which was much deeper than Auden's). The portrait of David Protetch, Kallman's roommate at the University of Michigan and Auden's physician thereafter, is totally wrong. So far from being "plump with a rosy complexion, a merry face, ever warm with animal joy," Protetch was tall, not heavy, very dark complexioned, and puffy faced (as a result of illness). He was also suicidal, especially after his marriage (in April 1968). His death shortly afterward—by fire, evidently while in a diabetic coma—might be compared to those of Sylvia Plath and Ingeborg Bachmann.

* * *

"*We're a funny pair, you and I.*"
Auden to Kallman, March 15, 1949

Auden in Love[1] is the biography of Chester Kallman, the "love" of the title and the poet's closest friend for thirty-four years. The author, Dorothy Farnan, had first known Auden while he was guest professor at the University of Michigan in 1941, and Kallman as a fellow student there a year later. During the following three decades in New York, she was in a better position than anyone else to observe the two of them together, incontestably so after 1948, when she became the consort of Kallman's father. In addition to her vantage as a member of the family, she has been able to quote extensively from Auden's letters to Kallman and from Kallman's to her, and to use the testimony of hitherto unknown friends and lovers of both men. The resulting story is of a relationship as strange and disturbing as any in all the lives of the poets.

Earlier writers on Auden have already established Kallman as the central figure in the second half of the poet's life. Farnan supplies the Kallman side of the connection, and by means of new sources, of which she herself—named only in passing in other books on the subject—is the most important, together with fifteen or so men referred to pseudonymously and interviewed by her only recently. The role of one of these, "Keith Callaghan," readjusts the picture of Auden's life in the years 1948 to 1953.

Farnan's thesis, if she has one, is that despite the anguish which Auden endured during all but the first two years of his marriage to Kallman, "Chester was good for him." She quotes Irving Weiss, a friend of Kallman's since undergraduate days and a neighbor in Ischia during four

---

[1] By Dorothy J. Farnan. New York, 1984.

of the summers that Auden and Kallman spent there together. (Though not mentioned in any of the Auden biographies, Professor Weiss and his wife were closer to the Ischian Auden than any other outsider except Hans Werner Henze, who is not a contributor to the book.)

> Chester frequently directed, or at least influenced, Wystan's taste. Because they were both intellectually powerful, each in his own right, they could talk to each other and have a lasting relationship: Chester was the only one in the world who could have had such a relationship with Wystan. One felt between them an instant electrical connection, particularly when they were talking about literature or music.

From my own observations of both men, this seems true, though of course no options are available concerning "the only one in the world who could have had such a relationship": we do not know what might have been. It should also be emphasized that Auden's philosophical and theological preoccupations were of little interest to Kallman, who knew and loved music and poetry but disliked "intellectuals," and who considered Auden's erudition and range of reading—as displayed in his Greek and Kierkegaard anthologies, and the essay on the Protestant Mystics—a liability in a poet.

Farnan is more generous to Auden than to her stepson, though she contends that Chester's deficiencies of character, which she exposes in painful detail, were outweighed by his charm. When she expresses the hope, in a story involving the disappearance of some money, "that Chester was not lying," I feel that even the possibility should not have been raised: Chester became a debauchee, but not, I feel certain, a thief.

Farnan describes Chester's behavior straightforwardly, supporting her narrative with reports from other witnesses, and seldom pronouncing direct moral judgment. Her account suggests, though the verdicts are not always spelled out, that Chester was a sociopathological personality, parasitical, irresponsible, selfish, spoiled, promiscuous, incapable of self-discipline or restraint. On the question of his financial dependence on Auden, and his taking this for granted, Farnan cites Mary Valentine, the closest to Chester of his female friends at the time: "I resented Auden, because I believed that [he] wanted Chester to be dependent on him." Most such dependencies are mutual, of course, but this is not true of Chester's exploitation of Auden's love for him. Long before the end,

> Wystan had reached that point at which he was willing to endure Chester's infidelity, his petulance, his periodic black depressions, . . . his often unwise choice of friends . . . as long as Chester remained at his side.

Farnan is more indulgent of Chester's sexual predatoriness than some readers might be, especially when it begins to override any consideration for the welfare of its objects. He seems to have confused love and sexual gratification in his last, comparatively enduring, affair with the young Greek, Yannis Boras (a practicing heterosexual like the others, Auden excepted), which can be said because Boras seems not to have been able to simulate any reciprocity of Chester's feelings. Moreover, Chester bequeathed his (*i.e.* Auden's) estate to Boras, apparently indifferent to the irony that this heir was ignorant of the poet and even of the language in which he wrote. Here, not for the first time, the reader is tempted to blame Auden for abdicating responsibility.

As it happened, Boras predeceased (1968) both Auden and Kallman. After Auden's death (1973), Kallman, who had not recovered from the first loss, lived only sixteen months, in a state of alcoholic *non compos mentis*. He squandered and mislaid—and was robbed by male prostitutes—the money received from Auden, and, through carelessness, or inadvertence, lost Auden's house in Austria. Thirteen days after Kallman's death, Farnan married his father and became the ultimate beneficiary. In the final chapter, "Last Days in Athens," she seems to be more appalled by the material waste than saddened by the human one.

Chester Kallman's mother died when he was four. His father remarried, and his stepmother was mean, even cruel to him. He hated this "simple," "pedestrian," "unimaginative," "intensely jealous" woman "until the day she died," Farnan writes, admitting that this is Chester's "side of the story." In any case, "mothers," Auden wrote to Kallman (December 25, 1941), "have much to do with your queerness and mine." Yet a mother is what Auden became after their short, initial period as lovers. In the letters, Auden refers to himself as "your mother," and in actuality he behaved like an overly apolaustic one, forever giving in, coming to the rescue, fretting about his feckless "daughter's" every need.

Farnan's chronicle of the Kallman family and of Chester's early years is largely new. So is her portrait of the precocious and personally appealing eighteen-year-old Brooklyn College student who bewitched the thirty-two-year-old poet (New York, April 1939), and of the slightly older student at Ann Arbor, who, like someone out of *La Cage aux folles*, would spend "the entire day before the prom taking foam baths and putting on mudpacks." Farnan is no less informative about the subsequent years in New York and on Fire Island, by which time Kallman had become the personal and artistic confidante of the spokesman—first-person-plural—poet of the age. Was Chester's rise too rapid? Was it, as Farnan speculates, that "now that he had Wystan, he had all the fruits of fame without the work it entailed"? Except that work alone cannot make a poet, my answer would be that Chester suffered from the reflected glory more than he basked in it.

Chester saw himself "as a victim of Wystan's fame: 'They think I can't do it on my own,'" Farnan quotes him as saying. The statement is revealing in an unintended way. Did Kallman actually regard himself as a poet of promise handicapped by the overshadowing figure of Auden? I believe, rather, that Kallman was perfectly aware of the insignificance of his powers compared to Auden's, and that only this can explain, as manifestations of subconscious envy, the humiliations to which the younger man continually subjected the older. Some of the symptoms are that Kallman was much too sensitive to the lack of recognition accorded his poems, as well as too bitter about writers he thought overrated—Lowell, for one, especially after he received a grant to study and report on aspects of opera in America, Chester's private preserve. And Chester was tormented by jealousies. Christopher Isherwood was one target of them: "That's an Isherwood remark," Chester would say of any comment that he suspected of being booby-trapped. Farnan reveals that "Keith Callaghan" was another, not as a rival for Auden's affections or esteem, but because of the fear of the interloper's possible ascendancy over him.

Kallman's inclusion as a collaborator on *The Rake's Progress* was the happiest event of his life. Here he merged with Auden so completely that only the two of them could say for certain which member of the coalition had written what. Moreover, Auden's colleagues believed that he probably would not have undertaken the libretto by himself, since his interest in opera was inseparable from his interest in Kallman, and since Kallman understood the structure of the Mozartian-Italian libretto that Stravinsky required. Though fond of Kallman and fully appreciative of his talents, Stravinsky could have worked alone with Auden who had written in praise of "metrical rules" that forbade "automatic responses" and offered freedom "from the fetters of self." Farnan writes that at the American premiere of *The Rake*, in February 1953,

> Chester and Wystan took their bow along with the brightly costumed singers on the stage of the beloved Old Met, and all the diamond horseshoe applauded. For Chester it was a dream come true.

Unfortunately, the later operas were failures musically, and the libretto of the most ambitious of them, *The Bassarids*, is dramatically convoluted and unmanageably baroque. Of the Auden-Kallman opera translations, that of *The Magic Flute*, which could have been the most useful, does not fit the music. For only one example, the English syllables in Papageno's first song outnumber the German and destroy Mozart's phrasing, besides which the itinerant bird-seller's vocabulary makes him sound like an ornithologist.

Of the lovers referred to by aliases and introduced by the footnote "not his real name," the identity of "Keith Callaghan" is the least carefully disguised. Farnan tells us that he was a Juilliard student (he wasn't) who played the violin, which is somewhat too close to his real instrument, the cello. (I mention this for the reason that when Auden invited me to meet "Callaghan" after a concert I had conducted in Town Hall, October 22, 1949, I found Auden utterly transformed—unrecognizably jovial and horribly solicitous.) "Callaghan" now confirms that Auden's sexual preferences were oral ("I don't think Wystan was interested in anal sex"), gives his timing ("about one half-hour"), and provides other performance details (he did not want "to cuddle . . . for hours"). Farnan supplements this with a remark from a 1948 Auden-to-Kallman letter: "Deciding that there ought to be [a pornographic poem] in the Auden Corpus, I am writing . . . *The Platonic Blow*. You should do one on the other Major Act."

Auden in Love is a contribution to the homosexual history, 1940s to 1960s, of the United States, Italy, Austria, Greece, and en route. The book defines the beginning of the period with the story of Auden applying for a job at the University of Michigan and telling the assembled dean, chairman, and professors: "I am queer, you know. I like boys." "If faces fell at this," Farnan writes, "it was not because they did not know . . . They just did not expect him to say it out loud." Later she says that Auden's 1948–52 letters to Kallman in Ischia convey

> the tone of the . . . relationship more than any other source . . . One glimpses through them the conversations Wystan and Chester must have had when they were alone together. With Chester, Auden did

> not need to strike an attitude . . . With Chester he was most truly himself.

What might disconcert some readers is the lavishing of terms of endearment—"my angel," "sweetie," "darling," "I adore you," "*tanti baci*"—as well as Auden's habit of referring to Kallman as "miss" and to himself as female ("You do keep a girl on edge," "You ask a lot of a girl in my present whirl").

Mother figures excepted, Auden was uncomfortable in the society of most women. I remember an evening in his New York apartment (March 2, 1958) with Margaret Mead and Danilo Dolci, when an English girl, traveling with Dolci as a translator, casually helped her skirt to stray above her knee-length stocking. Chester was amused—"I haven't seen so much thigh on that couch since the paratrooper last month"—but Wystan was mortified and scarcely able to control his indignation. Chester enjoyed female company as much as male, a difference in temperament that extended to other tastes as well. Yet Auden's affair with Rhoda Jaffe is believable, while rumors of Chester's affairs with women are not. "Most of Chester's friends who knew his sexual habits would have found such a revelation incredible," Farnan states and Mary Valentine corroborates.

The strangest incident of the Ischia decade is Auden's invitation to the Gestalt psychologist Wolfgang Köhler and his wife to stay in the house as paying guests. Wystan asked Chester to evict his friend Bill Aalto during the visit. This left the housekeeper, Giocondo—like Lulu's lovers in Dr. Schön's residence in Berlin, Chester's included the servants—and, according to Farnan, a prototype Boy George, with a hemp wig and false eyelashes. Whether because of him or the living conditions, the Köhlers soon left. Farnan justifiably wonders:

> How [Wystan] could have invited this very conventional . . . couple . . . to share a house . . . where the plumbing was crude and the electricity almost non-existent—managed by Chester, of all people, staggers the imagination . . . Did he not, after [more than] ten years' close association with Chester, know him better than to expect things to run smoothly?

Farnan might have told us something about the guardian-angel role of Lincoln Kirstein, who brought about the collaboration with Balanchine, secured commissions (including the one for the translation of *The Seven*

Deadly Sins), and delivered and collected Wystan at airports. But she does provide an accurate portrait of David Protetch, "the young man who was to become the physician of Auden and Stravinsky." Protetch was actually one of the three doctors attending the composer in New York and then only in the summers of 1957–61; in the following year, Protetch's request to accompany Stravinsky as personal physician on his forthcoming trip to the USSR and to observe drug abuse there, brought the relationship to an end. Anticipating complications—David's office on East Seventy-seventh Street was a kind of halfway house for homosexual junkies—the composer curtly refused. Six years later, Protetch impulsively married a drug-addicted patient whom he mistakenly believed he could cure, and a year later he and she were dead.

David and Chester were competitive friends in their devotion to opera—long after the final curtain of *La Gioconda* they would go on shouting "*Brava* Zinka [Milanov]"—in their pathological self-destructiveness, and in their relationships with the Stravinskys. Wystan accused David of subverting Chester's friendship with the composer and his wife, but the truth is simply that David had the means to chauffeur them around New York, and that Stravinsky was unduly susceptible to doctors (and lawyers and concert agents) who exchanged "free" professional service for such social favors as accepting dinner and theater invitations. David made almost daily house calls to give Stravinsky vitamin injections.

Farnan substantially adds to Auden folklore, though her version of the acceptance of the 1937 Gold Medal for Poetry from King George VI omits the part that Auden liked best, the reaction of his cabby when given the address: "Buckingham Palace." She repeats "Callaghan's" vignette of Auden "At Town Hall reciting his poems and blowing his nose into his hand" (a story I can vouch for, the reading having been part of my March 26, 1949 concert there). From the later New York years, she quotes one of his letters to a friend in Greenland: "How I envy you at this time [December] up there in total darkness," and describes his retiring at 9 o'clock with a plate of boiled potatoes and a bottle of wine on the floor next to his bed. The squalor of the Twenty-third Street and St Mark's Place apartments inspires set pieces:

> . . . the same dust . . . the same kind of anonymous makeshift furniture . . . bought second-hand from a Lower East Side flea market or the Salvation Army . . . Either the drains were clogged or the toilet would not flush; either a window would not open or an electrical socket had gone dead . . .

> Someone, probably Chester, frequently used the kitchen curtains to wipe the grease off his hands. No one ever bothered to clean the kitchen floor, take out the empty bottles, or pack up the garbage.

One hopes that the inevitable "Collected Eccentricities" does not neglect Auden the good citizen who always voted and obliged his friends to do the same, did not shirk jury duty, responded regularly to calls to donate blood, kept his telephone number in the book, and contributed generously to charities.

Among the errors and omissions that should be rectified in future editions, one might begin with the description of Sir William Walton as a "tourist" in Ischia (actually his permanent home), or point out that Chester and Wystan did not "return to New York after the premiere of *The Rake's Progress* in Venice." Chester remained in Europe until 1952. But the chronology is confused in other places as well. Farnan has Chester arriving in New York for the last time on December 29, 1972 (actually 1971), attending a New Year's Eve party at his father's, and a "day or so" later announcing his intention of going back to Greece. "The next day [he] returned to Athens." In fact he came to dinner at Vera Stravinsky's on January 11, which I mention because he telephoned her on the day of Wystan's death, twenty months later. (Wystan had always loved her, even given her English lessons and guided her reading—to the novels of George MacDonald, for instance—and on March 25 he had taken the trouble to write to her: "This is just to say that you will be very much in my thoughts on the 6th," the anniversary of Stravinsky's death.) Farnan duly notes Auden's farewell birthday party at the Coffee House, New York, February 21, 1972, and his departure for Europe on April 15, but not his poetry reading in mid-March at the State University of New York at New Paltz, arranged by Irving Weiss.

Other omissions include any reference to the Holliday Bookshop fire which destroyed Auden's notebooks (he had been accustomed to leaving them there during trips abroad); to Kallman's translation of *The Nightingale*; and to *Delia*, in the list of Auden-Kallman libretti (p. 191)—to which I call attention out of pride in the authors' inscription "To Bob, with love pure as the driven snow."

Amorous in Amherst

Polly Longsworth's *Austin and Mabel*,[1] which includes more than 250 of the one thousand or so extant love letters between Emily Dickinson's brother and Mrs. David Todd, is one of the most explosive books ever published about social and sexual mores in nineteenth-century America. Not surprisingly, its scandalous revelations have been ignored by protective Emily-ites. Richard B. Sewall, the poet's principal biographer, is an exception: "Since it happened so close to Emily Dickinson, it is important."

Almost none of the publications timed to the centenary of Dickinson's death discusses the Mabel and Austin episode, and few even mention it. Cynthia Griffin Wolff,[2] not naming Longsworth's book, issues the verdict that "this all-too-well documented love affair" is "entirely irrelevant save for one fact: Mabel Loomis Todd played a crucial role in getting Emily Dickinson's poems into print." (*The* role, surely, since Mabel accurately transcribed the poems from the manuscripts, a feat in itself, and persuaded her by-no-means convinced co-editor, T.W. Higginson, of their worth.) Precisely because, as Wolff writes, Dickinson's biography offers so little "in the way of striking occurrence," her brother's liaison has to have been a larger episode in her life than it would have been in almost anyone else's.

Sewall goes on to say that the diary of Millicent Todd Bingham, Mabel's daughter, takes us farther:

"The effect on Emily? She was glad that Austin had found some comfort after his all but ruined life. In my mother's words, 'Emily always respected real emotion.'" "Some comfort," translated, amounts to twelve crowded years of sexual intercourse. But the statement was

---

1 *Austin and Mabel. The Amherst Affair & Love Letters of Austin Dickinson and Mabel Loomis Todd*. New York, 1984.

2 *Emily Dickinson*. New York, 1986.

written sixty-five years after Emily Dickinson's death, and it was Bingham herself who for so long suppressed the Austin-Mabel correspondence.

Sewall also assures us of the solid basis for Longsworth's comment that "The Dickinson sisters were not only aware of their brother's intimacy with Mabel, they were accessory to it." No supporting evidence is offered, however, either here or in connection with the claims that "Emily, fully aware of what was occurring in her house, rejoiced in Austin's renewed happiness," and that "dozens of notes exchanged attest to Emily and Mabel's mutual affection." At least one such note might have been vouchsafed, especially since, in the only one given, Emily greets Mabel as "Brother's and Sister's Friend," not as her own. Of the fewer than a dozen published communications from Emily to Mabel, five are single sentences or incomplete sentences and only two can be called letters.

Mabel was determined to meet Emily. After playing the piano and singing in the Dickinson Homestead, September 10, 1882, Mabel wrote: "Miss Emily in her weird white dress was outside in the shadow hearing every word . . . I know I shall see her." She did not see her until, four years later, Emily was in her weird white casket. That Mabel asked Austin to arrange a meeting can be safely inferred, partly because it is in Mabel's character to do so and, the more concrete part, because of a remark in her journal: "No one has seen her in all these years except her own family." Austin would have had to give this untruthful excuse, since Emily received the people she wished to receive. After December 13, 1883, a face-to-face encounter would have been unthinkable, but the reasons for Emily's refusal before that date can only be conjectured. Did she sense that worldly, gregarious, self-assured, literary-dabbling Mabel was her exact opposite?

On that December 13, Austin Dickinson, fifty-four, married for twenty-six years and the father of three, became the lover of Mabel Loomis Todd, thirty years younger, married for four years and the mother of Millicent. The consummation took place in Emily's and her sister Lavinia's dining room, in which Emily sometimes wrote. The diaries of Austin and Mabel reveal that their extra-marital rites were repeated thereafter about twelve times a month, then somewhat less frequently from 1886 until Austin's death in 1895. The testimony of Maggie Maher, the sisters' housekeeper, in Lavinia's 1896 lawsuit against the Todds, places a higher estimate on the number of rendezvous and adds that they took place "sometimes in the afternoon and sometimes in the fore-noon

. . . Sometimes for three or four hours just as their consciences allowed them." (Who said anything about consciences?)

On two occasions, Maggie apparently stumbled on the pair *in flagrante delicto*. Why Austin's wife, Susan, never did the same can only be attributed to fear of her husband and to the powerlessness of a wife at the time. Susan rarely crossed the yard from her home, the Evergreens, to the Homestead, only a few hundred feet away, but to enter or leave the latter unobserved from the window of the former must have been even more difficult a century ago than it is today. Guarded by Emily and Lavinia, the Homestead dining room was to remain the scene of the assignations, except for Austin's carriage during a fair-weather turn in the great outdoors, and, when his and Mabel's spouses were away—and for a time when hers was not—in each other's houses. Even before the love affair was consummated, Emily wrote, perhaps not entirely without irony: "My brother is with us so often each Day, one almost forgets he passed to a wedded Home."

The correspondence monotonously supports the true-love view of the affair as well as its—what Yeats said the worst of us are full off—passionate intensity. But Mabel's diary, which also records her continuing, some eight-times-a-month, cohabitation with her husband, David, blights any aura of romance, at least for non-Mormon readers. Since she usually confined her sexual activity to the "safe" last ten days of her menstrual cycle, Mabel was perforce entertaining both men on several of the same days. Longsworth straight-facedly calls attention to Mabel's "energetic physical commitment," but does not elaborate on her remark that Mabel's diary—destined, no doubt, to appear in a lurid paperback with preface by Peter Gay—is less specific about lovemaking with Austin than with David. Nor are particulars given of arrangements in the Homestead dining room (was the table used, or would this have inhibited the saying of grace at mealtimes?), except that the pious lovers recited a prayer in unison.[1]

"Home is a Holy Thing," Emily once wrote to Austin, and "nothing of doubt or distrust can enter its sacred portals." Lares and penates. Love, moreover, must be "consecrated," and laws obeyed. "We die, said the Deathless of Thermopylae, in obedience to the Law." So Emily wrote to

---

[1] After 1875, "meals were eaten in the kitchen, or at a little table set up in the hallway," Mrs Longsworth wrote to me, May 12, 1987. The same letter reveals that "in winter, when the parlors were closed off, the dining room, with its couch, fireplace and desk, became a sort of winter parlor handy to the kitchen."

Mabel, after brother and brother's friend had broken the Seventh Commandment, upheld by law, society, religion, and private moral codes.

At a precocious age Mabel had discovered that she "was born with a certain lack of something in my moral nature." She was quick to recognize, as well, that her "strength & attractive power & magnetism" were "enough to fascinate a room full of people." In addition to being a talented painter, actress in amateur theatricals, musician—she had studied at the New England Conservatory—Mabel was endowed with a sense of literary discernment, perhaps cultivated by her father, who had known Thoreau and Whitman. She read and she wrote, publishing short stories and accounts of her travels—she was the first woman to climb Mt. Fujiyama. Whereas Emily, in Washington, D.C. with her Congressman father, avoided every social function, Mabel, thirty years later, was a hostess at a reception in Chester A. Arthur's White House.

Unlike Mabel, Austin had no inkling of his sister's genius. Said to be Emily's "closest confidant" ("Tho *all others* do, yet *I* will not forsake thee," she wrote to him, but what did she foresee as provocations from the others?), he nevertheless wrote irritably to Mabel, when she was about to leave for Boston in connection with the publication of Emily's poems, inquiring what she meant by "the poems" and dismissing them as of "no consequence." And when Emily was grieving over the death of her friend Judge Otis Lord, Mabel, but not Austin, seems to have had compunctions about using the dining room. Still, Austin must be believed when, expressing reservations about the publication of Emily's letters, he said that she "posed" in some of them.

Barton Levi St. Armand's chapter[1] on Austin as an art collector reveals that his father, Edward Dickinson, while executor of his brother-in-law's estate, "loaned" himself more than enough from the trust to pay for expensive renovations in his own house and to construct a new one for his son. As St. Armand says, Dickinson *père* played "fast and loose" with his sister's money. Or call it extortion. Longsworth's statement that Edward Dickinson "had the most irreproachable"—like most unique?—"record in the region" only indicates what the region did not know.

Austin bequeathed half of his patrimony to Mabel but instead of making the gift part of his will relied on Lavinia to carry out his wishes—this after he had described her to Mabel as "utterly slippery and

---

[1] *Emily Dickinson and Her Culture: The Soul's Society*. Cambridge, 1986.

treacherous"—evidently failing to realize that his death would unleash his wife's vindictiveness toward Mabel and that families in such situations traditionally close ranks against the outsider. Lavinia went back on her word—and on her promise to burn Mabel's letters to him—then relented to the extent of giving Mabel and David a plot of Dickinson land, whereupon Susan convinced her to sue the Todds on grounds that they had obtained her signature on the deed by misrepresentation and fraud. The Todds lost the trial, Mabel unaccountably failing to produce Austin's note to her confirming his intentions, but the Dickinsons lost too, morally, for Lavinia repeatedly perjured herself.

Dickinson biographers agree that Susan became "spiteful" with age, which raises the question of whether Austin might in some way have contributed to this unhappy development. Before the inaugural date in the dining room, Mabel said that "Susan stimulates me intellectually more than any woman I ever knew," but soon after, disappointed that Susan did not surrender as David had done, prayed for her demise. Emily, as well, held Susan's intellect in good opinion and, over the years, sent her nearly 300 poems. Longsworth classifies Emily's communications to Susan as "love letters" that "do not far exceed"—*i.e.*, they exceed, nevertheless—"the nineteenth-century tolerance for intimacy between unmarried females." But to form a firm impression of Susan is as difficult as Emily's unflattering verse about her warns:

> *To pity those that know her not*
> *Is helped by the regret*
> *That those who know her, know her less*
> *The nearer her they get.*

David Todd, the oddest character of the quadrangle, a direct descendant of Jonathan Edwards and of the New England of scarlet letters, was perversely, perhaps kinkily, acquiescent, even taking into account a history of mental illness in his mother's family. (Like her, he was eventually institutionalized.) During the last three days of the countdown to December 13, he and Mabel decided together that she would become Austin's mistress. David may have been concerned about his tenure as professor of astronomy at Amherst College, where Austin was all-powerful, but the main consideration was that as a philanderer himself, during as well as before his marriage, he was not in a position to insist on the fidelity of his spouse. Mabel noted in a journal of 1890 that he was capable of "falling immensely in love" and of "having a piquant time of it." Three years earlier he had begun to receive other women in the Todd home, and he once used "lustful language" in a letter to one of them that he failed to seal so that Mabel could read it—which somewhat redeemingly suggests that he might have been jealous.

When the Todds moved into a new house in the autumn of 1885, Mabel and Austin made love there on ten or more Sundays (celebrating black mass?) in the presence of, as Austin recorded, "a witness," who could only have been David. A few months earlier, while Mabel was in Europe and the two grass widowers were constantly together, Austin wrote to her—his letters to her were addressed to David to thwart post office gossip—"I think we three would have no trouble in a house together in living as you and I should wish." David seems not to have objected to Mabel wearing Austin's wedding ring on her right hand. Like his wife and her lover, he kept a diary, a record of his masturbations.

* * *

The Homestead today is "one of this country's landmarks," Wolff's book begins, but Emily Dickinson's bedroom

> is unrefurbished with the lingering personality of its former occupant. It is something of a puzzle . . . that so many readers regard this House almost as a holy place, making the trek to western Massachusetts as if to a saint's shrine . . . What they ask about is seldom the work. They want to know about the *woman.*

Is the literary persona not related to the woman who created it, despite artists paring fingernails and poetry as an escape from personality, despite the gap between human frailty and the strength of art, mortality and immortality?

And what is so puzzling about the pilgrimage? The Dickinson story, as Wolff herself says, "seems to have become central to American life." And though the poet's ever-ascending reputation has already overtaken those of every other great American writer, Wolff's own landmark book, showing that the poems lend themselves to depths, and sometimes merely to tangles, of interpretation, indicates that appreciation is still at a comparatively early stage. Feminist critics are clearly not finished with a poet who, conquering the barrier against women ("America is now wholly given over to a d----d mob of scribbling women," Hawthorne wrote in 1855), identifying with female novelists and poets, female nature and female love, is a legitimate feminist cause;[1] and more will be said, as well, by historians of modernism, for as Oscar Williams and other anthologists of modern poetry understood as long ago as the 1940s, she may have been the first of the movement, while transcending it.

If Dickinson's "personality" does not haunt her bedroom, the visitor there can still divine her physical presence. The white dress displayed in a glass case, now as much a part of American lore as Melville's white whale, is even smaller than expected from her own and other people's descriptions: "I have a little shape"; "I am . . . small, like the Wren"; "A little plain woman . . . in a clean white piqué"; "A tiny figure in white." Whether she began to wear white after her father's death, or because of a religious association—the multitude in white "who stood before the throne in Revelation" (Wolff); white was the dress "of her inner 'Calvary' drama of renunciation" (Northrop Frye)—she considered it the proper attire for death:

This sufferer polite—
Dressed to meet you
See—in white.

Some perspectives of Dickinson's solitary existence can be experienced in her bedroom, too, in the west window view toward the Evergreens and, on the south side, Main Street, where once "a circus passes the house. Still I feel the red in my mind." (She might have been taking mescaline.) The poignancy of her life as a recluse is most intensely felt at the sight in one of the window sills of a small basket with a string for lowering her gingerbread and cookies to her niece and other children. By 1876, Emily "looked ill . . . white and mothlike," from "living away from the sunlight," as Helen Hunt Jackson told her during a visit.

Wolff regards Dickinson's reclusiveness as both unexceptional and of little significance. There were precedents, she says, and in support quotes George Whicher's *This Was a Poet*: "[Reclusiveness] has always been a possible way of life for New England spinsters." (As well as for J.D. Salinger, Thomas Pynchon, and countless others far from there.) Moreover, Emily and Lavinia could, in the monetary sense, "afford not to marry," and, unmarried, they "would not have to confront the rigors of childbearing"—as if to remain single were strictly a matter of choice.

---

[1] See *Emily Dickinson* by Helen McNeil. London, 1986.

Susan's obituary for Emily in the *Springfield Republican* suggests that their Amherst contemporaries did not see the self-sequestration as ordinary, otherwise her "seclusion," Susan's word, need not have been mentioned and excused. By attributing it to "the rare mesh of her soul" and to "the realization that the sacred quiet of her own home proved the fit atmosphere for her worth and work," Susan may have been trying to bury speculation about nervous or mental illnesses ("the mad woman in the attic"). Amherst residents who had glimpsed the ghostly woman in white apparently writing by candlelight next to her window must have wondered about the nature of the work. If tongues wagged that "the intimacy existing between [Austin] and Mrs. Todd is as great as ever," they must also have talked about Emily's eccentricities. Almost no one, after all, knew that she was a poet.

Emily was no longer "a regular churchgoer" by 1867–68, Wolff tells us, even though Emily seems to have stopped being a churchgoer at all at a still earlier date. Her absence from her father's funeral disturbed her niece: "And where was Aunt Emily? Why did she not sit in the library with the family . . .?" That Emily did not appear at her mother's funeral can be established from the fact of her invitation to Mabel to attend.

Dickinson seems to have been withdrawing from society—"Society for me my misery"—as early as July 1853: "I sat in Professor Tyler's woods and saw the train off and then ran home again for fear somebody would see me." This suggests a physical stigma, blemish or disfigurement, as does her habit of talking to guests from behind a partly closed door or from the top of the stairs; psychological roots and causes are more apparent in later years, in, for example, her wish to have her letters addressed in someone else's handwriting. But whatever it was, including an experience that exceeds the known facts, *something* had happened to this 22-year-old girl who had been socially active only shortly before—"Amherst is alive with fun this winter," she wrote in 1850—participating in church gatherings and cooking contests, attending lectures and concerts. Yet before the end of the decade, she wrote that "someone rang the bell and I ran, as is my custom." A prison, as she said, "gets to be a friend."

Recent analysis of the daguerreotype portrait of the teenage Dickinson[1] indicates that she suffered from divergent strabismus (right

---

[1] See "Eyes Be Blind, Heart Be Still," by Sewall and Dr Martin Wand in *The New England Quarterly*, Fall 1979: "Dickinson frequently wrote by candlelight; sometimes a line would go off the page, as if she were writing in the dark."

exotropia), a congenital condition of the eye more prevalent in women than in men: her mother and sister were also afflicted but less severely than the estimated 15° deviation in Emily. Wolff mentions the diagnosis, but not that the Boston ophthalmologist Henry Williard Williams, whose patient Emily became in 1864 and 1865, had written papers on the subject, and not in connection with the reclusiveness but solely in relation to the "eye contact deprivation" that is one of Wolff's theories about the far from perfect relationship between the infant Emily and her mother. The seven-month length of Emily's first Boston visit—she stayed with her cousins in a Cambridge boarding house—is astonishing in the light of her unhappiness and homesickness nine years earlier during the few weeks with her father and sister in Washington.[1] Quite apart from what happened in Boston—her doctor asked her not to write (only ten letters represent the entire period) and even not to walk alone—the extended time there must have been traumatic.[2]

No biographer, not even St. Armand in his comprehensive treatment of the sun and sunset poems, seems to have attached any significance to the lines

Before I got my eye put out—
With just my soul—
Upon the window pane—
Where other Creatures put their eyes—
Incautious—of the sun—

But if Dickinson was walleyed, or had some other very evident eye impairment, why did Austin not mention it to Mabel, and the poet herself to T.W. Higginson in that first letter, as well known now as any of her poems, in which she mentions the color of her eyes? Clara Green, who saw her in 1877, wrote that "We were chiefly aware of a pair of great dark eyes set in a small, pale, delicately chiselled face and a little body." Whatever the other factors behind Dickinson's withdrawal, the decisive one is that her creative genius required it.

---

[1] *Emily Dickinson: Letter to the World*, published by the Folger Shakespeare Library, establishes the dates of Dickinson's arrival in Washington and visit to the National Gallery. The booklet also includes a fascinating account of railroad travel from New York to Washington in 1855, and a beautiful poem by Richard Wilbur.

[2] After the second visit she wrote to a friend: "a woe, the only one that ever made me tremble . . . was the shutting out of all the dearest ones of time, the strongest friends of the soul—BOOKS."

Was Dickinson a "Puritan to the last," as Northrop Frye believed? Wolff's well-documented argument is that by 1850 the Puritan tradition had been supplanted by Unitarianism, Revivalism, and the Trinitarian belief in "natural theology" that dominated the academic milieu to which the young Emily belonged. However this may be, the reader is obliged to accept Wolff's conclusion that Dickinson sought "a true covenant of faith . . . not in . . . Christianity, but in . . . the passion between a man and a woman," both because Dickinson herself says so

The Sweetest Heresy received
That Man and Woman know
Each other's Covenant
Though the Faith accommodate but Two—

and because no other explanation can account for the secrets of the dining room in the Tanglewood tale of Mabel and Austin.

"The Bible was the text she most consistently sought to undermine," Wolff goes on. Not "the Bible," one thinks, but its unreliable Christ

I say to you, said Jesus—
That there by standing here—
A Sort, that shall not taste of Death—
If Jesus was sincere—

and vindictive, arbitrary, even cowardly God, who, after wrestling with Jacob at Peniel,"retreated from us forever rather than risk combat again." The upside of this is that "Dickinson was deeply moved by the fact that God, in apparent humility, had elected to become one of us" ("When Christ was divine, he was uncontented till he had been human"). By the mid-1860s or early 1870s a "poetry of faith had emerged." Looking back, "the poetry described a long pilgrimage to faith."

The first critic to engage the larger structure of the poet's imagination, Wolff is also good on American history, medical history (pre-anaesthetic childbirth), social history, and Dickinson family history, in which she explores the psychological relationships more thoroughly than any predecessor. Finally, she succeeds, on her own lofty terms, in baring the "dynamic of Dickinson's interior life that infused her poetry with power and passes through the verse to readers."

Dickinson's preoccupation with death has been dismissed as a "natural compliment of an intense love of life." It is more than that, an obsession not found to the same extent in other intensely life-loving poets. Death, the deep Stranger, is her abiding theme, the overwhelmingly predominant one both in frequency of references and in the inspiration of some of her greatest poetry. Her vocation for dying began at an early age—

I noticed people disappearing
When but a little child—

She wrote conventional verse about it, even nodding toward *Cymbeline*,

This quiet Dust was Gentlemen and Ladies
And Lads and Girls—
Was laughter and ability and Sighing
And Frocks and Curls

observed details of burial ceremonies,

And even when with Cords
'Twas lowered like a Weight—

and wondered

Do People moulder equally,
They bury, in the Grave?

She knew the pain of loss: "Father does not live with us now—he lives in a new house. Though it was built in an hour it is better than this. He hasn't any garden because he moved after gardens were made, so we take him the best flowers, and if we only knew he knew, perhaps we could stop crying." She rehearsed her own dying

To die—takes but a little while—
They say it doesn't hurt—
It's only fainter—by degrees—
And then—it's out of sight—

and recognized the sensation of it

A Wounded Deer—leaps highest—
I've heard the Hunter tell—
'Tis but the Ecstacy of death—

You'll find it—when you try to die—
The easier to let go—

She knew that death and love go together: "*is* there more? More than Love and Death? Then tell me its name."

If just as soon as Breath's out
It shall belong to me

. . .

Think of it Lover! I and thee
Permitted—face to face to be—

But the greatest of her poems of death are those from the other side,[1] from within the upholstered coffin with the "rafter of satin—and roof of stone," in the quiet of the tomb:

Let no Sunrise' yellow noise
Interrupt this Ground—

Here is absolute genius of the word:

I died for Beauty—but was scarce
Adjusted in the Tomb
When One who died for Truth was lain
In an adjoining Room

. . .

And we talked between the Rooms
Until the Moss had reached our Lips

And here the persona of the poem and the persona of the poet unite, the mortal Emily Dickinson in her white dress and white casket—Higginson said that the fifty-five-year-old looked no more than thirty, her face without a wrinkle, head without a grey hair—carried "through the grass field to the family plot" by the six Irish retainers who had worked at the Homestead:

'Twas just this time last year, I died
I know I heard the Corn
When I was carried by the Farms

---

[1] See St. Armand, *op.cit.*, on Harriet Prescott Spofford's "I Must Have Died at Ten Minutes Past One."

PAINTERS

Munch in the Movies

The Norwegian film *Edvard Munch*[1] succeeds brilliantly in portraying the painter's apparent diffidence, impassivity, and failure to respond appropriately. He remains a silent observer during discussions in which others react with animation and spontaneity, thereby provoking the incidental thought that not many protagonists in three-hour films can have so few lines to learn or a smaller histrionic range to display than the actor who plays the painter. Successful, too, is the footage, about a third of the whole, devoted to the artist's childhood and to the harsh pieties and gruesome maladies of the Munch family. The scenes of the artist's consumptive sister frothing blood at the mouth, and of his own pulmonary hemorrhage at age fifteen, convince the viewer that the blood-smeared skies in *Anxiety* and *The Scream* are related to these traumatic experiences.

Whenever Munch's biography provides an opportunity for dramatization, the film does so effectively. Thus Munch's beliefs that he was "subject to unusual persecution"—one pathetic diary entry expresses the hope that a particular enemy "doesn't imagine that I take any notice of him"—and that the critics were in league against him, have been adroitly transposed to the screen. In one scene he enters an Oslo gallery where people are laughing at his pictures, and in the street afterward he hears himself called "fake painter" by the most esteemed artist of the day. His symptoms are the psychotic ones of a paranoid type schizophrenic characterized, in Arieti's terminology, by "unrealistic, illogical, hallucinatory thinking, and by bizarre delusions of being persecuted." In fact, Arieti's instance of paranoid hallucination might have been suggested by *The Scream*: "The individual [reports] 'voices' that no one else seems to hear, but the 'reality' of which he accepts."

---

[1] Directed, and with English titles and narration, by Peter Watkins. Distributed by New York Films.

Writers on Munch are continually trying to relate his aberrations to his work but rarely to each other or to physical causes. Agoraphobia is evident in his treatment of space, in the way in which his crowds huddle together and close to buildings, and in the extreme foreground position of individual figures. Rycroft (*Anxiety and Neurosis*) believes that this phobia can be traced to excessive fears of reality, of death, of leaving the mother, and Munch was subject to all three. He was five when his mother died, an event he may have portrayed in the horrifying *The Dead Mother* (1901). The child in this etching, though dressed as a girl, could be Munch, and the woman's clenched hands at the sides of her face are reminiscent of the figure in *The Scream*.

Munch's narcissism undoubtedly originated in ego bruises dating from infancy and his mother's death. It developed rapidly when he began to exhibit his pictures, at which time it would have been a protective response to the feeling that his art was under attack. But the sense of persecution is balanced by the fascination with the face in the mirror. Like Schiele, the number of self-portraits, overt, hidden, incipient, transferred—the artist as John the Baptist, as the bisexual Sphinx—is proportionately among the highest in any artist's *catalogue raisonné*. Even as an old man, Munch was still painting his self-portrait in the nude. His self-absorption may be the most important fact about him, his breakdown having been the consequence, apart from other physical and parataxic causes, of his inability to see the world except as it pertained to himself.

Munch's terror of women was very real, as, at the same time, were his fantasies of masochistic abasement at their hands, shown in his symbolic use of Salome and Charlotte Corday. The fear of losing his identity in women is made explicit when the lips of his kissing couple form a single repulsive snout. He was obsessed, too, with women's long hair (*Young Girl on the Shore* and *Summer Night*), especially the threat of being drowned in its coils as in the waves of the sea. And a case can be made that he was a latent necrophiliac (*The Madonna*). Sir Kenneth Clark once wrote that "No doubt [Munch] had strange experiences with the opposite sex," which, surely, should be the other way around: "No doubt the opposite sex had some strange experiences with Munch."

To project and illuminate mental states is much easier than to show a great painter painting. Only once does the film attempt to present "Munch" in artistic action, and this amounts to no more than a few glimpses of him setting up his easel and posing a sitter, after which his pencil and brush make chipping and scratching sounds strangely like those of scaupers or incising tools. Perhaps out of frustration in this regard, the camera towards the end is allowed to stray to the lakes and forests of Norway, thereby betraying Munch's creed that nature and art are enemies.

But in general the film is less reliable on Munch's art than on his life. "Perspective vanishes from Munch's pictures," a narrator says, but it has not done so in those chosen to illustrate the statements. Other observations are questionable. *Is* Munch's early withdrawal into himself "signified by the veiled eyes in a *Self-Portrait*"? *Is The Sick Child* "the first great Expressionist picture in modern art"?

The film's researchers have uncovered new facts, one of them that part of Munch's color symbolism can be traced to the phrase in the *Iliad*, "Blue death closes the eyes," another that Munch was given naphtha injections to relieve his coughing spells and stridulous breathing, still another that Dagny Juell was the model for *The Madonna*. Most important, Munch's grandfather had syphilis, which could account for the paresis of another of the painter's sisters, and raise the likelihood of the same disease in the artist himself.

Egon and Alter Egons

Though known in the 1950s only to admirers of the Viennese Secession, the art of Egon Schiele would probably draw as well at the Metropolitan Museum today as "Van Gogh in Arles," and for some of the same reasons: the "romantically" premature death—Schiele at twenty-eight—and the "mad" intensity of the pictures.

The Schiele exhibition at the Ca' Pesaro, though smaller than the one in Munich in 1975, offered a denser concentration of masterpieces, one of which, a seminude of 1911, seems not to have been shown heretofore and apparently has never been reproduced.[1] But a comprehensive presentation of Schiele, one that would include the sketchbooks in the Albertina, the woodcuts and other graphic work, and all known photographs[2] of this artist who endowed the people in his pictures with his own postures and even physical features, has yet to be organized.

The Ca' Pesaro show did not enable the viewer to form an appreciation of the profound changes in Schiele's work during his last three years (1915–18), when the portraits became increasingly naturalistic, the irregularly undulating lines of the female nudes tending to be reduced to convex curves, and the color to uniformity. Too few late pictures were displayed, and those of all periods were grouped according to medium, a standard approach to Schiele but unhelpful for the chronological study of his development. Furthermore, Edith Schiele, the artist's wife, was represented in Venice by only one innocuous drawing. It is true that her role as a model was much less significant than that of Valerie Neuzil, the painter's mistress during the more fecund preceding period, 1911–14, but the 1915 picture of the seminude Edith embracing her spouse,[3] and his

---

[1] Plate 82 in *Egon Schiele* by Serge Sabarsky, the catalog of the exhibition (1984).

[2] Nebehay's *Egon Schiele* (Salzburg and Vienna, 1980) and Alessandra Comini's *Egon Schiele Portraits* (Berkeley, CA, 1975) contain the fullest photographic archive.

[3] Plate 87 in Rudolph Leopold's *Egon Schiele*, London, 1971.

powerful drawing of her as a dying woman, offset the comparatively tensionless portraits and are essential to an understanding of the artist's final period.

The catalog does not improve on its predecessors in the quality of color reproductions, and Rudolph Leopold's *Egon Schiele* of 1971 is still the superior album both in this regard and in intelligent commentary. To compare the reproductions of *Three Standing Women* (1918), one of the best-known pictures, in Sabarsky's catalog of the exhibition and in Leopold's book, is to juxtapose a pink beige picture with dark brown background and a yellowish beige one with light red patches on a background dominated by dark green; both are false, but the latter contains more of the original and is therefore useful as an aide-memoire. Throughout his book, Leopold candidly points to the shortcomings of its reproductions, even in uncolored soft-lead drawings that fail to convey the effects of the originals.

Scale is an obstacle in all art books, some miniatures and collages (Schwitters) excepted, but a Schiele bookshelf is an impossibility. The townscapes and landscapes cannot be reduced to page size because color alone does not provide sufficient differentiation in these flat-surface and generally crowded pictures. Moreover, many of Schiele's eerily deserted cities and countrysides were conceived horizontally, in "geological" layers: clouds, mountain peaks, green foothills, shingled roofs, windows, walls, lines of laundry, grass, a street, more grass on the other side—which is to say, below. But in Sabarsky's book, Schiele's oblong becomes a perfect square, with a corresponding vertical thrust. And when the reproduction does preserve the proportions, as in the March 1913 self-portrait with Frl. Neuzil, the shrinking to postcard size of this near-largest (70 × 240 cm) of Schiele's pictures drains it of the moods of the two figures, which is nearly everything.

Schiele's primary subject is the human body as sexual object. For centuries paintings of nudes were concerned largely with *morbidezza* and the stylizing-idealizing of female forms. Thus the shock when, *c.* 1910, Schiele focused on the genitalia, painting them red and further concentrating sight lines by mutilating the remaining anatomy, colored cadaverous greens and yellows. Furthermore, his most emphasized secondary sexual feature is pubic and underarm hair, tufted in females, frizzed in males.

As a rule, and so far as possible allowing for subjective differences in the spectator, erotic attraction in Schiele's women is in inverse ratio to the degree of undress, with the exception of his entwining, totally nude

Sapphic pairs. The seminudes with exotically colored hosiery (one of them with nipples in matching orange) and Félicien Rops garters are more provoking than the stark-naked ones, but less so than the women with skirts and petticoats lifted above spread, stockinged knees, revealing only small patches of flesh. By this token, the most "pornographic" picture is that of the *Cardinal and Nun*, in which everything is left to facial expressions, body positions, and viewers' imaginations, intromission being completely hidden beneath the garments of the lovers.

The strain of kneeling, crouching, twisting, stretching, writhing, and the other contortions that Schiele obliged his models to perform shows in their eyes, along with desire, acquiescence, fear, vacancy (during intercourse), all of which charge these scenes with immediacy. Here it might be said that Schiele's anxious lovers are at the extreme opposite from the smiling ones in Taoist paintings, or the choreographed copulating figures in Indian temple sculpture, playfully following a by-the-numbers Art of Love. "I believe that man must suffer from sexual torture as long as he is capable of sexual feelings," Schiele wrote.

The seminude of 1911 reproduced in Sabarsky's book reminds the viewer of Balthus: a young girl, with no undergarments, lies on her stomach, legs spread, skirt billowing above the waist. But the brilliant red, orange, yellow, and blue stripes of her skirt, like a corolla around the pistil of the lower body, is remote from Balthus or any other artist. The upper body is not perspectively related to the lower, which is true of some of Schiele's other recumbent figures, and this is not a mannerism but a fault—which may also be said of the simultaneous front and profile faces that do not integrate with the portraits as wholes. In one 1913 drawing of a copulating couple, the head of the straddling male might have been borrowed from Picasso.

Schiele suffered from "unconditional omnipotence," in the language of the ego psychology of his time, and the neurosis never seems to have entered any less extreme stage. Alessandra Comini[1] contends that his life was profoundly altered by his twenty-four-day incarceration in the spring of 1912, and that he saw himself thereafter as a martyr and social outcast. But surely he *always* saw himself that way, and his verbal and graphic record of the experience only confirms that it inflated his supremacy feelings still more. In one "De Profundis," in his prison diary, he sanely observes that "to be in control, to be ready to endure . . . is a self-evident

---

[1] *Schiele in Prison*. New York, 1973.

duty," and he demands of God whether He wishes to tolerate such an indignity to an artist. In the final entry, Schiele remarks triumphantly that "anyone who has not suffered as I have—how ashamed he will have to feel before me from now on."

Schiele's dandyism, narcissism, dependence on mirrors, high proportion of self-portraits (some of them as Saint Sebastian, Death, Joseph in *The Holy Family*), and the infantile fascination with his sexual parts (in one drawing of masturbation, he portrays his face as conventionally handsome) can only be described as morbid. But his compulsion to transpose his own head, hands, eyes, and poses to the people he painted sometimes requires a stronger word: in the 1910 *Baby*, for instance, in which the infant's arms terminate in Schiele's long, spidery fingers, the effect is macabre. No one, not the unborn Christ, not even Arnold Schoenberg, the portrait of whom, unlike Kokoschka's, captures the composer's personality as well as his likeness, seems to have escaped the grouping of the fingers—as most photographs show *him* doing.

Sabarsky quotes the late Erich Lederer, whom Schiele drew several times: "Of all the people I have known in my life Egon Schiele was the most normal." No artist of Schiele's stature is "normal," of course, but if the statement was intended to demythicize him, it has validity. For one thing, Schiele continued to function and to paint during his three years in the Austrian Army, apparently adjusting to the radical change in his personal life. For another, he was remarkably successful in the worldly way, attracting influential friends and patrons, quickly gaining recognition, exhibiting throughout Central and Northern Europe, and finding buyers for his work. In this he doubtless exploited the voyeurist element in his art: but he did not, in his lifetime—the time of Weininger, of Musil's Moosbrugger, of Wedekind's Lulu plays—feel the wrath of moral rectitude that descended on his work in the 1930s and 1940s.

The Balthus Boom

Balthus has not been represented to advantage in exhibitions limited to his oil paintings: the 1958 and 1961 Turin shows, three of the four shows at the Pierre Matisse Gallery (1938, 1957, 1962), and the "Exposition Balthus" in the Louvre in May 1966. The crucial sharing of the Museum of Modern Art in 1956 with Jackson Pollock, a tortoise-and-hare race of mid-twentieth-century art that is still being run, displayed paintings and drawings side-by-side. But this cannot have pleased the artist, whose notorious indifference to his drawings has not helped to promote them. *Pace* Balthus, some of the paintings are better understood when seen together with their preliminary drawings, even when these are finished works in themselves.

Similarly, the most popular publications about the artist either exclude the drawings, as in the monograph by Stanislas Klossowski de Rola,[1] Balthus's elder son, or, Jean Leymarie's option,[2] separate them, as if they were a mere sideshow to the development of the easel painter. Neither volume is satisfactory. Despite the publisher's claim, Stanislas Klossowski de Rola does not provide "a unique insight into the true aim and meaning of his father's work," but, rather, adds to the mystification. Leymarie, though indispensable as a source of information, lacks a critical point of view, which may account for his choosing to open his book with the 1933 version of *La Rue*. (It may be worth noting that Marcel Duchamp owned the vastly superior 1929 original.)

Professor Carandente[3] gets off to a bad start even sooner than M. Leymarie, thanks to the selection of *Three Apples and a Quince* for the cover. Like most of Balthus's fruit and flower compositions, this one is

---

[1] *Balthus*. New York/London, 1983.

[2] *Balthus*. New York, 1979.

[3] *Balthus: Drawings and Watercolors* by Giovanni Carandente. New York/London, 1983.

sweet, pretty, academic, and not so much a still-life as lifeless. True, Carandente makes important comparisons, such as that in Balthus's portraits, as in Marino Marini's sculpted ones, "likeness is a completely secondary consideration." But the professor is overenthusiastic in rating Cézanne, Seurat, and Picasso "among the few names in modern art which can be placed in the same class."

Moreover, Carandente takes Balthus on his own terms: "Balthus considers the eroticism in his work to be sacred and for this reason he likes it to be neither publicized nor commented on." Amen. The viewer, of course, is not concerned with Balthus's personal relationship with this eroticism, and whether or not he may be a kind of Lewis Carroll or Nabokov of painters. No matter how remarkable Balthus's best portraits and landscapes are, his pictures of nude nymphets, with legs spread, are much more so because of the dramatic overtones—Camus saw many of the supine ones as "victims"—or active drama, as when the pictures include predatory presences such as the dwarf in the mysterious and terrifying *The Room*.

The novelty of the Carandente book is in the inclusion of Balthus's work as scenographer, though the three graphite and India ink stage designs for Artaud's *The Cenci*, and the two watercolors, the stage design and the costume sketch for *Così fan tutte* are insufficient for us to imagine what Balthus might have accomplished in theater design. The *Cenci* set (1935) seems to owe something to decors from Bibbiena to Berman (in whom the debt would be the other way around). Professor Carandente praises the "Parthenopean vista" for *Così fan tutte*, but to this opera-goer the view is like many others.

The Balthus question at present centers on the two-dimensionality of his late painting, which is to say from about 1964. Are the canvases and watercolors after he renounced the perspective of depth as powerful as the best of the earlier ones? Considered as a portrait, the *Turkish Room* (1966) is virtually an icon, since the background appears to be on the same optic level as the subject; a background, it should be mentioned, that in reality—the Turkish room, in the Villa Medici, painted by Horace Vernet, *c.* 1830—includes an alcove of a yard or so that Balthus telescopes to the foreground surface. Theoretically, the merging into space should make the figure "timeless." But only time will tell.

Balthus's admirers are divided over the recent work. Perhaps they should look more closely at such early pictures as *Place de l'Odéon*, in which scarcely any attempt is made to simulate the third dimension. The artist might be flirting with the fourth, as his son's references to mystics and alchemists seem to hint, but in any case the Balthus boom has increased by several decibels since the Metropolitan Museum's 1983 acquisition of *The Mountain*.

Uccello and Kenneth Clark

This collection of five of the late Lord Clark's lectures and essays[1] is in dire need of editorial revision. The Donatello chapter is spoiled by an illustration of a *Lamentation Over the Dead Christ* that is not the one under discussion by Donatello. The Botticelli chapter, among other defects, exposes the author to the charge of innumeracy: "of the 85 drawings (originally over a hundred, for ten from the *Inferno* and four from the *Paradiso* are missing"), eight "were bought by Queen Christina . . . the remaining 76 . . ." But 10 plus 4 plus 85 equals 99, and 85 minus 8 equals 77. The chapter "Mantegna and Classical Antiquity" is marred by empty comparisons between different arts: the "frieze-like treatment" in Mantegna's Roman frescoes in the Eremitani is said to be the "equivalent of a Latin metre," while the *Triumphs* are "the nearest thing in painting to Latin poetry after Petrarch." In what ways does a verbal metre resemble a frieze, and what is the connection between Classical Antiquity and Latin poetry *after* Petrarch, whose influential poetry is in Italian?

Worse still is the essay on Alberti, quite apart from the run-together sentences, the mis-spelling and typos. His "*Della Pittura* is the first treatise on the art of painting ever written," Clark asserts, though Tsung Ping's essay on landscape painting is a thousand years older. When Clark says that the "only Italian text" of the *Della Pittura* is "now in the Bibl. Nat., Florence," an editor should have explained that more than one text existed, as is proven by the extensive influence of the book, and Clark's own assumption that Leonardo "had a copy of [it] beside him," since his *Trattato* borrows from it "almost word for word." Clark charges Alberti with exaggeration, "the national weakness." But Italy was not a nation in the *quattrocento*, and even at that time "exaggeration" had not been established as a characteristic of the people as a whole.

---

[1] *The Art of Humanism* by Kenneth Clark. London, 1983.

The remaining essay, "Paolo Uccello and Abstract Painting," contains a number of shrewd perceptions and deserves a place in the artist's still remarkably slender bibliography. Though not dated, it may have been provoked in part by John Pope-Hennessy's 1949 monograph, which rejects the surrealist *St. George and the Dragon* in the Jacquemart-André, a picture that Clark enthusiastically accepts.

"Abstract" in the title refers to Uccello's use of pure geometric forms, and to his perspectivism. The former is illustrated by the familiar comparison of the horse in the Hawkwood memorial fresco (Cathedral of Florence) and the horse in the drawing of it (Uffizi). The animal's hindquarters and belly, perfect arcs in the drawing, are naturalistic in the painting, which may have been deformed by its restorers. But surely the geometry came first, the modifications later, and, if scale is not ignored, the round rump of the drawing would be grotesquely unreal in the fresco. If the drawing is more "beautiful," the painting presents the more convincing horse.

The Hawkwood memorial attests Uccello's mastery of perspective at a comparatively early date in his career, which must be said because, for him, the science of perspective is not necessarily related to the art of painting pictures. Though he had successfully adjusted the circle, the cylinder, and the sphere to perfect perspective, Uccello, in his later paintings, was evidently not tempted to create the illusion of depth to provide an imitation of reality. But not all of his perspectivist work is confined to technical exercises divorced from pictures. The *mazzocchi* (a kind of circular hat) in *The Deluge* are islands of geometry. One of them, ringed like a life-preserver around the neck of a man in the foreground, far from being a detail—as, realistically, it should have been, in the midst of drowned bodies and in the *sauve qui peut* situation—is the picture's inescapable focus.

The same headgear is worn by some of the battling knights in the *Rout of San Romano*, no less conspicuously and inappropriately (helmets would be in order). Here Uccello is painting *mazzocchi* for their own sakes, as well as pieces of armor, plumage, pennons, and the Solomon's knot. Nor is he concerned to relate these and other objects and figures to the space that he comparts into separate nooks for separate events, or even much concerned about their juxtaposition in the composition.

Consider Uccello's disregard of perspective in all three *San Romano* pictures. In the one in the National Gallery, London, the individual planes of foreground and background do not recede successively toward a vanishing point, and no semblance of natural relationships obtains among the stage-front objects, where a still-life of assorted segments of armor in the center occupies more space than the body of a fallen warrior only a horse's length away. The picture is a Gothic fantasy with Surrealist horses, for the white steed of Niccolò da Tolentino, the condottiere who directs the battle, might have come from a carousel in a Fellini film.

In the Uffizi picture, the featured weapons are different—crossbows and halberds—and the lances, unlike those in the London version, are distributed on both sides, thereby providing balance as well as a scheme of orthogonals and a traversal, because of a direct thrust across the center of the picture. The positioning of the equestrian target and the curvetted horse to the right, though the two are not perspectively related, endows the whole scene with dramatic coherence, but the fore- and backgrounds are even further removed from a perspectival relationship than they are in the National Gallery panel.

The third picture, in the Louvre, has no background at all, which is part of its superiority, for it is a better composition in other ways as well, with Niccolò and his horse in the center of the scene symmetrically dividing it. Attention, otherwise, is drawn to the thickets of lances at the top of the picture space and, at the bottom, to the innumerable legs of horses, the remainders of whose bodies are not only invisible but also unimaginable. Unlike the London *San Romano* and the one in Florence, in which the carnage, like casualties in a boys' war of tin soldiers, conveys no sense of tragedy, this one, with its faceless men in helmets, is haunting.

Uccello was only marginally a humanist, and, in his indifference to Classicism, no humanist at all. For contrast, and to choose the most extreme contemporary example, consider Donatello's horrifying, in its human truthfulness, *Mary Magdalene*. Though much of Uccello's work is lost, it is unlikely that, after the pedestal in the Hawkwood monument, classical architecture makes any appearance in it. Few or none of his heads, faces, and bodies are modelled on antique sculpture. Uccello's most beautiful "human" figures are blonde, snub-nosed angels, like the one in San Miniato. The effect of Alberti's classicism on Uccello was short-lived but pernicious, as, for example, in the absurd wind-god prop in the background of *The Deluge*.

What Uccello did love was the Gothic. Clark traces this taste from the artist's apprenticeship in Ghiberti's workshop to his early employment as a mosaicist in St. Mark's in Venice, and his work as a designer of stained-glass windows in the Duomo in Florence. Another influence seems to be that of the Gothic miniaturists, one of whom, Pope-Hennessy believes, may have been the Rohan Master. Uccello's greatest art, Clark concludes, achieves "a synthesis of his Gothic fantasy and Euclidean logic."

The sonorous dimension in Uccello's action scenes is never mentioned, but *The Rout of San Romano* is loud with the clash of arms, blare of trumpets, neighing of horses, as is the hunt scene at Oxford with the hallooing of the horsemen, the shouting of the beaters, the barking of the hounds. The *caccia*, it should be said, is a major musical form of the time, especially in Florence.

* * *

Meryle Secrest's disadvantage in undertaking a life of Kenneth Clark[1] would be the same for almost anyone with the same ambition: the unlikelihood of being able to write as well as Clark does in his autobiographies, even though these are not among his enduring achievements. That Clark himself failed suggests that he is not a subject for a biography, not an exploitable personality apart from his work, which in turn seems to defy critical study, perhaps for the reason that his mandarin style is inseparable from his "art appreciation."

Clark would quickly have removed the skin-deep blemishes in Secrest's style—the redundancies ("one could never predict which mood K. would be in and when"), the mis-use of the subjunctive ("if drinking were her attempt at self-cure"), the pomposities ("peacocks from the castle were wont to make their appearance")—but how would he have dealt with her rhapsodies about art ("Botticelli . . . that exquisite sensualist and poet of the beautiful line")?

The chapters on Clark's immensely wealthy but otherwise unremarkable ancestors, on the association with Berenson, on the years as Director of the National Gallery and on the TV culture huckster add little to his own account. Of new subjects, the most prominent are the related ones of his philanderings and his first wife's alcoholism, for the balance of speculation leans to the conclusion that he drove her to drink, the testimony of household retainers affirming that even in late years the intake was far less when he was absent. Whatever the full story, and the scenes from her dipsomaniac life recorded here do not tell it, Jane Clark inspires more sympathy than her husband.

---

[1] *Kenneth Clark*. New York, 1985.

"K. found the attentions of an intelligent attractive woman thirty years his junior hard to resist," Secrest writes, thereby begging a question about herself, since she was at least that much younger than K. when they first met, fourteen years before his death, and since "By the time he had definitely decided that I should write his biography we were on easy terms." At that time, another woman recalls, K. was still "his fun-loving, bottom-pinching self."

BALLETS

Lopokova in Bloomsbury

Lydia Lopokova (1892–1981) was "not really a great ballerina, nor was she among the most technically expert," Sir Frederick Ashton concedes in this volume of tributes[1] to the Diaghilev dancer. Neither does the book add to ballet history, some of which, instead, is subtracted, thanks to the introduction of mistaken or misleading versions of such well-documented history as the conception of *Petrushka*. What Milo Keynes does offer is the story of the unlikely but nevertheless successful marriage of Lopokova and John Maynard Keynes. The Lady Keynes side of the book much outweighs the Lydia Lopokova side.

In the one entirely candid contribution, Quentin Bell reveals that until shortly before the marriage, Keynes's constant companion was a certain Professor Sprott, "a very elegant and seductive youth" sometimes referred to as "Maynard's wife." Sprott's "union with Maynard never caused the slightest difficulty with Maynard's other friends," Bell goes on—unnecessarily, since these were the Bloomsbury set. And though Lopokova's arrival did create a fuss, Lytton Strachey, describing her as a "half-witted canary" and remarking that having children would be "*too* improbable," nevertheless reported that "Maynard actually seemed to be in love with her—and she with him."

The true subject of the book is not how Keynes could have lived conjugally with Loppy, as he called her, but how this gamine of unexceptional intellect, limited education, and incompatible social background could have provided companionship for one of the most brilliant men of his time. Assuming that he could not have considered the consequences of marriage, his friends plotted to extricate him from the "catastrophe," as Virginia Woolf foresaw it, adding that "I should rather like her for a mistress myself," a wish that seems to be on the way to

---

[1] *Lydia Lopokova*. Edited and with an introduction by Milo Keynes. New York, 1984.

fulfillment in a 1923 photograph of the two women together. The wedding took place on August 25, 1925, and was immediately followed by a honeymoon in Russia. The reader is not told what became of Professor Sprott.

Milo Keynes, nephew of the great economist, refers to the twenty-five-year marriage as a "happy association," and the book convinces the reader of the truth of the claim. Loppy not only diverted and charmed her husband, but she also nursed him, and before as well as after the heart attack that left him partially incapacitated during the last nine years of his life. His niece, Polly Hill, quotes a friend: "He enjoyed a nursery atmosphere." Speaking for herself, she says that he never outgrew "his own precocity." Even after his marriage, he would "call for his mother when ill."

Though the book's nineteen authors are kindly intentioned toward Lady Keynes, their obeisances are less memorable than the criticisms implied in their anecdotes about her. Isaiah Berlin, avowing that Keynes was "certainly the cleverest man I have ever met," describes a scene in the British Embassy in Washington on the night of Roosevelt's election to a fourth term. As a group listened to radio reports of the election returns, Loppy was bored and restless:

> Do you like the President? Roosevelt? Rosie? Do you like Rosie? I like Rosie. Everybody here likes Rosie. Do you like Rosie, too? Shoosh, Lydia, not now, said Keynes . . . She turned to me again, Do you like Lord Halifax? The Ambassador was sitting about a yard from me at the time . . . Keynes did not shoosh her this time, but stared straight in front of him with a faint smile on his lips . . . Lord Halifax looked faintly, very faintly, embarrassed, rose from his place, patted his little dachshund . . . and . . . strode from the room.

Quentin Bell tells a similar story, expressing amazement that Keynes "made not the slightest attempt to stop Lydia from making a fool of herself, [when with] some very slight exercise of that incredibly brilliant mind of his, he could have set everything straight." Clive Bell, Quentin's father, offers a clue: Keynes's hubris (read "arrogance") was as dominating as his brain.

In such situations, Lady Keynes seems to have been less to blame than her husband, being not so much tactless as without any notion of the meaning of the term. Her insensitivity, vanity, exhibitionism, and, as Frederick Ashton says, fiendish rudeness, are more difficult to excuse.

Many of the contributors agree that she was "witty," but their illustrations of this are generally confined to some not-that-amusing misuse of English. David Garnett gushes about her "enchanting use" of the language, but the reader can judge this for himself in the excerpts from her letters to her husband and in the reprinted radio scripts and newspaper articles—the reader, that is, undeterred by malapropisms, non sequiturs and digressions.

John Gielgud remembers that Lopokova had a strong accent, but does not identify it as Russian. What kind was it? We learn that she had studied English in, of all places, the Catskills. None of this would matter except that she pursued a career as an actress and appeared on stage in English-language plays, including Shakespeare's. She received favorable reviews in the publications that Keynes owned, the other kind elsewhere. But why did he encourage her?

Loppy seems to have provided aggravations on the opposite side of the footlights as well, as a member of the audience talking not only audibly but also embarrassingly. Ashton remembers an occasion when "The curtain went up and all was quiet until Lydia's voice rang out: 'Oh, Maynard, look at her mouth. It is indecent. It looks as though it belongs somewhere else.'" Yet E.M. Forster, a "favorite friend," sitting directly behind Lydia during a stage-adaptation of *A Room With a View*, is said to have been amused by her comments "made in a fairly loud voice during the performance."

A prodigious number of errors will be noticed by readers acquainted with ballet history, and who but the editor could fail to see that the reproduction of Picasso's portrait of Lopokova on the dust jacket is signed by him "Londres 1919" but described on the infold as made "in Rome in 1917"? The level of much of the book is exemplified in a remark about "the first public performance in English of Stravinsky's *The Soldier's Tale*, called at that time *The Tale of the Soldier*."[1]

---

1 Reprinted from *New York Times*. April 29, 1984.

Tchaikovsky's Ballets

The book one has always hoped for about the ballets one loves most matches the highest expectations.[1] Wiley presents the fruits of his research with utmost clarity. He has made the original scenarios and Petipa's notes available for the first time in English, fully described the original productions (including both the Moscow and the St. Petersburg stagings of *Swan Lake*), and translated the relevant documents, including excerpts from Russian newspapers and periodicals of the time, and critical commentaries by Russian scholars of Tchaikovsky's time and ours. The result is a virtually complete history of *Swan Lake*, *Sleeping Beauty*, and *Nutcracker*. Wiley also provides the first adequate analyses of the music of all three ballets, fills gaps in Tchaikovsky's biography with well-chosen verbal close-ups of the composer, and conveys an enthusiasm that recharges the reader's.

The introductory essays on late nineteenth-century Russian social, as well as cultural, history; on the ballet audience; the subordinate relationship of composer to choreographer; and the growth of ballet from operatic models—Aurora's solo as choreographic coloratura aria, mime as recitative—are of sufficient general interest to warrant separate publication. By means of quotations from newspaper articles, memoirs and letters, Wiley portrays the ballet public in the two Russian cities as fanatically partisan and rich in eccentrics. The vignettes of theater directors, bureaucrats and officials, choreographers and dancers, costume designers, composers, conductors and critics could hardly be more vivid.

Wiley dissects the Petipa-Minkus *La Bayadère* as a representative ballet at the time of Tchaikovsky's debut in this category of theater. Performed four weeks before the premiere of *Swan Lake*, the musically

---

[1] *Tchaikovsky's Ballets* by Roland John Wiley. Oxford, 1985.

trivial Petipa-Minkus was immeasurably more successful than the musically unforgettable Reisiger-Tchaikovsky, but when we learn how poorly the second ballet was prepared, the audience and the critical reactions are understandable. The triumph was to come later, in St. Petersburg, after managerial and artistic theatrical reforms, comprehensively described by Wiley, had been instituted on every level.

The chapters on *Swan Lake* reveal the extent of the composer's subservience to the choreographer. The success of the former was measured "first in the opera house, second in the concert hall, and not at all in the ballet theater." The ballet master ordered the form, character, length, meter, tempo, and even the features of instrumentation of each musical number, and if the finished product did not meet with his approval, another composer would be asked to substitute new pieces. This nearly happened to Tchaikovsky, when a ballerina wished to introduce a pas de deux by Minkus in *Swan Lake*. "Whether my ballet is good or bad," Tchaikovsky protested, "I alone would like to take responsibility for its music," and to avoid mutilation and humiliation he wrote new music that agreed bar for bar with Minkus's.

"Tchaikovsky never surpassed *Sleeping Beauty*," Wiley writes. In some ways *Nutcracker* surpasses it, though Wiley rightly says that *Nutcracker* "remains simply a child's tale, without significance as an allegory or parable." *Sleeping Beauty* sprawls, and the hunting music in Act II and the dances that follow for the duchesses, baronesses, countesses, marquises are tediously protracted. Not even the best of the character dances in *Sleeping Beauty* can compare to the Arabian, Chinese, Spanish, and Russian dances in *Nutcracker*, whose instrumentation is also more original and transparent.

Readers drawn to the book because of Tchaikovsky can skip the chapters on staging, but ballet buffs cannot ignore the musical discussions, and they must be able to read the scores; every gesture and movement in *Sleeping Beauty* and *Nutcracker* is identified by measure numbers. Wiley's comments on the interlocking of drama and music, the most valuable parts of his book, cannot be understood without a knowledge of musical terms. Some of these, it must be admitted, are confusing, as when, referring to a chart of tonality relationships, he says that "the keys opposite one another are the most distant," meaning, in this instance, a tritone apart. Later he writes that "E flat major lies between Siegfried's D and Odette's E, practically opposite both in the circle of fifths." But here he means equidistant, not opposite. Nor are the music examples free of errors: cacophonies mar pp. 123 and 251.

All the same, the book never slows the reader with grammatical perplexities, and such oddities as occur in the translations might well be faithful renderings of the originals ("Odette tells how she could be saved in F#"). Otherwise Wiley's only fault, a tendency to lapse into a form of the pathetic fallacy, stems from a virtue: the admirable predominance of the musician in him over the critic. "One cannot imagine what could better convey the image and sense of atmosphere . . . of a group of swans coming to rest on a lake in the forest at nightfall than Tchaikovsky's famous oboe solo." But the image is conveyed by association after the fact. It could fit a lonely lover no less adeptly.

In Balanchine's Footsteps

None of the books about George Balanchine discussed below will present him to more than a small fraction of the readers of Shana Alexander's best-selling *Nutcracker.*[1] This much-publicized story of Balanchine's involvement with Frances Schreuder, his "last patron"—and coincidentally the psychopathic instigator of her father's murder by her son—does not change the perspectives of his life, but the connection cannot be dismissed as simply another grotesque act of "fate." After Mrs. Schreuder's arrest, "George," as she referred to him, supported her with his belief in her innocence. "He cried with joy, when I was released from prison," she claimed. "He even offered to testify for me."

True, other New York City Ballet officials weathering the scandal were sympathetic—if that is the word for Robert Gottlieb's gift to the then Rikers Island inmate of a "slim volume of Igor Stravinsky's letters." But Balanchine was closer to her. That he seems not to have been disturbed by manifestations of her "bipolar mood disorders" may not be surprising, in view of his long experience of the same condition in others. What does elude explanation is that even during her most stable periods, Mrs. Schreuder must have offended Balanchine's natural delicacy and sense of decorum. Reliable, as a rule, in his evaluation of character, was he blinded in this odd instance, or confused by the contradictions and by his own illness? What can be said is that his death a year before Mrs. Schreuder's trial (and conviction) was merciful in other respects than were known at the time.

Shana Alexander is less than reverential toward Balanchine, and she does not hesitate to expose his, well, orgulous side—as in his remark that if audiences were unable to pronounce *Davidsbundlertänze*, a ballet Mrs. Schreuder sponsored, they could stay away. For the rest, the book's

---

[1] *Nutcracker* by Shana Alexander. New York, 1985.

account of ballet-school life in relation to Mrs. Schreuder's career as Balanchine's underwriter is overwritten:

> The crackle and hiss of neurotic mothers and their anorexic daughters . . . wracked bodies, fevered imaginations, Balkan intrigue, and sulfurous hatreds . . . when the prima ballerina found ground glass in her toe slipper—every other dancer was equally suspect.

* * *

Solomon Volkov's title[1] is misleading: his subject is Balanchine, not Tchaikovsky, on whom Mr. B.'s comments are largely familiar and rarely remarkable. Far more valuable and almost as voluminous—if the word can be used in connection with so slender a book—are Balanchine's reflections concerning his relationship with Stravinsky. Tchaikovsky's craftsmanship, one of Balanchine's main themes, had been inculcated by Stravinsky from the time of *Apollo*. Moreover, the collaboration between the contemporaries provokes Balanchine's most acute insights about himself: "Stravinsky planned, and I improvised, that may be my great fault." And under whatever heading, Volkov has preserved a few marvelous moments with the living Balanchine, for which this reader, at least, is grateful.

Anyone who knew the choreographer will be nonplussed at the outset to read that he was "a relaxed, gray-haired man" who "identified with Tchaikovsky." Balanchine's intensity was always close to the surface; his hair was the least noticeable feature of his majestic head; and not at any time could this deeply restrained artist have felt an affinity with Tchaikovsky's self-pitying and sentimentality. After the Preface, and from the moment Balanchine begins to speak, the voice is unmistakable, the language characteristic. With few exceptions, Ms. Bouis's translation is indistinguishable from Balanchine's own highly idiomatic English.

Volkov's insistence on the Tchaikovsky-Petipa and Stravinsky-Balanchine parallel does not yield rich returns, perhaps because of the unsuitable form of the questioning. Volkov makes a statement about Tchaikovsky, Balanchine takes the bait and starts out with the equivalent of "Tchaikovsky used to say . . .," whereupon Volkov supplies verbatim

[1] *Balanchine's Tchaikovsky: Interviews with George Balanchine*. New York, 1985.

what Tchaikovsky did say. Balanchine soon moves away from the subject but is never allowed to stray far enough before being called back from possibly rewarding digressions ("When you dance, there are no erotic impulses at all") to some grindingly dull factual point about Tchaikovsky.

Nor does Volkov provide sufficient background information. Here is part of Balanchine's description of a visit to Stravinsky in Nice (undated, but early April 1928; Balanchine had already been there in January, with Diaghilev):

> So the Stravinsky table is set: At the head of the table a priest, Father Nikolai, because Stravinsky was very religious and he kept to that . . . The children are at the table too, and they resemble each other terribly. Svetik looks like Fedya and Fedya looks like his father. They're all sitting at the table and munching some salad, then spaghetti, and so on. All the faces are the same, and Stravinsky sees himself in them. Do you think that's interesting—looking at yourself all the time? I don't.
>
> And then I always had the feeling that his wife was in his way . . . He did not divorce his wife. When she died, he married a second time. So, as I remember, life in Nice was alien for Stravinsky, he didn't belong to it. He had nothing to look at.

The grim household atmosphere and the narrator's attitudes toward parenthood, cloning, and the desirability of divorce (followed by marriage to a younger woman) could hardly be more vividly conveyed. But nothing is said about the purpose of the visit, to study the music of *Apollon Musagète*, the cornerstone ballet of Balanchine's career. Surely Volkov must have asked Balanchine for his impressions of Stravinsky playing the score at the piano, asked whether mention was made of the derivation of rhythmic patterns from verse meters, and asked what was said concerning the staging and the set. Surely two such rich visual imaginations brought forth *something*.

Perhaps because he could not write, Balanchine vehemently denied that he had a verbal gift. But his story of the visit to Nice contradicts the contention. "They resemble each other terribly" is devastating, and so is the operative *mot juste* in "Isadora Duncan didn't care to which music she jumped." His language is always direct and concrete—"Stravinsky's music is like a corset; it's very good to have someone to hold you tight"—and it seemed to be on the tip of his tongue, as when he snapped back at an interviewer who wondered why he preferred Stravinsky to others: "Who are the others?" The ballerinas' books now in spate will remain in print if only for their quotations from Balanchine.

Volkov has not steeped himself in his material. When Balanchine says that he loves *The Magic Flute* above the other Mozart operas, Volkov fails to pick up on this and ask Balanchine about his 1956 televised version of the opera, or about his early stagings of *Figaro* and *Don Giovanni* at Monte Carlo. So, too, Volkov says that at the time of these interviews (1981), Balanchine was "bent on debunking the myth of the glamorous Diaghilev era." Even before Diaghilev's death, Balanchine had been criticizing him, above all for his highhandedness in ordering cuts in *Apollo*. Odder still, in view of the book's ostensible subject, Volkov does not ask Balanchine about his experience conducting the orchestra for his Tchaikovsky ballet *Theme and Variations* in April 1948.

Volkov leads Balanchine through the history of his Stravinsky ballets, probably for the reason that a tour of the Tchaikovsky ballets would not go very far: Balanchine did not choreograph *Sleeping Beauty*—which, as a ballet, he rates "second" to *Giselle*!—or even the complete *Swan Lake*. We learn that at fourteen Georgi Balanchivadze "participated," but not in what capacity, in Meyerhold's Maryinsky production of *Nightingale*. (Jennifer Dunning's source[1] states only that Balanchine regarded the piece as "cacophonous.") The *Petrushka* in the same theater two years later is not mentioned, though both the ballet and the ballerina, Karsavina, had a powerful effect on Balanchine. Some bitterness is evident in his reference to *Pulcinella* at the Maryinsky, of having been refused permission, for financial reasons, to stage it there himself: "After I left Petersburg for Europe, I learned that *Pulcinella* had indeed been done . . . So they found the hard currency . . . but without me."

Nothing is said of disappointments in France, of the *Noces* that "I probably would have done differently from what [Nijinska] did," of her *Baiser de la fée* and Lifar's *Renard*, though Balanchine's exclusion of these ballets (the complete *Fée*, that is) from his 1972 and 1982 Stravinsky festivals may be interpreted as an indication of still unhealed wounds. Balanchine's truncated *Fée*, like his streamlined semifinal version of *Apollo*, destroys the recapitulatory form of the work, and his 1947 *Renard* is a comic masterpiece that today's audiences should be given an opportunity to see.

---

[1] *But First a School* by Jennifer Dunning. New York, 1985.

The story of the visit to Nice conceals reactions to Stravinsky himself that Balanchine never divulged. The regrettable truth is that Stravinsky, before his second marriage (1940), could be overbearing even to Balanchine. An interview with Balanchine's friend Lucia Davidova, filmed in 1980 and recently made available at the Paul Sacher Foundation in Basel, bears witness to this. Reminiscing about the rehearsal period of *Jeu de cartes* (April 1937), Mme Davidova describes a social evening[1] in the course of which the composer spoke to his young collaborator with a tactlessness all too believable for the date—which may help to explain why Balanchine, vulnerable and easily wounded as he was, did not like to talk about this ballet in later years.

Volkov's Balanchine makes two remarks about Stravinsky that can only be explained as errors in transcription. No one knew better than Balanchine that Stravinsky did not "cry" when he "listened to his own music." Nor was Stravinsky ever "a gambler," except in the sense of artistic risks so minutely calculated, of bets so carefully hedged, that the word loses its applicability. (In a Las Vegas casino, Stravinsky's attention was confined to the skill of the croupiers and to the denouements of the dramas taking place around the tables.) But then, Volkov also credits Balanchine with Stravinsky's well-known artistic advice: "If you like something of someone else's, why not take it?"

Balanchine's recollections of life in Russia in his earliest years support the theory that memory is the creative part of the mind, at least of the mind that staged *Nutcracker*; even in 1981 Mr. B. remembered details about his childhood Christmas presents. And it must be said that the anecdotes about Russia and Russians—the musical compositions of the poet Kuzmin (one of them is included in the Prideaux Press edition of Kuzmin's comedy *Evdokia*), Prokofiev's meanness about royalties for *Prodigal Son*—are the most delectable in the book.

But if Balanchine's audiences are the target of his hardest-hitting observation ("Whatever you do is good enough, and if you do it better, they won't even understand that it's better"), the subject of the most painful; about being in a group of young girls, is himself:

> If you're interested in one of them a lot [their indifference] can hurt . . . Love is a very important thing in a man's life, especially toward the end. More than art.

---

[1] Wrongly ascribed in Richard Buckle's *George Balanchine* (see below).

Anyone in search of a broad-outline version of the life, must turn to Bernard Taper's twice-updated and revised 1963 biography of Balanchine,[1] but it is a skimpy book for one that claims to be comprehensive. Obviously Mr. Taper was closer to the New York City Ballet twenty years ago than at any subsequent time. Much of his chronicle of the Seventies is crammed into diary entries of a few meetings with the choreographer during the company's 1974 summer season in the Greek Theater, Los Angeles. Much, too, is secondhand, including the accounts of the Russian tours of 1962 and 1972.

Mr. Taper does not always explain the significance of the important points that he observes. Thus Merrill Ashley quotes Balanchine to the effect that if he could have one wish granted, it would be "to have perfect tempos all the time." Taper is well aware of this. He describes Balanchine and his music director, Robert Irving, fixing tempos metronomically weeks before a ballet was to be videotaped. But the several aspects of the question are left unexplored. If live orchestras are involved, tempo, to some degree, must be circumstantial, subject to psychological factors, the weather, acoustics. Clearly, too, the tempos of a ballet created to a difficult piece of new music cannot be set at the first performance and remain unalterable thereafter. Years may elapse before the true tempos, which may differ from the metronome markings, have been established, and the ballet master who works with a recording made at the time of the premiere may misconstrue the spirit of the music.

Balanchine himself avoided tape-embalmed peformances, and his instinctive sense of tempo was more reliable than that of most conductors—one of the reasons that his performance of *Theme and Variations* was so memorable. Yet he composed dances to tempos as he first learned them. When in the 1965 Leacock-Liebermann film of Stravinsky conducting, Suzanne Farrell dancing, the Terpsichore Variation in *Apollo*, the composer's pulsation is impossibly fast, Balanchine demonstrates the exact fit of his choreography to the speed of the 1928 original. Still, Stravinsky's argument that "the times" had changed, as well as his experience with the work, has its truths.

Taper does not linger over such aspects of Balanchine's personal history as his larger-than-normal quota of wives and close female friends, and his habit of referring to the spouse of a favorite ballerina as "my husband-in-law." He describes the gruesome premonitory incident of

---

[1] *Balanchine: A Biography*. New York, 1985.

Balanchine dancing the role of The Threat of Polio in his 1944 March of Dimes benefit ballet, of reaching out and touching a healthy young girl, danced by Tanaquil Le Clercq, who then falls paralyzed to the floor; and the same girl, twelve years later, actually crippled by polio. But we are not told that the Eurydice in *Orpheus* (1948), played by Balanchine's wife, Maria Tallchief, died and was borne off just as the leader of the Bacchantes, played by his future wife, Tanaquil Le Clercq, leaped onstage. Not only are the symbolic and real-life successions overlooked, but so is Le Clercq's participation in this ballet, though in the view of many her staccato style had stolen the show.

Mr. Taper quotes one of Balanchine's intimates: "The only time Balanchine loses that air of calm, complete authority . . . is when he's with Stravinsky. Then he's like a boy with his father." Father and son were together several times each year from October 1939 to June 1970. What seems not to be known is that, in crises, Balanchine turned to Stravinsky, flying to California for a week, or even a day, in search of inspiration, consolation, renewal, assurance of the continuing existence of creative genius.

After his humiliating treatment in Paris in 1947, Balanchine literally recovered in the Stravinsky home. "Thin as a wick," Mrs. Stravinsky described him in her diary, and "complaining of the same cracked toilet seat at the Opéra as in 1927." Balanchine's California visits were productive beyond the collaborations. His ballet-score choices of the Brahms-Schoenberg Quartet, of the music for *Episodes* and *Opus 34*, and of the Bizet and Gounod symphonies, extended from playing and listening sessions there. It should also be said that on anniversaries of Stravinsky's death, Balanchine observed the Panikhida services on his knees, in the New York church where his own funeral was to be held in 1983.

Referring to Robert Garis's article "Balanchine-Stravinsky Facts and Problems," in *Ballet Review*, Taper writes that "only late in Stravinsky's life, Garis thinks, [did] Stravinsky come to a true recognition of Balanchine's genius, not merely mastery. That was when he saw Balanchine's choreography for *Movements*." If I understand the distinction, I believe that Stravinsky first became aware of new dimensions in Balanchine's powers of imagination a year earlier, during discussions of *The Flood*. Stravinsky chose to publicize his discovery after *Movements* precisely because this ballet was not a collaboration and the score not one he would have proposed for choreography. In New York, April 5, 1963, Stravinsky came back from a *Movements* rehearsal not only stunned by the invasion and conquest of his musical mind but also overwhelmed by the autonomous beauty of Balanchine's "movements." An eye for an ear, one might say.

If the music of the great collaborations, *Orpheus*, *Agon*, and *Apollo*, seems less successful today in concert form, the reason is that these pieces gain so much as ballets—though *Orpheus* was always too episodic and visually explicit for orchestral programs, and even in the theater its very moving slow sections suffer from the alternation with fast ones containing, as Taper writes, a touch of "music hall high-kicking." To what extent was *Apollo* a collaboration? All that can be said for certain is that Stravinsky chose the subject—the divine nature of inspiration—that he supervised rehearsals, and that Balanchine, though only twenty-four and with no safety net of previous achievements under him, was his own master. For what it is worth, the one criticism of the staging that this reader ever heard from Stravinsky was, characteristically, of the stool on which Apollo sits to judge the Muses: "He looks as if enthroned on the WC."

Since Taper's biography is certain to remain in demand, a new edition might be foreseen that would correct a few errors. The subheading of a famous ballet is "inspired by the muse," not "by the music," of Tchaikovsky. The name of the Russian Easter cake is not "pascha," as in a seraglio—Valerie Brooks[1] writes it "pasha"—but with a "k" in place of the "ch". In need of revision, too, is Nicolas Nabokov's tale of a cross-country trip with Balanchine in 1947 to join Maria Tallchief, who is part Osage: "Balanchine was quite agog when the train, passing through Oklahoma, went by an Indian reservation. 'Look, those are my new relatives!' " The *Super Chief* has never detoured to Oklahoma.

Finally, the statement that Noguchi's designs for *Orpheus* "seemed absolutely right to Balanchine and Stravinsky" is true, but in the theater the authors of the ballet were dismayed by the overstrained schlepping of obviously featherweight boulders in the Sisyphean underworld, and by Orpheus' mask, which was remade after the dancer complained of being unable to see the floor. The most stunning effect in the decor was the silk curtain with the slit of light in the top center streaming downward like liquid metal.

* * *

---

[1] *Balanchine's "Mozartiana"* by Robert Maiorano and Valerie Brooks. New York, 1985.

Jennifer Dunning covers some of the same ground as Bernard Taper, but her last chapters, "The School Today" and "Approaching the Stage," are post-Balanchine. Kirstein is still a presence, but a lonely one, a "Drosselmeyer" to the youngest students.

But First a School is first of all a biography of Lincoln Kirstein, founding father of the American School of Ballet—not a school of *dance*— the genius who recognized the genius of Balanchine, and the David (hiding in a Goliath) who fought and defeated critical as well as financial odds: none of the literature has given a true picture of the years of abuse that Balanchine's ballets suffered in the New York press. If the turn-around ultimately went too far in adulation and fideism, this can only be explained as a natural tipping of the balance to extremes.

Dunning fills many gaps, including the history of Kirstein's own brief training as a dancer in Fokine's New York studio. She also ignores vital ones, as when she mentions Kirstein's "mystical turn of mind" but fails to name Gurdjieff. "I am still his student," Kirstein wrote in 1980, and, "work done with George Balanchine since 1933, as far as my part goes, was determined by what I gained from Gurdjieff's notions." This reader has not seen the Gurdjieff dance films (or heard the recordings of him playing the harmonium; his composer was Thomas von Hartmann, Kandinsky's collaborator on *Der gelbe Klang*), but the impression of them on Kirstein, and of his meeting with Gurdjieff, was profound.

* * *

Since the theme of this article is the aptness and enduring importance of Balanchine's own words, attention should be called to Jonathan Cott's two brilliant interviews (1978 and 1982) reprinted in Kirstein's book *Portrait of Mr B.*[1] Cott happily includes Balanchine's gestures in brackets, and in at least one case the gesture makes the meaning clear. Replying to a remark by Stravinsky about "the struggle between music and choreography," Balanchine says, "It's not so easy to unite and to be together. When you are *immediately* together it's [claps hands] and you evaporate." (Friar Laurence: "Fire and powder/which as they kiss, consume.") But when Balanchine sings "ta ta ta ta, ta tum ta tum," he can only be indicating the first two phrases of *Apollo*, not, as Cott writes, *Le Chant du rossignol*.

---

[1] *Portrait of Mr B.* by Lincoln Kirstein. New York, 1985.

From moment to moment, in session after session, *Balanchine's "Mozartiana"* describes the choreographing, rehearsing, costuming, and decorating of Balanchine's fourth and final ballet based on Tchaikovsky's suite. The Balanchine of Robert Maiorano and Valerie Brooks *is* the New York City Ballet, its creative source, the onlie begetter of its dances and dancers, the chooser of its music, the arbiter of the way its people shall be clothed, lighted, and placed in settings of his imagining. "Not until Balanchine walks onto the stage is anything resolved," the authors declare on one occasion, but the remark applies to all of them. The NYCB, moreover, is his family, children and grandchildren, cup bearers and acolytes, favorites, real-life ex-wives, "concubines" dreaming of advancement and fearing, but much more strongly wanting, the rivet of his eye. Balanchine is the destiny of everyone in the company, and he cannot be succeeded.

Merrill Ashley[1] sharply challenges this dead-end view, observing that in Balanchine's "contradictory attitudes toward the future of the Company, a small part of him found solace in the thought that it would all fall apart without him." Maiorano and Brooks do not raise such questions. They are action reporters intent on recording the birth of Balanchine's every step and sequence, as well as each of his words, expressions, gestures. They succeed extremely well, and not only in this but also in conveying the changing tensions and moods, the strains and frustrations, the constant awareness of the clock, the jokes and the short-lived, short-fused explosions, the exhaustion of dancers draped about the furniture, limp as Dali watches. Some of the narrative reads like a film script:

> Farrell kneels. The children flutter around, then softly join the prayer. The music envelops them. The ballerina's heart is open as she ascends and glides forward. Balanchine mirrors her movements. In time to Mozart, they pull together, expand and close. She shines under heavy lids of purple. Balanchine is intent. Farrell's brow creases, her mouth mourns. They separate, part, then close together.

The relationship between Balanchine and Farrell, the dancer who inspired him more deeply and for a longer period than any other, is the book's second subject, hardly less absorbing than the creation of

---

[1] *Dancing for Balanchine.* New York, 1985.

Mozartiana. The relationship has been "a glory of the New York City Ballet for twenty years," the authors rhapsodize, and the purple that they borrow from those lids becomes thicker as the ballet grows—"He opens her arms . . . baring her breast and tender throat"; "As she starts to kneel he has the children form a curve behind her. A saint in a niche"; "Balanchine and Farrell leave together with her supporting him around the waist. He drapes his arms over her shoulder and rests his head"—until the conclusion takes wing in iambics and alliteration: "as Farrell's final furl unfolds."

Balanchine made *Mozartiana* for Farrell, and the love story begins with her first entrance in the rehearsal hall, and with Balanchine indicating a place for a caesura because "we don't want the music to be drowned out by the applause of Suzanne's fans." We see Balanchine in the throes of composition, "head bowed in thought," "eyes excited, full of light," demonstrating each position and movement himself, copying Farrell in order "to sense in his own body which direction the weight will fall," incorporating an arm movement that Farrell had done naturally, modifying and embellishing her gestures. "Usually," we are told, "Balanchine's initial responses to music are his best," and a dancer "rarely felt he was being directed by Balanchine, only led or persuaded"; that "in Balanchine ballets, the steps themselves are not the most difficult part. It's the pace, precision, brief preparation and wide use of space that are unusual"; and that Balanchine, though seventy-seven, in poor health, and impeded by thick-soled street shoes, "moved more gracefully than the ballet dancers."

The chapter describing Farrell at a costume tryout shows Balanchine to have been as certain of what he wanted in the textures and colors of fabrics, the cut, dimensions, and fit of garments, in shoulder straps and hems and ornaments, as he was in his choreography. This contradicts his reputation of indifference to dress before he began to collaborate with the costume-maker Varvara Karinska in that masterpiece of gyration, *La Valse*. But Balanchine had devoted the same talents to the supervision of Vera Zorina's clothes in Hollywood films, more than once staying up all night to recobble a pair of her shoes. Some of the book's liveliest exchanges are between Balanchine and seamstresses, but the center of attention is always Suzanne: "Balanchine would not want sleeves to cover Farrell's lovely arms."

The best lines in *Balanchine's "Mozartiana"* are the quotations from Balanchine. He tells his very young dancing class: "Those who can't or are old, don't have to"; what an audience's applause really means is:

"You see how nice I am to you. What are you going to do for me next." Best of all is his admonition: "The mirror is another person. Don't rely on it."

Merrill Ashley rules out mirrors for the very different reason that "one sees in them only what one wants to see." *Dancing for Balanchine*, her autobiography to age thirty-five, is the full story of the making of a ballerina, from early childhood to New York City Ballet principal dancer. The first step, assuming the physical and other attributes and potentials, is to recognize one's vocation as a dancer at a precocious age, and to want to be a dancer with unwavering singularity of purpose. Step two is to be taught by the right teachers and schools. Step three is to renounce a normal life and education and embark on a ten-year apprenticeship of relentless and intensive work. Injuries are an inherent hazard of the profession, and a considerable part of Ashley's book is devoted to her ballet-related medical history, including an incapacitating hip pain that eventually required surgery. No less painful and rife is the mental and emotional anguish. The competitiveness is fierce, survival is from day to day, and a dancer's career is short.

Ashley's account of her background, artistic training, and acculturation in the company will be of immeasurable value to aspirant ballerinas. Useful, too, are the series of photographs in which she demonstrates correct and incorrect positions and movements, a manual of technique that even the keenest balletomanes should find helpful to their appreciation of the art. Ashley's technique, as she regularly reminds the reader—"I was growing into one of the strongest technicians in the company"; "[my] fast, clear footwork"—is second to none.

Yet Ashley seems to have been slow to understand what anyone else would suppose to have been immediately obvious, that her "only hope of stimulating Balanchine's interest was to learn to dance the way he wanted." Her ground plan was to observe Farrell: "I was intrigued that Balanchine found her unendingly fascinating, and I resolved to discover what it was in her that inspired him." The feline streak appears when Farrell returns to the company after a long absence, and "Balanchine again cast her in all her old roles and gave her a lot of attention. Gradually he catered to her more and more," though she "broke the rules both on the stage and, more surprisingly, in class: . . . As far as I could see, the few that found favor seemed to grasp the spirit of [Balanchine's] laws while violating the letter."

Colleen Neary is also seen as a preferentially treated rival. A certain role "required regal bearing, dignity, and elegance. In my mind those qualities were more evident in my dancing than in Colleen's," who was chosen for the part. In another ballet, "My variation turned out to be fiendishly difficult, but its subtleties impressed the other dancers more than the audience. Balanchine had also choreographed a variation for Colleen that was more easily appreciated by the audience [and that] spoiled my fun a bit . . ." Later, when Colleen left the company, "I derived no satisfaction from [her] defeat."

Obviously not! But the company's male dancers also inspire spite. They "had become involved in dance because they enjoyed jumping and turning, not because they looked forward to learning the difficult skills of partnering a woman." Successfully stalked at last, Balanchine finally begins to notice her, whereupon Ashley thinks the reason may be that he "liked my straightforward but quiet manner and uncomplaining nature." Straightforward, yes: she freely admits that the choice of her professional name "Ashley" was partly because "the Company lists its dancers alphabetically," and that "thoughts of promotion crossed my mind" (this is said halfway through the book, though from the beginning they have been crossing and recrossing as regularly as a palace guard). Uncomplaining, no: "Why had I been treated offhandedly?" she wonders. Should she "say something to Balanchine" about being passed over, she asks Peter Martins, who tells her to "Swallow it. Just swallow it." Seeing her react to Balanchine's arrival one day just before she goes onstage, Martins says: "Cool it. Just dance for yourself."

Balanchine is quoted infrequently, yet some of his words come out wrong: "Bigger! Stronger! There are English horns in this variation." Balanchine could not have mistaken the nationality of Mozart's wind instruments. Once, too, Balanchine is made to sound like a comic-strip Chinese laundryman: "They think is more clever. But never was . . . I tell them, but they never do."

Ashley's comments on Balanchine betray a strange remoteness from his world. "Many people, upon meeting him for the first time, expected to find a man full of false airs." Many people? But what could be the basis for such presuppositions even if they existed? And how can anyone say that "with Balanchine's death, an important period in the life of the Company . . . came to an end." *An* important period? There had been no other, nor is one likely to recur marked by greatness comparable to George Balanchine's.

* * *

No other European émigré artist of the 1930s had as great an effect on American culture and bequeathed a richer legacy to it than George Balanchine. When he arrived in New York in October 1933, architecture was flourishing in the United States, conservatories and fine arts academies existed, and painters, poets, sculptors, and composers somehow survived. But in this country, classical ballet, that international transplant, indigenous nowhere, was not for certainty considered an art at all, much less a respectable one.

At the time of his death fifty years later, the émigré with, more truly than the author of the phrase, nothing to declare except his genius, had won recognition for ballet as a great art, trained a company of nonpareil dancers for whom he created many masterpieces, and established a school. His New York City Ballet was the one American artistic enterprise consistently welcomed and applauded abroad, while his version of the Russian ballet *Nutcracker* became an American institution, as much a part of our holiday seasons as turkey. Now, in 1988, on the fifth anniversary of his death, no memorial has been raised to this man who gave us so much, nor, as yet, has the essential drama of his life been captured, if it has been perceived, by biographers.

Richard Buckle's *George Balanchine*[1] is an affectionate portrait of the great choreographer. Though not the anticipated sequel to his *Diaghilev* and *Nijinsky*, but a more selective, not to say sketchy, biography, that deals briefly with well-worked subjects and avoids twice-told tales, his survey of the ballets seeks, not always successfully, to place them in post-Balanchine perspectives. Even so, this is the Balanchine book, at least to date, for those who will read only one.

Balanchine history is largely, inevitably oral. He himself was a voluble interviewee, and the best lines in the book are excerpted from his talk ("music . . . I make dance that looks like it. I was born for that reason"). Though a non-writer—only a few of the letters from his American period published here sound like him ("Please, no *Sebastian*, . . . a dreadful ballet, lousy music, stinking story")—with no grammar, a limited vocabulary, a peculiar idiolect, an accent grossly misrendered in all orthographies, he nevertheless manages to be ringingly articulate.

Substantial portions of Buckle's text derive from spokespersons for specific periods, including widows of both the never-quite-married-to-him and the never-quite-unmarried-to-him kind. In the early Lincoln

---

[1] *George Balanchine: Ballet Master* by Richard Buckle in collaboration with John Taras. New York, 1988.

Kirstein years, and again at times in the late Thirties and Forties, the voice is more Kirstein's than Buckle's. But no matter. The quotations from Kirstein's writings, letters and telegrams, together with those from "groupie" ballerinas—"he always made a dance with one person in mind and if another person were to dance it he would change the steps"—bring us nearer to the living Balanchine than any amount of third-hand description.

The short chapter on Balanchine in Russia (1904–24) provides a smattering of political and cultural history, and as much as most readers will wish to know of his family background (half-Georgian, with a musical father and Orthodox priest paternal grandfather), his schooling (the Imperial Theater Ballet School, St. Petersburg, and musical studies in the Petrograd Conservatory), and his first theater experiences (attending performances from an early age in the Maryinsky Theater, and, while still a child, dancing a small part there in *Sleeping Beauty*). Little is known about Balanchine's first efforts to choreograph, but a precocious attraction to Stravinsky should be remarked: at eighteen Balanchine had devised dance movements for *Ragtime* and sought permission (not granted) to stage *Pulcinella*.

On the subject of the vexed relationship with Diaghilev, the chapter about the decade in Western Europe (1924–33) adds little more than a note to Diaghilev's friend Boris Kochno, in which Balanchine complains that Diaghilev owes him money, and a characteristic story: Diaghilev wanted to cut Terpsichore's variation. "He told me that the choreography . . . was no good. I said 'The choreography's fine. It's the dancer who is no good.' " In later life Balanchine criticized the quality of dancing in the Diaghilev company, the emphasis on décors and the preferential treatment of Serge Lifar as *premier mignon*, but these objections seem not to have been known at the time. Buckle's histories of *Apollo* and *Prodigal Son* are useful introductions to the two great ballets that Balanchine created for Diaghilev, but the inner path by which the choreographer reached this pinnacle of creativity at age twenty-four remains obscure.

In the "American" five-sixths of the book, the chapter "How Kirstein Brought Balanchine to America: June-December 1933" contains new material from Kirstein's letters and diaries that amplifies but does not significantly alter the by now familiar story. What we are given for the first time are the *pour parlers*, many of them by cable, between Balanchine and his American Maecenas to establish a ballet school and performing company in the United States. We learn that whereas

Kirstein's recognition of Balanchine's genius was by no means immediate, he was quick to remark that in ballets, as in life, Balanchine sees the relationship between men and women tragically, "always broken up by someone jumping in between." Kirstein kept cribs on Balanchine's observations as, for example, that Massine was "unmusical"; "that mime, gesture language, was antiquated"; that the greatest dancers of former periods were technically inferior "to any well trained modern dancer"; and that "Fokine can no longer compose [ballets]. He can teach, sitting down, but no one can compose long after they forget the actual movement . . . in their own bodies." Here Buckle interposes that Balanchine "could compose only with flesh and blood before him, 'like a sculptor with clay, putting off here, taking on there.' "

Only two months after Balanchine had settled in the United States, the School of American Ballet was duly opened in New York. Buckle's view of this event credits similar efforts by Mordkin, Bolm, Fokine, and others, it details the financial and other responsibilities of the founders, and it explains the organization and the curriculum. The first students are identified, too, and some of them contribute vivid reminiscences of Balanchine in his classes. But for an adequate discussion of his teaching methods, the reader must look elsewhere.[1]

Apart from teaching, Balanchine spent the decade and a half before the formation of the New York City Ballet (1948) making dances for the Metropolitan Opera, Broadway, Hollywood, and part-time and touring companies. In a 1936 letter to Stravinsky (not cited by Buckle) about commissioning a new work, Balanchine says, "I would not want the ballet to be strictly entertaining in character; I have been 'entertaining' here for two years already and now everybody has begun to copy me." The "two years" is an exaggeration, if he means *Slaughter on Tenth Avenue* and his dance numbers for *Ziegfield Follies*, but doubtless these and the later collaborations with Rodgers and Hart, *Babes in Arms* and *The Boys from Syracuse*, were widely imitated.

In the years 1938–42, Balanchine would set new standards for the movie musical in his films—no longer revivable at any hour of the night—for Vera Zorina, *The Goldwyn Follies*, *On Your Toes*, *I Was an Adventuress*, and *Star Spangled Rhythm*. But Buckle tells us no more

---

[1] See especially Nancy Goldner's "The School of American Ballet," in Nancy Reynolds's *Repertory in Review: 40 Years of the New York City Ballet*. New York, 1977.

about these standards than that Balanchine had brought the superior dancers of the American Ballet to Hollywood with him, and that his innovative mind was soon alerted to ways of making dancers more effective on the screen through the use of new camera angles.

The scene in *The Goldwyn Follies* of the water nymph rising slowly from a pool, dancing on the water, and mounting a white and rearing Chirico-like carousel horse seems to have been entirely his idea—though Moira Shearer[1] dismisses it as "a conventional water-nymph ballet (shades of *Swan Lake*) [with] conventional choreography." (Neither she nor Buckle mentions that this ballet became the model for the hippo-ostrich sequence in *Fantasia*, presumably with Balanchine's concurrence, since he was with Disney at the time, December 1939.) Whether or not Balanchine's later costume and fantasy ballets are in any way indebted to his cinema experience, what can be said with certainty is that his powers of invention on movie sets were not confined to choreography. But the range of Balanchine's theatrical imagination has not been generally understood, and this potential Aesop of the narrative ballet is now exclusively associated (shades of Bouvard and Pécuchet) with the plotless kind.

The pursuit of the female, with its entanglements and disentanglements, occupies the second largest part of Balanchine biography. Buckle, no latter-day saint-defrocker, introduces the subject with Byron's "My heart always alights on the nearest perch," meaning, in Balanchine's case, the latest, youngest, most gifted and attractive ballerina. His marriages to four of them follow a pattern of infatuation, rapid disinclination, the accession to the family circle of a third-party companion from among Balanchine's "slaves" (Nicholas Magallanes in the Maria Tallchief period), Balanchine's retreat to what anthropologists call secondary wives, divorce, and lasting friendship with the ex-spouse.

Balanchine's sexual predilections may be understood as a corollary of the flat-chested ballerina ideal. "He gave me a little pat on the behind," Ruthanna Boris recalls, and he "told me later 'You were . . . so cute . . . if you could not dance at all I would have taken you anyway. I wanted to bite your knees.' " Darci Kistler also confesses that he gave her "a slap on the rear," and one of his fantasies during World War II, so he told Stravinsky and Nicolas Nabokov, was to be a general of the Women's

---

[1] *Balletmaster: A Dancer's View of George Balanchine* by Moira Shearer. New York, 1987.

Army Auxiliary Corps, in order to stand a company of them to attention, command them to lift their skirts and lower their undergarments at the back, and, while inspecting the "ranks," concupiscently whack WAACs. Balanchine's old friend from Russia, V.P. Dmitriev, advised Kirstein that no young woman had ever been safe with "Georgian, heartless" George, and Buckle, remarking on what could be "the fulfillment of a personal fantasy," the "throes of stylized orgasm" in the *Bugaku* pas de deux, quotes one of Balanchine's close female friends: "If people could see into his mind he would be in prison."

Buckle gives ample space to several of the landmark ballets—more of it to *A Midsummer Night's Dream* than to any other—sometimes, as with *Symphony in Three Movements*, offering ingenious "interpretations" as well. But his omissions beg questions. Surely *Opus 34*, Balanchine's excursus into Expressionism, based on Schoenberg's score for an imaginary film, deserves mention, both in itself and as an experiment with two totally different choreographies, a composition of abstract dance movements followed by a Caligari's cabinet of surgical horrors, for the same music played twice consecutively. And why is the 1947 *Renard*, Balanchine's theater-of-comedy masterpiece, not listed among the achievements of Ballet Society, especially since John Taras, Buckle's coauthor, was in the original cast? Compared to *Four Temperaments*, Balanchine's most enduring creation of the late 1940s, the barnyard fable's pantomime centerpiece relegates it to the category of divergent work; but "the revelation of Balanchine's varied genius" is one of Buckle's themes.

Gaps also occur in Buckle's chronicle of the life. No explanation is given for Balanchine's return to Buenos Aires in 1942, so unexpected after the unsuccessful South American tour the year before, but important in that it provided opportunities to compose pure, complete-in-themselves ballets, as distinguished from incidental numbers for stage and movie spectacles. Balanchine would always recall with pleasure and pride the never-revived (in complete form) *Concierto de Mozart* (A-major Violin Concerto), choreographed in Argentina in the summer of 1942. Nor does Buckle say anything about the coengagement of Balanchine's friend Pavel Tchelitchev to execute new décors for the Teatro Colón *Apollo*, replacing the ones that had made the great ballet disappointing the year before. But even the biographical thread is lost after Balanchine's departure for the United States in mid-August 1942, Buckle mistakenly taking him to New York instead of to Hollywood and his then wife, Vera Zorina.

Other journeys have sunk without trace, including the one in September 1965 to Hamburg, where, after preparing Suzanne Farrell for a televised performance as Terpsichore, Balanchine heard Stravinsky's *Variations* and already began to think of it as a solo ballet for her—or three ballets, going *Opus 34* one better. Of the eight-country tour in 1956, we learn only that *La Valse* was received coolly in Vienna, but not that in Venice Balanchine became acquainted with the music of *Agon* as far as the "Bransle Gay" and some of the "Bransle de Poitou," two dances that inspired him. Perhaps Buckle felt that to discuss Balanchine's burst of new creativity at a time when Tanaquil Le Clercq, his young wife, had been stricken with polio might seem insensitive. But the transformation in Balanchine consequent to this tragedy, his religious "conversion," the return to God and strict Orthodoxy, and the faithful churchgoing that marked his life thereafter, is also not recorded in this book.

Of all the ballets that Buckle celebrates, *Agon* elicits his keenest appreciation:

> After nearly thirty years, we are still rediscovering, each time we see it performed, some breathtaking wonder that we had forgotten. Although the ballet ends as it begins, we are not left with a sense of QED—nothing has been proved—but of "Here we are again, back where we started and none the wiser."

Buckle is at his best and most moving describing Balanchine's cruel physical and mental decline, from the angina attacks that began in 1978 and the bypass operation a year later to the cataract removal, the increasing giddiness, falls and blackouts and the final six months of deterioration in the hospital. Though no one could have believed that he would recover, the death on April 30, 1983, came as a great shock. This reviewer heard the news in Venice, and went, for next of kin, to the Russian corner of the island cemetery, not learning until the next morning that, back in New York, Lincoln Kirstein had stepped before the curtain at the evening performance and said: "I don't have to tell you that Mr. B. is with Mozart and Tchaikovsky and Stravinsky."

* * *

Moira Shearer inevitably covers the same ground as Buckle, yet the overlap is minimal, partly because she devotes more than half of her book to Balanchine's earlier years. Her picture of his Russian childhood is more extensive than Buckle's because she imaginatively fills it out with what life in St. Petersburg and in a house in the Finnish forest must have been like in the years before the First World War. But she may be less reliable, as in her acceptance of Balanchine's statement that his father spent two years in a czarist prison after having been declared "a willful bankrupt," a story dismissed by Buckle as "romantic exaggeration" (what is romantic about that?). Her narrative often reads as though intended for the very young ("It is so easy to exaggerate in retrospect, we all do it") or part of a fairy tale ("Now something happened which is astonishing . . . "). And some of it, such as the compassionate portrait of the lonely little boy in school, and with his mother and sister in the train to St. Petersburg ("Sitting in their compartment, both children were excited and nervous"), is fictionalized; but harmlessly: the reality could hardly have been very different. So, too, the infusions of autobiography with which she regularly supplements her account are unobtrusive as well as pertinent.

Shearer reserves her more distinctive views and speculations for the shorter, American half of her "tribute." Switching to the first person to describe her adventures on the Balanchine trail in New York, she calls on Lincoln Kirstein, but, not surprisingly in 1985, without reaping rich rewards. What does take the reader aback are some of her comments after the meeting: "rather unbalanced—an unusual American dilettante . . . his writing is not for me . . . Kirstein's considerable erudition is given an airing in almost every sentence." Yet in a "happy final moment," Kirstein said, "George mentioned you often—oh yes, he talked about you a lot." Since George had last seen her nearly four decades earlier, "a lot" seems incredible. But not to Moira Shearer:

> We were on the stage [at Covent Garden] in the dreary working light waiting for him. I was very nervous. [Balanchine] arrived, elegant as always. We had never really met, so we all shook hands and he made some courteous small talk for a few minutes . . . Then, nodding to the pianist, he said, "So—let us begin." . . . Waiting for the first notes, I realized that I hadn't the least notion whether I could do what I was about to attempt . . . The cadenza begins quietly and slowly. I saw his face briefly, impassive, enigmatic. Then the tempo builds until one is a whirling mass and there is no time to be aware of anything. The pianist struck the final chord . . . He came towards me with a charming, surprised expression, put his hands round my face and kissed me.

> Looking back over thirty-seven years, I realize that the next few minutes of that day were the most important in my career as a dancer. This man, whom I hardly knew, gave me something invaluable, something I lacked totally—self-confidence . . . Did Mr. Balanchine sense this? I shall never know. I only know that he gave genuine praise for my efforts, showed his interest and pleasure and, above all, showed me that he believed in me.

Shearer's aversion to dance critics centers on the late Edwin Denby, to the extent that she quotes a preciously written passage from one of his reviews and follows it with her own "translation," as she calls it, though it does not say any of the same things. But she drubs British critics no less soundly: part of the purpose of her book is to secure a measure of appreciation and justice for Balanchine in Britain, and to referee the extreme views on both sides of the Atlantic, "close to total dismissal" in Britain and to "deification" in America, the former "blind," the latter "overblown." In the course of this she incidentally reveals that Balanchine's chief British detractor, though not in print, was the choreographer Frederick Ashton, whose homily to her on Balanchine she compares to "Mark Antony's famous speech of denigration, then eulogy, in *Julius Caesar*—but in reverse."

Shearer believes that Balanchine himself was fatalistic and optimistic, and that with age he became petty, rude, arrogant, autocratic, intolerant, vain, capable of humiliating a dancer, guilty of favoritism. To these charges even his most loyal friends would add that, young as well as old, he could be fickle, stubborn, prejudiced, grudge-bearing, childish—like other creative artists whose thought-processes outside of their work, and day-to-day social behavior, do not always match the high levels maintained by the uncreative. She also reminds us that Balanchine was a sometime dupe of the avant-garde, choosing not only Pierre Henry's *musique concrète* and Xenakis's *Metastaseis* and *Pithoprakta* for ballets that proved to be disasters, but also the score for *Episodes*, a work she does not regret having missed because "I have never yet been able to share a room with the music of Webern."

Still, she is shrewd about Balanchine's private life, and her suggestion that "a minimum of sex" might have had something to do with the undoing of the marriages may come close to the truth. This, at any rate, would explain that although "sexual jealousy can be such a strong force in women, one never senses the slightest breath of such feelings among the women he loved."

Shearer describes the autopsy from which it was discovered that Balanchine had died from Creutzfeldt-Jakob's disease, "a slow and so far untreatable condition . . . almost impossible to detect in a living person."

> An autopsy was performed and his brain removed . . . It was then sliced in layers and tissue removed and treated for study under a microscope . . . a pink circle called *kuru plaque* [was found], the sign of a rare family of virus diseases.

* * *

To turn from the dissection of the body to a post-mortem on the art and character, and from hearsay history to personal reminiscence, Gelsey Kirkland's autobiography[1] is not the book that rumor threatened. Her ongoing quarrel with Balanchine ("my greatest adversary") is in no way damaging to him. Nor does she accuse him, as publicized, of introducing her to drugs, but merely of giving her a single amphetamine when this seemed justified (at least to this reader). As she tells it, the late Patrick Bissell was responsible for the first stages of her cocaine addiction; but she was clearly ready for it and does not overtly blame him—at least not more than everybody else in her life, for this intolerably all-knowing, self-centered, and highly gifted dancer may be more deeply paranoid and self-destructive than even she suspects. One wishes Gelsey Kirkland, with her independence of mind, her talents, and her lively intelligence, a more peaceful future than the past recounted in this disturbing book.

In opposing her artistic philosophy to Balanchine's, Kirkland assumes—with what justification is not said—that the reader accords her equal status. She contends that ballets should have meanings beyond choreographic values and dancing for its own sake, that they must be about something besides technical perfection. Balanchine, she writes, failed to realize that in "extracting a code of movement from what he saw as the corpse of classical ballet . . . he thought he had isolated its soul." Balanchine, moreover, wanted only mechanically perfect dancers, while Kirkland wished to be an actress as well, or first of all. Not far along she asks, "What place did feeling and wit, love and reason, have in Mr. B.'s theater?" The answer of course is "every place," But Kirkland's perception of these qualities is a long way from Balanchine's.

---

[1] *Dancing on My Grave* by Gelsey Kirkland with Greg Lawrence. Garden City, New York, 1986.

At the age of ten, in the School of American Ballet, she thinks of Balanchine as a divinity. Shortly after, at a costume-fitting, he asks her in front of other males to change her clothes, which she does behind a screen. But something about the incident has embarrassed her—she is easily humiliated—in spite of which she remarks afterward: "I had caught the eye of George Balanchine." A few years later, seeing herself as "not pretty or sleek enough to fit the image of a 'Balanchine ballerina,' "she sets out "to alter my natural shape," to conform to "Balanchine's ideal female proportions," and to be "on my way to stardom." This involves crash diets, dental realignment, plastic surgery and silicone injections: "A fulsome [!] pair of breasts seemed the only attribute with which a ballerina could assert her sexuality."

Balanchine is duly blamed for her attendant sufferings, for ignoring the risks of injury, and for encouraging young dancers to "self-destruct." Nonetheless, "Mr. B. seemed to favor me, and I was determined to prove myself worthy of his affections." Even after she has exposed the ogre for what he is—a certain dancer "might receive a . . . gift if she allowed his fondling touch in private" (Kirkland herself was "relatively safe from the possibility of overt advances")—she can still say, dropping her guard and her "case": "I never knew what to do with my love for him."

One could "be banished from Mr. B.'s little empire" on the slightest provocation, Kirkland goes on, and, going too far: "All that he needed were dancers who could approximate some of the formal elements of classical technique." Conceding that Balanchine was "human enough to be jealous" of young male dancers, she accuses him, in one ballet, of "choreographically castrating" Peter Martins. Yet after venting all of this and much more, she cannot hide the rejection that seems to be her real grievance: "I continued to hope for some sign of approval from Balanchine."

Early on, the young liberator from "the Balanchine system" exposes a depth of incomprehension about the relationship between dance and music that makes the reader wonder why and how she became a ballerina in the first place: "As a dancer I rebelled against rhythm. I did not care for its effects, rhythm obscured meaning and constrained my movements." Obviously this was not lost on Balanchine:

> When I tried to extend a step in a phrase, lingering on a particular quality through the notes, Balanchine accelerated the tempo, throwing me off.

When glory is thrust upon her and she is chosen for the role of Firebird, Kirkland protests that Pavlova had hated the music, and "I would soon discover how wise she had been, how well she knew the score" (which, in truth, she could not learn). Seventy years later, the music—Kirkland's preferred ballet composers are Minkus and Adophe Adam—drove her "literally to place cotton in my ears." And as if it were not enough that Stravinsky and Balanchine had confronted her with an "approach" she "simply could not adopt," Chagall's sets threw her "off balance." She had been victimized by artistic bullying, and "Three Russian men against one American girl was not exactly a fair fight."

Balanchine does not entirely disappear from the book after this, but the reader who has come to it on his account, rather than out of curiosity about the details of front-page love affairs and the highs and lows of junkies, will be tempted to do just that.

"Sacre" at Seventy-Five: The Contrapuntal Conception of the Choreography

The music . . . struck me as possessing a quality of modernity which I missed from the ballet that accompanied it . . . The spirit of the music was modern, and the spirit of the ballet was primitive ceremony . . . In everything in Le Sacre du printemps, *except the music, one missed the sense of the present.* T.S. Eliot (1921)

The most written-about dance event of 1987, the Joffrey Ballet's restoration of *Le Sacre du printemps*, requires still more comment. Important historical aspects of the work have been lost in the critical aftermath, which, moreover, has shown no comprehension of what is wrong with the choreographic syntax. If the great ballet of 1913 is to have a future, its present form must undergo major repairs.

The New York Times, October 25, 1987, reported that Millicent Hodson, the dance historian and choreographer who guided the reconstruction, found two documents especially valuable, one of them the score in which Marie Rambert wrote down "as much of Nijinsky's choreography as possible," the other the score in which "Stravinsky had written descriptions of stage action above the music." Having seen no more of the Rambert score than the portion of a page reproduced in her autobiography, I have nothing to say about it except that her notes were not made "during rehearsals," as claimed in the Sotheby sale catalog of July 16, 1968, but at a distance of several months.

Concerning the score that Stravinsky prepared for Nijinsky, the *Times* quoted Hodson directly: "[The annotations] seldom mention specific dance steps, [but] they do indicate what happens by means of phrases such as 'the men group together,' 'here they fall to the floor.' " Let me add that the notes also describe movements, such as, for the women in Part Two: "Walk in a bell-swinging rhythm." But the real importance of the score is that it provides a map to the *musical* design of the choreography which shows that in rhythmic emphasis and phrasing, music and dance, as a rule, are in counterpoint to each other.

The score itself, as distinguished from verbal descriptions of its contents in a 1969 facsimile volume of the musical sketches, has yet to be mined for the full yield of its performance information. The reasons for this are that much of it is in coded or graphic form, and that the faded pencilling can be read only with the help of photographic boosting of contrasts. The score was shown to Jerome Robbins—for guidance, not reconstruction, which is for archeologists, not artists—during the planning stages of the New York City Ballet's 1972 Stravinsky Festival, a *Sacre* ballet having been momentarily considered with Robbins choreographing the groups, Balanchine the solo dance, the presumed division of labor in their *Firebird* collaboration. But Balanchine believed that *Sacre* should be heard and not seen.

The October 25 *Times* further reported that Kenneth Archer, the art historian, described the *Sacre* as

> Roerich's brainchild: Stravinsky often claimed that the idea for it came to him in a dream. Yet interviews in Russian newspapers of the time reveal that when Stravinsky finished composing *Firebird* in 1910 and sought ideas for a new ballet, Roerich suggested two scenarios. One concerned chess. The other was *Sacre*.

Hodson herself had written in the *Dance Research Journal* that

> an interview with Roerich in the St. Petersburg press and other documentation show that he had already written a scenario when Stravinsky approached him with the notion of a ballet about archaic Russia. Roerich's scenario was entitled "The Great Sacrifice" and it survives as the second act of what we know as *Le Sacre du printemps*.

Actually the interview with Roerich,[1] in *The St. Petersburg Gazette*, in

[1] Roerich's veracity is nearly always in question. See the detailed investigation of this monumental con artist in R.C. Williams's *Russian Art and American Money*, Cambridge, MA, 1980, and Karl E. Meyer's "The Two Roerichs are One" in the editorial column of *The New York Times*, January 22, 1988.

which he refers to the ballet-in-progress as "The Sacred Night of the Ancient Slavs"—what we know as Part Two—appeared two months *after* Stravinsky had written to him, July 2, 1910, discussing their plans for the "Great Sacrifice"—and, incidentally, revealing (to us) that work on the new ballet had begun even before *Firebird* was performed. Writing again on August 9, 1910, Stravinsky mentions the existence of musical sketches and not one but two versions of the libretto, in the second of which Fokine had participated. Fokine is never mentioned in connection with *Sacre*, even though as late as May 1912 he was to have been its choreographer. Whatever his contribution to the ballet, the "mysterious circles" of Part Two are clearly descended from his Enchanted Princesses in *Firebird*, and so is the hand-to-cheek gesture (those shouts for "*dentistes*" from the first *Sacre* audience). Stravinsky might even have had Kastchei's court in mind when he wrote that aforementioned "Fall to the floor" direction in the 4-hand score. And some musico-dramatic axials between *Sacre* and the end of *Firebird*—ritual (celebration), dance form (rounds), rhythm (shifting meters) and even sonority (swooping horns)—are real and powerful.

Granted that Stravinsky's recollections were not always reliable, and that in the case of his mid-1930s condemnation of Nijinsky's *Sacre* they amounted to a betrayal of his on-the-spot judgments of 1913. But his story of the vision of *Sacre* coming to him as he completed *Firebird*, and of seeking out Roerich, is documented in letters and interviews at the time: To Andrey Rimsky-Korsakov, March 7, 1912: "I am working on the piece that I conceived after *Firebird*"; to N.F. Findeizen, December 15, 1912: "My first thoughts about my new choreodrama *Vesna Sviaschennaya* came to me as I was finishing *Firebird* . . . I wanted to compose the libretto together with N.K. Roerich, because who else could help me . . .?"

Whatever the contents of the 1910 libretto, the authors rewrote it a year later—at Talashkino, the Princess Tenisheva's estate near Smolyensk, which is described in her memoirs as having burned down before that time and she herself as already living in Paris. What concerns us is that the July 1911 libretto is the one Stravinsky followed, and that it differs significantly from the two subsequent versions Roerich gave to Diaghilev, the first in the spring of 1912, the second undated but not earlier than March 1913. Whereas Stravinsky's copy of the 1911 scenario does not refer to Yarilo the sun god, Roerich's second version begins with him and excludes any mention of maidens with painted faces and even a ritual of abduction.

In November 1912, in Berlin, only days after completing the ballet in sketch-score form, Stravinsky received a letter from Roerich, in St. Petersburg, announcing that he had "changed the first act, and it is better now." But of course the music could not be changed or revisions introduced, except to add programmatic significance. As surely as Roerich's knowledge of Russian prehistory had originally inspired Stravinsky, so was the composer deaf to his colibrettist's later alterations. The statements on the title page of the 4-hand score that *Le Sacre du printemps* is *by* "Stravinsky and Roerich," the "*mise-en-scène by* Stravinsky and Nijinsky," confirm both that Roerich had no role in translating the libretto into action and that Stravinsky shared responsibility for the staging, a fact apparently unknown to ballet historians.

Bronislava Nijinska's memoirs attest to Roerich's influence on Nijinsky. We know from her and from Stravinsky-Nijinsky-Diaghilev correspondence that Nijinsky insisted on seeing Roerich's set and costume designs before beginning the choreography. No less certainly, Roerich's art and anthropology inspired Nijinsky far more than Stravinsky's bewilderingly new and terrifyingly difficult music.

* * *

In recent years, the *music* of *Le Sacre du printemps* has been measured by new critical and analytical tools. One result is that its harmonic organization has been quantified, revealing the fundamental combinations and structures, and the interrelationships and frequency of usage, of its vocabulary of chords. Another result is that the folkloric origins of its archaic melodies have been traced. Still another is that some light, but not enough, has been shed on the rhythmic element, that unprecedented and unsucceeded feature of the work. Publications of a more familiar kind have accumulated, as well, offering fresh and not so fresh appraisals of the influence of *Sacre* on the other arts, along with speculations about its significance as *the* representative creation of the modern period, for no contender, not *Erwartung*, or *Pierrot Lunaire*, not *Les Demoiselles*, Munch's *Scream*, or Mondrian's trees, not even *Ulysses* has attained the universality of Stravinsky's masterpiece, and maintained it for seventy-five years.

Historical and other documenting has also proceeded apace. Press dossiers of the first performance have appeared, from which further information has been gleaned about the staging, the dancing and the décors. Editions and revisions of the music have been minutely compared, as have musical interpretations, notably of Stravinsky's recordings and player-piano rolls, and arrangements for different instrumental combinations, from the disastrously misconceived orchestral version by Robert Rudolph to the illuminating transcription by Maarten Bon for four pianos, which shows that harmonic perspectives change with the different weights and prominences of the same notes in the orchestra and in the piano.

Exhibitions of the set and costume designs have also been presented, as well as of the costumes themselves, the latter most spectacularly in the Basel Kunstmuseum, where they were suspended in a circle from the ceiling. And the Joffrey Ballet has in places skillfully re-realized the pictorial dimension, aided by Roerich's *Sacre* legacy, photographs of the dancers taken at the time of the premiere, descriptions by participants and observers, Emmanuel Barcet's drawings and Valentine Hugo's drawings and pastels—though the promise in the pastels of stage depth, of diminutive figures in a spacious landscape, ill prepared the viewer at City Center, where the dance groups were too close to the audience and to each other. So, too, from the same visual and verbal sources the Joffrey has reconstructed movements, the jumps and jerks, the shiverings and tremblings—with the entrance of the Sage—and dance postures, the legs and feet of the men, as Bronislava Nijinska recalled, "turned inward, their fists clenched, their heads held hunched between their shoulders, and their walk on slightly bent knees."

The Joffrey staging is exciting at the very end, where the paroxysms of the Chosen One are inevitably intensified by the music but also, and often, it is academic, that danger of revivals even of ballets with choreographies intact. At times, too, Russia forgotten, the viewer has the impression of watching Sioux Indians in a kitsch Western, to some extent a fault of the costumes, albeit those of the young girls looked too neat and trim even for the movies, while "the old men" wearing bear skins suggested a college fraternity caper with trophies borrowed from a hunting lodge. To these detriments must be added the scratch performance of the Rudolph version of the music—ragged ensembles, inaudible strings, a missing horn solo (a case of not giving a hoot?)— and the relentless synchronization between musical and stage event (except where necessary: the Sage planted his earth-kiss prematurely, during the creaky-knees music instead of with the celebrated string chord).

* * *

Marie Rambert does not date or locate the rehearsal she describes at which Stravinsky began playing the piano at double the speed the dancers had learned, but this could only have been at the beginning of February 1913 in London. Her account seems to imply that a 2-hand arrangement was used, but Bronia Nijinska remembered Stravinsky playing 4-hands with one Steinman, actually Michael Osipovitch Shteinman, whom Diaghilev had engaged as second conductor in St. Petersburg in October 1912. Nijinska recalled that Shteinman played alone only when trying to bang out the "Sacrificial Dance" from the sketch for the full score, the only available version of the music before late March 1913, as a telegram from Nijinsky to Stravinsky asking for a piano score establishes. The sketch-score, which Serge Lifar finally surfaced and sold in 1982, ends with a note in Stravinsky's hand: "That idiot Nijinsky has not returned the 'Sacrificial Dance'."[1] The four-hand score, from which Stravinsky and Debussy played the not quite complete *Sacre* months before dance rehearsals began, served for all other rehearsals.

On January 4, 1913, Emile Jaques-Dalcroze wrote Stravinsky urging him to teach the music to his assistant Marie Rambert directly, sidestepping Nijinsky. But Stravinsky, preoccupied with the orchestration, did not answer. In a conversation with Romain Rolland after the premiere, the composer objected to the "rhythmic gymnastics of Dalcroze" in the choreography, yet a trace and more of Dalcroze can be seen in Stravinsky's own instructions about counting beats. The autobiography of Nijinska, who opposed Diaghilev's decision to introduce Dalcrozian eurhythmics to help the dancers learn the music, reveals that her brother did not have recourse to counting beats aloud until he came under the influence of the Dalcroze system. The annotated score shows how these beats were tallied. It also proves, if proof is still necessary, that Nijinsky was perfectly able to read the *musical* notation of beats and rhythms.

Decades after the premiere, Mme Rambert wrote:

> There was no melody to hold on to—so the only way to learn it was to count the bars all the time. The movements in themselves were simple and so was the floor pattern. But . . . the mastering of that rhythm was almost impossible.

---

[1] Pierre Monteux's reference to "Nijinsky's two-hand score" (letter to Stravinsky, February 22, 1913) evidently refers to the sketch-score.

This suggests that the radical rhythmic and harmonic newness had distracted the dancers to the extent that they could not hear melodies that were simple and far from new in kind. But surely, after three months of piano rehearsals, the greatest difficulty for the dancers was in the last-minute switch to the orchestra. The sonorities were entirely new, some of the figurations had either not been *in* the piano score or were unrecognizably transformed, and the dynamic and volumetric ranges were without precedent in music history. Shortly before the first performance, Stravinsky told an interviewer that "[At times] the dynamic power of the orchestra is more important than the melodic line itself."

The Joffrey production follows the score in allowing the orchestral Introduction to be heard with the curtain closed, thereby obtaining the maximum contrast between the rhythmically free beginning—so supple in the first measures that even the notation is only approximate[1]—and the isochronous dance beat of the "Augurs of Spring." In this first section of the ballet, however and unfortunately, the dancers hop *with* each note and emphasize none of them. A glance at the following extract from the score shows that not only are the pencilled-in dance accents (∧) *against* the orchestral accents (>), but that the first accent is in the choreography. The music imitates the dancers' jump, and a *hoquetus* is set in motion between them, though not in the Joffrey performance, which leaves the orchestra to hiccup by itself.

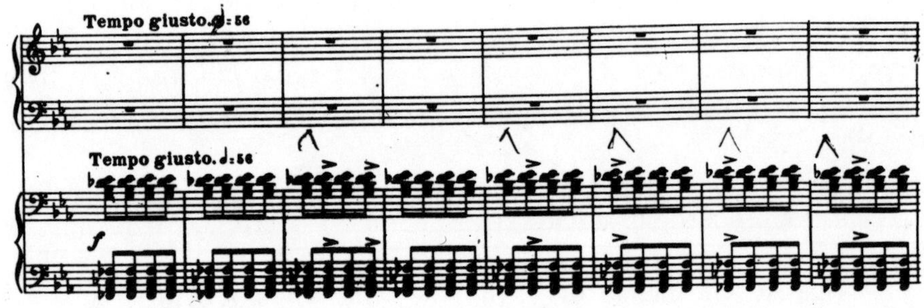

[1] See the essay by Carl Dahlhaus, "Problems of Rhythm in the New Music," in *Schoenberg and the New Music*. New York, 1987.

The script at the top of the next extract, the beginning of "The Ritual of Abduction," says "4 important accents" (found at the beginning of measures 1, 2, 3, and 7), and the Russian word in measures 2 and 3 identifies them as "jumps." As in "Augurs of Spring," the dance accents are on, the musical accents off, the beat. The perspicacious London *Times* critic H.C. Collis noted in July 1913: "What is really of chief interest in the dancing is the employment of rhythmical counterpoint in the mass for group movement." The Joffrey reconstruction is totally devoid of rhythmical counterpoint. (The words in the first measure say that "a large group of men begin.")

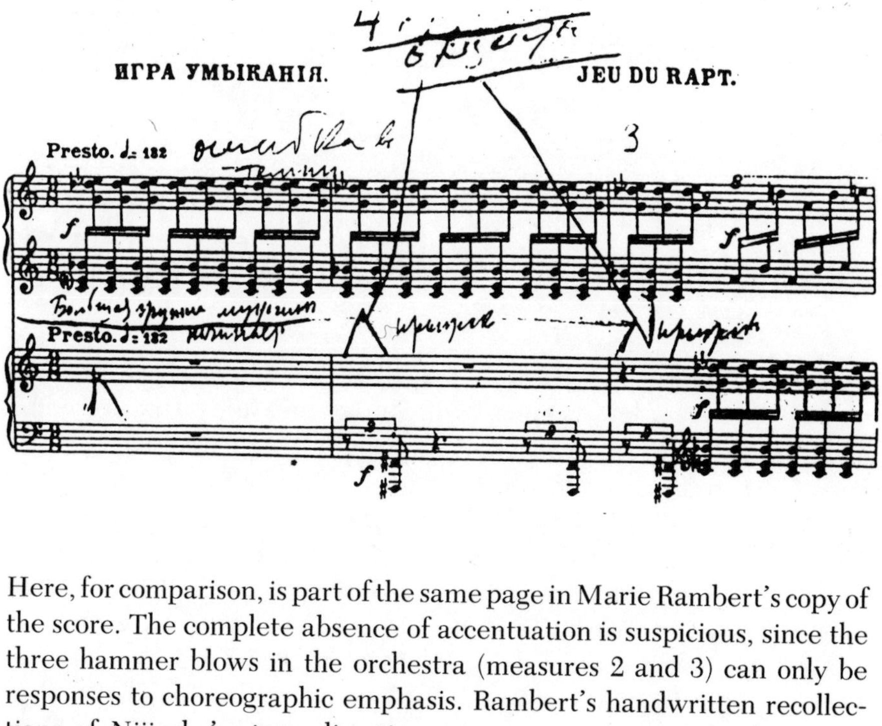

Here, for comparison, is part of the same page in Marie Rambert's copy of the score. The complete absence of accentuation is suspicious, since the three hammer blows in the orchestra (measures 2 and 3) can only be responses to choreographic emphasis. Rambert's handwritten recollections of Nijinsky's stage direction seem to support Stravinsky's later criticism that Nijinsky "had complicated and encumbered his dances beyond all reason": the furiously fast music is too short for the stage business.

In the next extract, Stravinsky's pencilled-in notation above the first measure (which he had combined with the last measure on the preceding page) shows a different rhythmic grouping for the choreography: "Cut these two measures in half," the Russian says. The half-note tied to a 16th and the 16th tied to a half form a retrograde rhythm (one that remains identical read backwards or forwards), a favorite Stravinsky construction, found in music as remote from *Sacre* as *Mavra* and *Apollo*. The direction in the next (and again in the fifth) measure is "The answer of the women," and in the measure after that, "Rhythm of the men in two parts." Remembering that Stravinsky later objected to the "parallelism" in Nijinsky's choreography, we should note that parallels are specified here, and that these associations of music for male and female dancers, back and forth from groups of one sex to the other, are as traditional—masculine horn-call in the lower part, feminine skitterings in the higher—as in the ballets of Tchaikovsky.

The next two extracts, showing the polyphonic construction of the choreography in *Spring Rounds*, suggest that Stravinsky had composed the choreography at the same time as the music. The dancers are divided into three groups entering at different time-intervals, like voices in a fugue; each group, moreover, is identified with a different rhythm. The written-in accents in the upper score define rhythm number one, those on the right side of the lower score rhythm number two. The word above measures 4, 7, and 8 says that all movement stops during them, thereby dividing the otherwise monotonous dance into interesting period-lengths. The Joffrey performance ignored this.

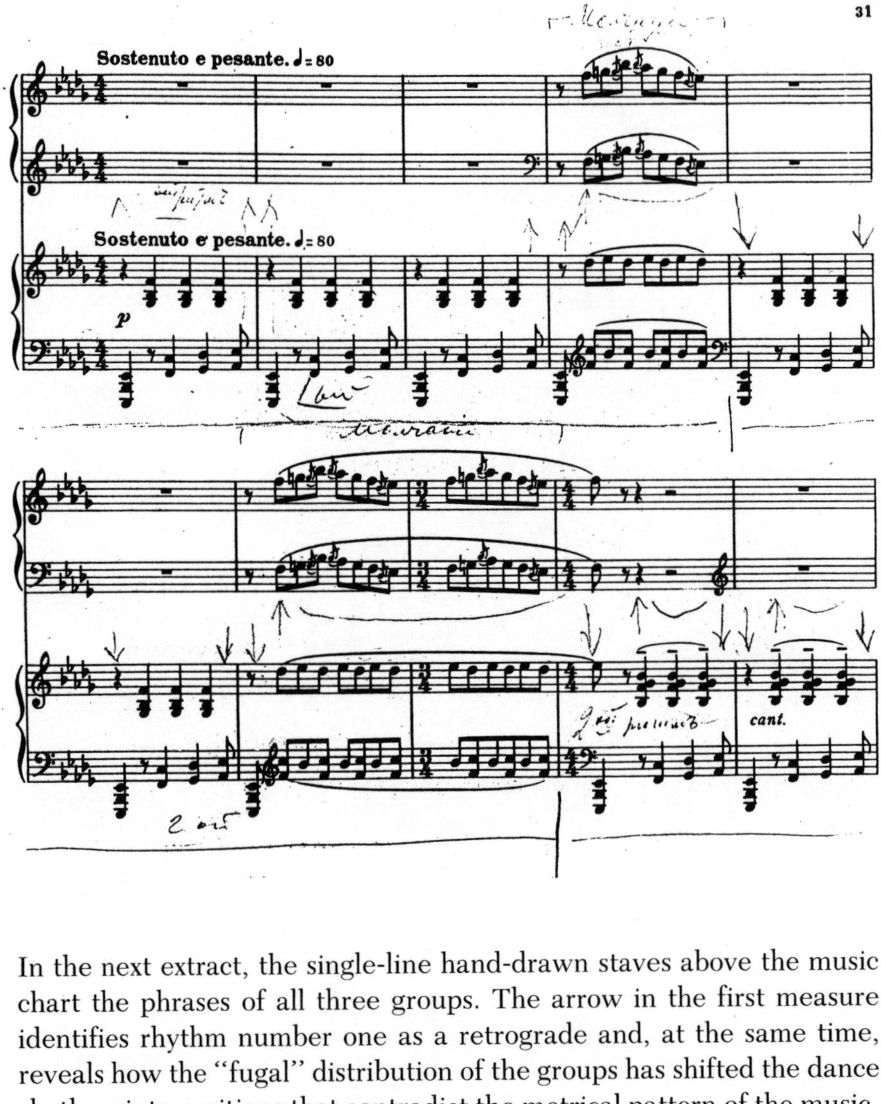

In the next extract, the single-line hand-drawn staves above the music chart the phrases of all three groups. The arrow in the first measure identifies rhythm number one as a retrograde and, at the same time, reveals how the "fugal" distribution of the groups has shifted the dance rhythms into positions that contradict the metrical pattern of the music.

In the next extract, the Russian words assign the music to female dancers whose 4-beat phrases are counterpointed against the musical meter. (The quarter-note melody in the lower part, bracketed by twos, reappears seven years later in Stravinsky's *Symphonies of Wind Instruments.*)

"Music exists when there is rhythm, as life exist when there is a pulse," Stravinsky wrote above one of his *Sacre* sketches, and, in a letter, "I sought to give the feeling of closeness between men and earth through a lapidary rhythm." Sometimes, as in the following sketch for the most lapidary rhythm in the history of dance music, his first idea may have been purely rhythmic:

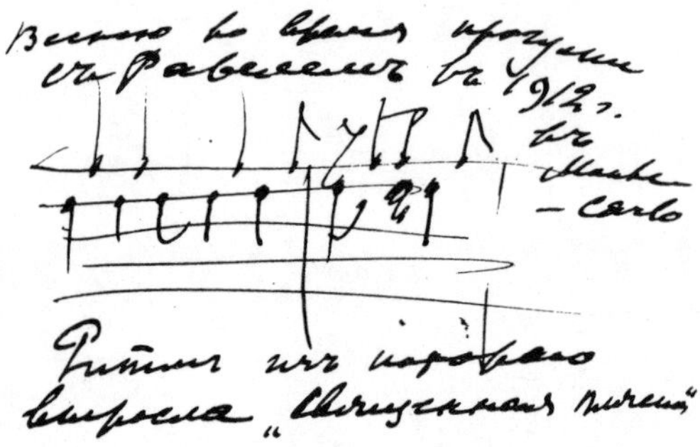

His Russian script says: "In the spring of 1912 during a walk with Ravel in Monte Carlo. This is the rhythm from which the Sacred Dance grew." The music that "grew" is in the next excerpt.

The composition of the "Sacred Dance," a dance piece from its inception, coincided with Fokine's departure and Nijinsky's arrival. All evidence indicates that the choreography was created in close collaboration between Stravinsky and Nijinsky during meetings in Bayreuth (!), Venice, Lugano, Monte Carlo, and Berlin: after returning to Switzerland from Berlin in mid-December, Stravinsky wrote: "Nijinsky directs it with passionate zeal." As in no other movement in the ballet, the orchestra in the second section has an accompanying role. The strong choreographic first beats in the following excerpt further show that Stravinsky adjusted his metrical system to the dance, since the corresponding place earlier in the movement is differently metered.[1]

[1] See Dahlhaus, *op. cit.*

Needless to say, the rhythmic pattern of the solo dance ($\frac{7}{8}$ ♪♪♪♪) is in counterpoint to the pattern of the orchestral rhythm. Regrettably, the Joffrey performance indicated no awareness of these ingenious designs.

The music was apparently heard for the first time in any form when Stravinsky and Claude Debussy played it 4-hands, June 9, 1912. Did the solo-instrument beginning, on this mind-boggling occasion, seem to the French master—as it still does to us—indebted to the example of *Afternoon of a Faun*? And what did Debussy, whose fluid music is forever overflowing its meters, think of the metrical tyrannies of the Russian master?

The reading took place in the home of Debussy's friend Louis Laloy, who wrote: "We were dumbfounded, flattened as though by a hurricane from the roots of time."

MUSICIANS

Saint Lambert

One of the most useful and enjoyable music books to appear in some time is the first English version of Saint Lambert's 1702 classic, *Les Principes du Clavecin Contenant une Explication exact de tout ce qui concerne la Tablature et le Clavier.*[1] The translation is felicitous, the introduction and notes are uncommon instances of musical scholarship lucidly presented, and the volume is elegantly produced—format, cover (Thomas Hill's painting *Garton Orme at the Spinet*), quality of paper, print, and music examples (both in facsimile and, for those containing more than one part, modern notation). This second publication in the Cambridge Musical Texts and Monographs series deserves high praise.

Saint Lambert's title does not claim enough. Besides a treatise on playing the harpsichord, the twenty-eight brief chapters are an authentic guide, as distinguished from a latter-day commentary, to musical performance generally in the time of Lully. The author, about whom the only known fact is that he had been called from Paris to the provinces to teach the clavecin, writes as if his lessons were intended for children. However that may be, professionals as well as amateurs, and of dance as well as music—the principal forms are chaconnes, gavottes, passepieds, rigaudons, sarabandes—should enroll in Saint Lambert's course today.

Harris-Warrick believes that François Couperin's dictum, "The difference between notation and performance is immense" (*L'Art de toucher le clavecin*, 1716), may have been aimed at Saint Lambert's literalism. Yet the *Principes* acknowledges the player's considerable freedom in choosing *agréments*, while demonstrating that the object of the strict rules, such as the one for starting a trill with the upper note on the beat, is to achieve the grace which is Saint Lambert's aesthetic ideal.

---

1 *Principles of the Harpsichord* by Monsieur de Saint Lambert, translated and edited by Rebecca Harris-Warrick. London, 1984.

The most absorbing pages are devoted to the relationship between meter and tempo, but Saint Lambert's unit of measurement must set a record for vagueness: "the step of a man of average height who walks one and a quarter leagues in an hour." All that can be said for certain about average height in 1702 is that it was smaller than today. With the help of Pascal Boyer's *Lettre à Monsieur Diderot* (1767), and Ronald Zupko's *French Weights and Measures Before the Revolution* (1978), Harris-Warrick establishes that the league most likely intended by Saint Lambert was the "*lieue de Paris*," which is equivalent to 2.4222 miles, and that the stride, if not of "a man of average height," then of a French regiment, was ♩= 107 per 2 $\frac{1}{2}$ feet or ♩= 125 for "*deux pieds*."

Wagner in Action

In 1864 Richard Wagner invited Heinrich Porges, musician and writer, to become his live-in secretary. Porges declined, but later accepted the composer's request to take down his remarks at rehearsals for the premiere of *Der Ring des Nibelungen* concerning the musical and stage performance. The importance of Porges's notes, published in 1896 as *Die Bühnenproben zu den Bayreuther Festspielen des Jahres 1876*,[1] has only recently been acknowledged, partly because Cosima Wagner, believing that she remembered the same dicta that Porges had recorded, did not want his book to be reprinted, and partly because it could not have been in the Hitler period, since Porges was Jewish. Ernest Newman did not even mention the *Bühnenproben*, having had an aversion to its reverential tone and high-flown literary style—or so Robert Jacobs speculates, though some of Newman's other sources are no less floridly devout.

Many of the instructions that Porges preserved are simply to the effect that in certain places the words and music should be properly emphasized and articulated, obvious requirements that a conscientious conductor would carry out without prompting. More valuable are Wagner's indications with regard to inflections of tempo, *viz.*, that it should be accelerated when the rhythmic tension slackens, as in the rests between the thinly-spread notes of a tympani solo in a slow passage in *Die Walküre*.

Porges tells us that Wagner's "directions pertaining to the action—the gestures, the positioning, the articulation of the sung words—were governed by . . . the basic principle of Shakespearean drama, namely mimic-dramatic naturalness." Non-existent Shakespearean principles apart, Wagner wanted his characters to create themselves in movements

---

[1] *Wagner Rehearsing the "Ring": An Eye-Witness Account of the Stage Rehearsals of the First Bayreuth Festival* by Heinrich Porges. Translated by Robert L. Jacobs. Cambridge, 1983.

having "the quality of living sculpture." He asked the Loge, for example, to enter from a cleft in the rocks in center stage, to sway his upper body, and, as he approached Nibelheim, to try to express "the cheerful mockery of a superior intellect pursuing a goal within certain reach," an attitude that no one could have understood better than Wagner himself. During rehearsals Wagner demonstrated stances for his singers, and even sang passages for them, rendering one of Brünnhilde's lines "with thrilling power in his voice."

The first English translation of Porges's book leaves its numerous quotations from the libretto in German, though anyone who can read them would surely be able to manage the whole book in that language. In one instance (a footnote on page 25) Jacobs inconsistently provides them in English, and in another (page 16) he translates Wagner's "expression marks" followed by the German in parenthesis—the method that should have been adopted throughout. The extracts from the reduced score of the *Ring* are said to be "as given by Porges," but this cannot be true, since the indications for instrumentation are in English. Not having the original to hand, I cannot tell whether the wrongly pluralized "protagonists," the mixing of past and present tenses, and the confusion of modifiers ("the sequence of chromatic six-four figures" should be "the chromatic sequence of . . . ") are faults of the translation. But Porges, not Robert Jacobs, is undoubtedly responsible for the statement: "In Wagner's works the pace of every syllable is determined by note-values." And not in other operas?

Nicolai Andreyevitch and Igor Fyodorovitch

"That blockhead," Igor Stravinsky wrote to a friend who had called his attention to the publication (1959–1960) of Vasily Vasilyevich Yastrebtsev's *Reminiscences of Rimsky-Korsakov*,[1] nor was this verdict changed on acquaintance with the book. Twenty-five years later, this much abbreviated English version will attract as many readers for the glimpses it contains of the young Stravinsky as for the portrait of his teacher, the composer of, and now almost exclusively known by, *Sheherazade*. Yastrebtsev, a well-to-do amateur, had briefly been a Rimsky pupil.

The *Reminiscences* cover the last sixteen years of Rimsky-Korsakov's life. In these pages, Stravinsky enters five years before the end, on January 26, 1903 (whether Old or New Style is not specified), with some "very charming and witty musical jokes of his own invention" performed for a gathering in the Rimsky-Korsakov home. Yastrebtsev's comment that the twenty-year-old composer was "a man of undoubted talent" stirs a suspicion that it was not written at the time but added at a later date (Yastrebtsev died in 1934), both because remarks of the kind are out of character in the book, and since Stravinsky's juvenilia is remarkable precisely for the absence of indications of an unusual gift. Nothing in his music before 1907 points in the direction of the masterpieces that came immediately after and were to bury the works of Rimsky-Korsakov.

Yastrebtsev glimpses Stravinsky in the summer of 1904, living with the Rimsky-Korsakovs in their summer vacation home and scoring wind parts in the master's new opera. The pupil is also seen taking an active part in musical evenings in the Rimsky-Korsakov St. Petersburg home, playing operas and symphonies at the piano, introducing a birthday cantata of his own composition for his teacher, even dancing the cakewalk. No close-up

[1] *Reminiscences of Rimsky-Korsakov* by V.V. Yastrebtsev. Edited and translated by Florence Jonas, foreword by Gerald Abraham. New York, 1986.

of Stravinsky's appearance is offered and no observation about his personality. But the book is short on description, and, as Gerald Abraham notes, Yastrebtsev's ears were "pricked only for Rimsky-Korsakov." The *Reminiscences* record Rimsky-Korsakov's musical opinions and not much else.

Yet how many of Stravinsky's opinions sound like echoes of those of his teacher! "Beethoven was not a great melodist," Rimsky declares, as the composer of *Firebird* did after him, no less inanely. When Rimsky berates a conductor for introducing "an absurd ritard" and for beginning "to sentimentalize" in the *Eroica*, even the voice reminds us of Stravinsky, who would also have said, with his teacher, albeit in sharper language and with a hand-on-bosom gesture, "I'm no admirer of heart-rending sounds." So, too, Rimsky's claim, while improvising a parody of Wagner, that "given a certain facility for harmonization, there is nothing easier than to write recitatives in this style," was Stravinsky's as well. Stravinsky's irony must also owe something to Rimsky's example, but Yastrebtsev, totally lacking the quality himself, is not alert to it in his idol.

Most of Rimsky-Korsakov's obiter dicta will appall the reader unfamiliar with the identity struggles of the Russian Nationalist School. In opera, Rimsky says, "Wagner and Glinka achieved heights unattainable by Mozart [in *Don Giovanni*]." And though "Beethoven and Glinka possessed inexhaustible technical resources," in the domain of rhythm "Berlioz is the only indisputable genius in all music." A symphony by Rimsky-Korsakov should be played for the reason that it is "no worse than those by Brahms." Some of the "technical" talk is equally naive—on relationships between tonalities and colors, for instance, where E minor is "bluish," and A flat major, as the dominant of D flat minor, "grayish violet." No reader can help noticing that while Rimsky-Korsakov is primarily a composer of operas, he says virtually nothing about dramatic concepts and construction, but discusses at length musical effects that usually prove to be no more than orchestral ones. And what is meant by good orchestration is, on the whole, simply the use of a novel instrument or combination of instruments.

Rimsky-Korsakov was commonsensical, and the *Reminiscences* should be read for this and his other earthbound qualities. A certain piece by Arensky "is boring not because it's long but, on the contrary, long because it's boring." To cut Schubert's "heavenly-length" symphony is actually to prolong it because "the elimination of the modulation or development section compels the listener to remain longer in the same key."

When the musicologists of the younger generation publish their

Russian-oriented books on Stravinsky, the debt of the composer of *Sacre* to Rimsky-Korsakov may be exposed as more profound than anyone has so far been aware, and, along with this readjustment, we may expect a new and higher appreciation of Rimsky-Korsakov himself.

Fouling the Firebird's Nest

John Kobler's *Firebird*,[1] falsely advertised as a "full-length biography," provides further unneeded proof that the life of an artist with the art left out, the man minus the mind, is of little value. In addition, or subtraction, Kobler makes no original contribution, passes off speculations and allegations as certified truths, and compounds distortions with errors of fact and opinion several to the page. True, he pays the present reviewer the dubious compliment of acknowledging the appropriation of thousands of words from his writings, but says nothing about the remainder of the contents, more than half of which have been filched from the same source and ineptly paraphrased.

Part of Kobler's preparatory training for his portrait of one of the makers of the century was in the biographizing of Al Capone. This background work shows most effectively in a re-enactment of the St. Valentine's Day Massacre in which the gunned-down Chicago bootleggers are replaced by the Stravinsky family. The target most often hit, shot so full of holes that no recognizable picture emerges, is the composer himself. In Kobler's drum-head court, Stravinsky is convicted of dishonesty and fraud ("Stravinsky fabricated various fictions about marriage and divorce"); of avarice and lack of integrity ("Career and money took place over ideology"; "While Stravinsky despised the Germans and particularly the Nazis, his concern for performances of his own work transcended his antipathy"); of exploiting friends ("he had no compunction about using others—in fact, seemed to consider it his right"); of philandering and leading a double life ("'I am a bigamist'"); of mean-spiritedness ("Stravinsky gave a dinner party . . . When the

---

[1] *Firebird*. A Biography of Igor Stravinsky by John Kobler. Macmillan Publishing Company. The book reviewed here was blocked by Judge Pierre Laval in Federal District Court, Manhattan, August 6, 1987 (*New York Times*, August 7, 1987) in a copyright infringement suit by the present writer. The review is based on the widely distributed page proofs.

check was presented, he excused himself to make a telephone call . . ."); of vanity and vulgarity ("I am very famous and I must own expensive cars"); even of boorishness ("I will bring my own [wine] and so he did, consuming it to the last drop himself"). Worst of all, Kobler's account of Stravinsky's selfishness in the neglect of his sick and dying first wife makes him a monster.

Much, if not quite everything, remains to be said in extenuation and amplification of these and similar indictments, but even in these examples, Kobler, who never, not even accidentally, gets Stravinsky's measure, demonstrates that he cannot distinguish an out-and-out lie (Stravinsky would not even have known how to make a call from a restaurant), recognize a joke ("expensive automobiles"), imagine the circumstances of a bring-it-yourself dinner, and perceive the extent to which the composer's first wife spent twenty years punishing him with his guilt and paying him back with her illness for having deserted her. Nevertheless, and momentarily to pretend that such things could be of any importance in comparison with the creation of masterpieces, Stravinsky, wherever he is, must be thinking of Anna Akhmatova's: "Worship the night/Lest you wake up famous."

Kobler's principal victim is not *the* Stravinsky, however, but his defenseless son, Soulima. While pretending to clear him of the taint of collaborating with the Nazis in France during World War II, Kobler insidiously delves further into the family disgrace, reveals much more than had been made public before, and underlines the charges in a mock justification: "What he did to sustain himself . . . seems trifling in comparison with the collaboration of many a celebrated Frenchman." Pierre Laval, for example. Even more damning is Kobler's show of whitewashing Soulima's appeal to high-ups inside the Third Reich to arrange concerts for him there and thus enlarge the scope of a career confined until then to Collaborationist circles in Paris. Kobler goes through the motions of excusing this on grounds that "He failed," while in truth he is deliberately publicizing the story, perhaps to bring it to the attention of the Simon Wiesenthal Center and eventually effect a deportation.

Most damaging of all, Kobler describes a backstage encounter between Soulima and the conductor Manuel Rosenthal at a performance of *Noces* in Paris immediately after the War. Why was he not invited to play one of the piano parts, Soulima asked, and Kobler does not even attempt to rebut Rosenthal's answer: "Because of your conduct during the Occupation." One other episode in this chapter provides the book with a much needed dramatic moment. In Los Angeles, toward the end of the War, Darius Milhaud received a letter from Francis Poulenc describing the activities of French musicians during the Occupation, and began reading it to a group of friends that included Hindemith and Stravinsky. "Milhaud evidently did not realize what was coming," Kobler says, "for despite Stravinsky's presence he read how Soulima behaved. Stravinsky covered his face with his hands."

But Kobler's treatment of all the Stravinsky children is much the same. While ostensibly sympathizing with their position vis-à-vis their father and stepmother—"A reproof [from father] sufficed to reduce Milena to tears and send her hurrying to Vera for consolation"—he constantly exposes them as devious and conniving, of showing "outward amiability" and "apparent affection," and of keeping up the duplicity for fifty years. In Kobler's presentation, the composer's progeny, like characters in Balzac, seem to have spent their entire lives foretasting their inheritances. No wonder Stravinsky had begun "to suspect that his children and their mates"—one of the latter is posthumously clobbered, or Koblered, as "stubborn, humorless, and unimaginative"—"were primarily concerned with what benefits they might receive from him."

Nor do Kobler's jumping in and mostly out of chronology, his long digressions (on Ida Rubinstein and D'Annunzio), and the omissions of essential events, help to present the children in a more favorable light. On the contrary, the avoidance of any reference to the crucial incident in the story, their alleged embezzlement of their father's lifetime savings from a Swiss bank in August 1969, inevitably draws attention to it and compels anyone wishing to pursue the subject to turn to other sources for the full explanation.

For a Kobler, all hypothetical attributions, no matter how flimsy, must be turned into established fact, no statement ever left under-exaggerated, no permanently lost link unsupplied. Thus Stravinsky's friend Gerald Heard is introduced as "the mystic . . . upon whom W. Somerset Maugham modeled the Hindu-converted hero of his *The Razor's Edge*;" after Christopher Isherwood had finally made clear that the character was *not* modeled on him, a "name" replacement was required instead of the actual but little-known real-life model identified by Maugham's biographer, Wilmon Menard.

The inflating process is automatic: Stravinsky "often" visited "Giacometti's Montparnasse studio where he sat for a great many drawings" (one visit, no drawings done there); "dined several times in Schoenberg's [Berlin] home" (not even once); "invited practically everyone he knew in Venice to a dinner party" at which there were "gallons of champagne"—"rivers" of it flow elsewhere in the book—and "kilos of caviar" (five guests, as photographs show, none from Venice, modest amounts of the liquid and the roe). Even the irruption at the premiere of *Sacre*, thoroughly documented years ago, is not sufficiently sensational for a gossip writer who has every regard for scandal and none for veracity. In the version that Kobler concocts, "some fifty pro-Stravinsky students stripped to the buff and [were] hauled off to police headquarters." 1960s-style protest nudity in 1913?

A volume of the same size would be required to correct the errors, but a few examples suffice to indicate that nothing in the present one is reliable. Quite apart from the scores of easily rectifiable mistakes—"the spring of 1925 found him in Venice where he played his *Piano Sonata*" (it didn't and he didn't); "in 1917, following a trip to Madrid" (not *in* Spain that year); his mother, leaving Russia, "arrived in August 1922" (arrived *where*?, and it was November)—what is the reader to make of such diametrically contradictory statements as, 1) "They all crossed themselves before each meal, knelt and prayed at bedtime . . . Except Stravinsky . . . Disaffected from the church in his youth, he still remained outside of it" (p. 113), and 2) "Stravinsky prayed often, crossed himself continually and made the sign of the cross over others . . . [he] remained a committed communicant" (p. 121).

By disclaiming any competence in music, Kobler assumes that he is licensed to write nonsense about it. Perhaps a musicologist might be able to sort out the confusion between the Credos of 1932 and 1948, and between them and a non-existent third one (which might be the Te Deum), but what will ordinary lovers of Stravinsky's music make of those "sudden atonalities" in *The Rake's Progress*, and of descriptions of the Serenade as "Mozartian," of the *Cinq Doigts* as "children's exercises for the fingers of the right hand," and of "The Owl and the Pussy-Cat" as a "giddy flight" (try "calm sea and prosperous voyage")?

Al Capone, indeed.

Stravinsky Centenary

This much-need *Stravinsky*[1] for the general audience is an intelligent, sensitive and fair-minded guide, musically perceptive in a non- or only minimally-technical way. The music is always the center of focus, with the biography interspersed, a more engaging method than the strict separation of life and work that had become a formula in Stravinsky's case. So, too, the presentation of the music is more integrated than that by most earlier commentators, more attuned to the features that unite than to those that divide the creations of earlier and later periods.

Admittedly, errors of fact occur on an average of about two per page, but they do not detract from the book's theses, and many readers will pick up on some of the misinformation: *viz.* Nora Kaye was "married in turn to Balanchine" (neither in nor out of turn); Stravinsky's tombstone bears his "name and two dates" (no dates). Even Boucourechliev's discovery of a correspondence between "a basic Balinese mode" and the theme, actually a Russian folk tune, of the middle movement of the 1944 Sonata is not so much wrong as irrelevant.

The perspective is that of the generation of French musicians who came to maturity after the Second World War, the radical evolutionists for whom Stravinsky had ceased to exist as a creative artist at about 1920, then, "after forty years in the desert . . . found his salvation in Webern." We can believe Boucourechliev that this has changed, and that in Paris, as in New York, "Music now enjoys a multiplicity . . . Nothing is obligatory, nothing is banned and the 'common grammar' based on Schoenberg and Webern has even been questioned . . . in its basic assumptions (atonality)." Meanwhile, during those decades in the wilderness, and after, Stravinsky had been regarding history "as *permanence*, as his property and his *instrument*. He saw the whole course of history as available to him, and he criss-crossed over it with abandon and delight . . . to

---

[1] *Stravinsky* by Andre Boucourechliev. Translated from the French by Martin Cooper. New York, 1987.

rediscover, perpetually recurring down the ages, certain active *constants.*"

Vestiges of the older French attitude toward the American Stravinsky show through, nevertheless. Why did he "choose to go to the United States, to relinquish his French nationality . . .? These were questions that Stravinsky's French friends asked themselves, not without bitterness, as they found themselves faced with . . . the Occupation." The answers are that he went to the United States to fulfill conducting and lecturing engagements contracted before the War, that he changed citizenships because of restrictions imposed on Russian-born French nationals after the debacle of May 1940, and that any *real* friend would have rejoiced in his escape from the Nazis.

Boucourechliev loves the late works almost as much as the popular Russian theater pieces, and he brings new insights to all the music without prejudice of category. His enlightening discussion of *Mavra*, for instance, is independent of the side-taking that this "stylistic exercise" inevitably provokes. And the favorable things that he finds to say about some of the shorter works of the early California period—*Circus Polka, Danses concertantes, Scènes de Ballet, Ebony Concerto*—are more surprising from a critic of his background than the unfavorable judgments on the Symphony in C ("the musical discourse is reduced to compulsive repetition") and *Orpheus* ("lacking in inner tension . . . One of Stravinsky's least successful works"). The Mass, which is "not . . . neo-classical," is the "masterpiece" of the late 1940s, Boucourechliev predicates. Whereas Beethoven was "trapped into the pitfall of theatricalizing the text" of the Credo, Stravinsky confines himself to "scanning it syllable by syllable, simply and humbly," the sound of his chanting voices "never rising above a murmur . . . except at . . . the reference to the Last Judgment . . . and on the word '*ecclesiam*,' where a dogma is being stated . . ."

The "crisis work" is *The Rake's Progress*. With it, Stravinsky had come to an impasse: "The tonal bases of his language seem . . . to be somehow off-center in their almost desperate affirmations," and when "the orchestra appears in the court dress worn by eighteenth-century Overtures," we are aware of a "vacuousness in the immaculate good manners of these acts of homage to the past." These criticisms are not without truth, and Boucourechliev's conclusions that Stravinsky's melody "leans to the hieratic rather than the dramatic," and that opera is not the medium for his "lofty distancing" and "purely musical structures," are astute.

In certain passages in the *Rake* the listener may wonder "Who is that by?," Boucourechliev asserts, while in all the works that follow "we are immediately back with the Stravinsky we have always known"—meaning that the continually exploring Stravinsky is the one we know. Perhaps, though the exact opposite was the case when the *Rake* and those later works were first performed. Here an illustration might have been provided of how new elements in, for example, rhythmic vocabulary (units of 7 for 6, 11 for 3, 12 for 5, and so forth) are joined to the syncopation, the irregular accents and meters, and the ostinati—in *The Flood* and *Requiem Canticles*—extending from the Stravinsky of yore.

In Boucourechliev's view, the *Canticum Sacrum*, in which Stravinsky abandoned "the style to which he had accustomed his admirers in order to follow his own inner promptings," is the pivotal work of the final period. The performance of this "most unified of his compositions," moreover, was "a 'milestone' in the public musical life of our time." Stravinsky was seventy-four then. *Threni*, his next work and "the most noble and the most inspiring of all the composer's religious music," concludes with words from the Prayer of Jeremiah that, Boucourechliev thinks, "might serve as a motto for Stravinsky's whole artistic career: *Innova dies nostros sicut a principio.*"

* * *

Before turning to collections of papers originally prepared for centenary symposia in San Diego[1] and Notre Dame,[2] I should mention the recent publication[3] of A.I. Klimovitsky's "Two Versions of the 'Song of the Flea'—by Beethoven and by Mussorgsky—in Stravinsky's Orchestrations." Klimovitsky fills gaps in the composer's pre-*Firebird* biography, provides guidelines for the study of his early manuscripts as a whole, and shows how, even in 1909, the young Stravinsky succeeded in imposing his inventiveness as well as elements of his style on the young Beethoven. No less remarkable than the essay itself is the fact of its appearance in the prestigious *Yearbook of the Academy of Sciences of the USSR*, surely a

---

1 *Confronting Stravinsky: Man, Musician, Modernist.* Edited by Jann Pasler. Berkeley, CA, 1986.

2 *Stravinsky Retrospectives.* Edited by Ethan Haimo and Paul Johnson. Lincoln, Nebraska/London, 1987.

3 *Monuments of Culture: New Discoveries.* 59 authors. Leningrad, 1986.

sign of the times (Gorbachev's). The music type is loud and clear, but the facsimiles of the manuscripts, now in the Institute of Theatre, Music and Cinema in Leningrad, have been reduced beyond legibility.

Recognizing that the relationship of Stravinsky's music to that of his Russian predecessors is still the largest blank in our knowledge of the composer, the editors of *Stravinsky Retrospectives*, much the shorter of the centenary volumes, give more than half of their space to two studies that stake out important areas in this vaguely charted territory. Since the one by Richard Taruskin is a chapter from a forthcoming book that connects Stravinsky with his cultural roots and provides the background perspectives for an understanding of his art, no more need be said at this point than that the subject here is Stravinsky's setting of Russian and other texts. Another Taruskin chapter, "Stravinsky and the Painters"—Russian painters—is included in the larger volume of symposia papers, *Confronting Stravinsky*.

In "The Influence of Russian Composers on Stravinsky," Claudio Spies compares family characteristics in Stravinsky's music and in Glinka's, Dargomyzhsky's, and Tchaikovsky's, the closest of kin among his musical ancestors. No less important, Professor Spies severs heretofore presumed lines of descent from Rimsky-Korsakov, claiming that the effect of teacher on pupil, apart from the tritone in *Firebird*, a Rimsky-inherited predilection, is no more than sporadic. Even here, in Stravinsky's first masterpiece, "procedural characteristics are," according to Spies, "a fair distance beyond the reaches of Rimsky-Korsakov's imagination." Also traced to Rimsky is a chromatic "parallel harmonic slithering" device found in, of all pieces, *Perséphone*. Spies concludes that on Stravinsky "Rimsky-Korsakov's music may be more accurately judged a deterrent, rather than an encouragement, to emulative efforts."

Spies's discoveries of Tchaikovsky in Stravinsky, and his discerning choice of music examples are special delights. For this reader, the most perceptive conjunction is between a passage in Tchaikovsky's *The Little Slippers* and the beginning of Stravinsky's *Le Baiser de la fée*, a work that contains "some of the best music Tchaikovsky never composed."

Professor Spies accurately recalls Stravinsky playing a passage from Act II, scene I of the *Rake* for him when the composer "came east sometime in 1949 or 50." (Actually April 29, 1950, four weeks after Stravinsky began work on Act II.) Partly accurate, too, is the recollection that Stravinsky had "conducted Tchaikovsky's Serenade in New York . . . a few days later . . . I was among the friends who saw him off at the then Idlewild Airport." (The seeing off was on April 13, 1955, but Stravinsky, only one night in New York, had not conducted there.) More doubtful is the speculation that a "performance of *Idomeneo* in Boston, in 1947" planted the Mozartian "seed" at the time of the *Rake*. *Idomeneo* was seen in Boston that year but not Stravinsky, who heard it there in February 1949 (before a dinner at the home of Winifred Johnstone, one of Nadia Boulanger's lieutenants, who tried to oblige Mr. Spies and this reviewer to wash the dishes). *Così fan tutte*, heard in Colorado in July 1948, continued to inspire Stravinsky throughout the composition of the *Rake*.

All three younger contributors, Joseph Straus, Paul Johnson, and Ethan Haimo, musically astute critics, would no doubt agree that Stravinsky mastered the "problems of structural coherence, hierarchy, and stylistic consistency imposed . . . by the abandonment of traditional tonality" (Haimo), and that his music has an "underlying unity" despite a "stylistic diversity . . . greater than that of any other composer preceding him" (Johnson).

* * *

Confronting Stravinsky explores little-known aspects of Stravinsky's music, his mind, and his Russian culture. The range of the book far exceeds that of any other on the composer, and some of the subjects—Stravinsky and Russian pre-literate theater, discontinuity and proportion in Stravinsky's music, Stravinsky and the pianola—are introduced for the first time. For the first time, too, the tallest peaks of analysis can be scaled by musical literates not trained in technical criticism.

A good starting point would be Elmer Schönberger's and Louis Andriessen's "The Utopian Unison," which isolates an important stylistic feature of Stravinsky's music, the intermittently wayward octave and unison doublings of melodic lines. The presentation is witty and the musical perception as "profound" as any in the academic studies implicitly mocked. This is music criticism of a rare kind, largely confined to music examples. But why was the best-known instance of not-quite-successive octaves, the opening of *Symphony of Psalms*, omitted?

In "The Significance of Stravinsky's Last Works," Charles Wuorinen and Jeffry Kresky contend that the late music, especially the 1966 fragments, the pediment of Wuorinen's own musical monument, *An Igor Stravinsky Reliquary*, will ultimately be seen as the most "significant." However that may be, "The remarkable spare last works [are] the precious link that may show the possibility of convergence and direct continuity between the diatonic past and what can in a very general way be called the chromatic present." In less precise words, Stravinsky's later "serial" music may point towards a synthesis of tonal and twelve-tone procedures.

Thanks in part to the use of letters, in addition to numerals and to a chord chart and letter name-graphs that anyone who can read music will have no trouble in following, Allen Forte's analyses of harmonic syntax and voice-leading in passages from five pre-World War I works including *Zvezdoliki* ("Wholly consistent with its predecessors" in both) are models of lucidity. He seems to be the first to remark the derivation of the "Infernal Dance" motive from the introductory music of *Firebird*, the first—at this date!—to point out that the villains in both *Firebird* (Kaschei) and *Petrushka* (the Moor) are evoked by simple whole-tone figures, and the first to identify one of Stravinsky's favorite chords, introduced at a crucial place in the stage action in the Fourth Tableau of *Petrushka*, as both another form of Scriabin's "mystic chord" and "the *Wozzeck* hexachord."

Pieter Van Den Toorn makes clear that an approach to Stravinsky must begin with the recognition that the music does not lend itself to traditional tonal, atonal, and serial analysis. Anyone puzzled by the identity of the "distinctive musical presence" that transcends the Russian, the neoclassical, and the serial periods will find part of the explanation in Van Den Toorn's divisions into music of "explicit diatonic intent," music wholly referable to the octatonic collection, and music fusing octatonic and diatonic contexts. As in his landmark book,[1] Van Den Toorn never loses sight of the consistency of Stravinsky's musical thought.

Accessible, with rather more effort, is the essay by Milton Babbitt—after a 120-word opening sentence containing a suspension as long as the Golden Gate Bridge—but his analysis of the same music (*Movements*) in *Stravinsky Perspectives* has more to recommend it, including a corrected musical example. In the spirit of the occasion, and letting his back and side hair down, Professor Babbitt indulges in some rare personal recollections, introducing them most aptly with : "[They are] intended to prove nothing, but I hope they will say something." They say, among other things, that Babbitt is no less perceptive about Stravinsky's words than about his music:

[1] *The Music of Igor Stravinsky*. New Haven, 1983.

> In 1962, when Stravinsky's eightieth birth year was being celebrated in Santa Fe and he was just beginning the composition of *Abraham and Isaac*, he spent an afternoon hearing and seeing the works of a group of young composers who had been imported for the occasion. He was unusually pensive and meditative during the journey back from the ceremony, and finally—with not, for him, exceptional insight and foresight—he quietly remarked that music already had and probably would continue to retreat from the kind of luxuriant complexity that now engaged him . . .

Jonathan Kramer notes that some of Stravinsky's music, most markedly in the second decade of the century, is "overtly sectionalized"; that these sections are harmonically static; that they "unfold more through permutation and variation than through progression and development"; that their lengths are "less internally predictable than are traditional tonal durations"; and that in juxtaposition they are discontinuous. In an effort to define "moment form," Kramer advances the notion that we are forced "to hear all moments as having equal importance regardless of their lengths." But since one measure does not have the same importance as fifty, this sounds like an over-extension of his valid argument that short sections in Stravinsky are not subsidiary to long ones as they are in traditional tonal music.

Kramer's most interesting suggestions are that the development of proportional consistencies in Stravinsky's later music might be seen as a parallel to his developing classical aesthetic, and that transitions do not exist in his sectional forms, or are themselves harmonically static sections. Thus the "modulation" back to the first subject in the third movement of the 1944 Sonata would be more accurately described as a brief, static interlude. A reference to *Agon* ("the most pervasive and elegant proportion I have found in Stravinsky's music") as an 18-minute composition—this is the duration of only three-fourths of the piece—tends to undermine confidence in the split-second timings on which Kramer's analyses of temporal ratios depend.

Some of Louis Cyr's assumptions in "Writing the *Rite* Right" are wrong. But first, he seems to be unaware that the 1943 "Sacrificial Dance" was not "made compulsory from 1945 onwards in all performances of *The Rite*" for the simple reason that the "original" was not protected by United States copyright. This also explains what he mistakenly interprets as Stravinsky's "approval" of Robert Rudolph's reduced instrumentation. Not being able to outlaw this grotesque transmogrification, the composer chose to improve it in a well-known problem passage. At this same place, Cyr writes, "Someone obviously advised Stravinsky in 1921 to strengthen the upper thirds by simply doubling them." Why "obviously"? Was Stravinsky incapable of making the simple adjustment himself?

Of the passage that Stravinsky reorchestrated in response to some comments by Pierre Monteux following his rehearsals in March 1913, Cyr says: "the amazing thing . . . is that none of the percussion instruments had a place in the original orchestral texture. It is interesting to speculate what prompted the composer to introduce such instrumental novelties at that late stage of rehearsing . . ." Late stage? The rehearsals, two months before the performance, were the first. But the speculation is of interest in that Ravel was with Stravinsky when he received Monteux's letter and could have influenced those instrumental choices.

Some of Cyr's other questions can be answered conclusively. The supposedly "inauthentic" timpani parts at [146] and [171] are found in Stravinsky's 1926 manuscript, as are the timpani notes at [167] and at one measure before [169] (deleted by Stravinsky in 1965). Who is responsible for altering the timpani parts at the beginning of "The Ritual of Abduction?" Cyr asks, and the answer is again "Stravinsky," in a 1922 manuscript. The 1967 score compounds the error here, incidentally, in that the timpano piccolo should play only the B, the other timpani the C and G (C and F sharp at [57]). Cyr frets about the restoration of the "col legno" indication for the second violins at [24] in the 1967 version, but Stravinsky red-inked it in his score after hearing a performance of it in Vancouver and London in 1965.

Curiously Cyr does not mention three even more glaring errors in the 1967 "definitive" edition: the missing indication for mute in the first trumpet part at [26] (the muted second trumpet is not an echo effect), corrected in Stravinsky's 1922 manuscript; the mistaken instructions for the basses at [90], where the two solos should play pizzicato, the others arco, as in the 1926 manuscript, and the E flat and G flat (instead F and G flat) in the first trumpet in the second measure of [148], also found in Stravinsky's 1926 manuscript (in music notation *and* writing).

Not all the papers can be mentioned here, though all contribute significantly to Stravinskyology. Pride of place has rightly been given to Karlinsky's essay on Russian pre-literate theater, but, like Roger Shattuck's essay, this has already been published and noticed. The chapter by the late Lawrence Morton makes us regret that he did not write a full-length book.

Since errors perpetrated by academics might well be repeated, the more parlous should be noted here. Titles are misspelled (*Tres sacra* [sic] *cantiones*), as are well-known names (Jacques-Dalcroze [sic]), while others are mysteriously gallicized (Théodor Adorno). Stravinsky did not come to New York in December 1958 "to conduct the first performance of *Threni*" (he had already conducted the piece in six other cities); the *Serenade en la* was not "completed in Venice on 9 September 1925"; "*Libera me*" is not one of his *a cappella* pieces; the second movement of *Le Marteau sans maître* is not likely to have reminded us of *Agon*, which was written three years later; Igor Markevitch did not prepare *The Rake's Progress* "for performances in Venice" (as *he* claims in a letter that should have been corrected in a footnote); and the Violin Concerto, said to be unperformable with piano, was performed with one several times by Stravinsky and Dushkin.

Sometimes errors of this kind are thick on the ground. To illustrate an article adding to the lore of Stravinsky-Schoenberg non-relations, a German newspaper interview with Stravinsky in New York in January 1925, shown in facsimile, is described as "a continuation of the feud that *began . . . in September 1925*." (Emphasis added.) The editor says that the interview was "Originally written in English," though it might have been written in Russian or French, and an ungrammatical caption identifies the interviewer as "R. Roerig," though the name in the facsimile is plainly "N. Roerig". After Roerig's words "Piano-Rag," the editor, or the author, has inserted the words "The Piano Concerto" in square brackets, as if this were an alternate title. Finally, the word "passacaglia," in Schoenberg's marginalia, becomes "passacagalia" in the book's transcription.

Many of the examples in music-type are seriously flawed, and not all are on the right pages (the last one on p. 237 belongs on p. 244). In the one on pp. 256–7, several pitches are wrong and some are absent; indications for instrumentation are misplaced (the trombones in the example at the top of p. 203); key signatures (p. 212) and changes of clef (top of p. 203) are missing; meters are wrong (pp. 212 and 227), and bizarre abbreviations introduced, as in "pizzi" for "pizzicato."

What *Confronting Stravinsky* lacks most is a contribution to biography. At a time when researchers have discovered that F.I. Stravinsky, the composer's father, is listed in the 1898 St. Petersburg telephone directory, we still know almost nothing about the composer I.F. Stravinsky's Greek-Russian Orthodoxy. How, for example, could a believer in the Pentecostal miracle of the restoration of language have chosen Babel as the text for a cantata? The answer may be simply that Stravinsky had forgotten this in 1944, as, two decades later, he definitely had forgotten that the Cumaean Sybil had been expurgated from the Requiem text (at about the same time as the dropping of Saint Christopher). Perhaps his correspondence with Father Nestor at Mount Athos in the terrible spring of 1939 will shed some light. A full, let alone a magisterial, biography of Stravinsky beyond his comings and goings in the beau monde is still some distance in the future.

* * *

Stephen Walsh's commentaries on the music of Igor Stravinsky[1] bring us nearer than ever before to an understanding of the composer's artistic philosophy and the nature of his achievement. The level of discourse is high and lucidly sustained, and the qualitative judgments, disputable in the case of individual works, reflect close inner and outer listening. Though the book appears in a popular series, "Companions to the Great Composers," it is far from simply introductory; ordinary music lovers will encounter momentary, but not insuperable difficulties. And any reader caught up in the end-of-century game of defining "modernism" can ill afford to ignore Professor Walsh's presentation of one of its greatest creators.

Biography, except when it bears directly on the conception and circumstances of a composition, is dispensed with. So is the formula which apportions space according to conventionally accepted importance, more words and more musical illustration being given to the early *Pastorale* and the short, lost-in-the-shuffle *Balmont Songs* than to the *Capriccio*, Violin Concerto, Duo concertant, and *Jeu de cartes* all together. Strict chronology is also suspended for side-by-side comparisons. This may momentarily confuse, as when we learn that one version of *The Wedding* employs a pianola before learning that Stravinsky had written an Etude for the machine two years earlier. But Walsh's unwavering focus on the larger features of Stravinsky's music justifies his methods.

The chapters on the early Russian ballets introduce new viewpoints, somewhat disconcerting in the case of *Firebird*, which Walsh classifies with the "pre-Stravinskian works"—despite the immense gap between it and all the earlier music. (Who, if not Stravinsky, could have written the

[1] *The Music of Stravinsky* by Stephen Walsh. London and New York, 1988.

"Infernal Dance," which Walsh considers less original in harmony and phrasing than Mussorgsky's *Night on Bare Mount*?) "*Firebird* is a work of synthesis rather than innovation," Walsh maintains. But surely it is both. Onward, then, to *Petrushka*, whose "most modern feature is its detachment." *Petrushka*, moreover, "exemplifies a new mood in the arts generally, in which the self-absorption and anguish of romanticism and expressionism begin to be opposed by an outward-looking objectivity . . . it is fitting that [Petrushka's] final gesture should be not an apotheosis or a transfiguration, but a nose-thumbing gesture at his tormentors."

The most pertinent of many astute observations about *The Rite of Spring*—"one of the greatest moulders of new sensibilities in the history of Western music"—is that "While Stravinsky's harmonic palette had certainly grown harsher and more complex—it is not atonal." To deny [*The Rite*] a tonal function "is misleading," Walsh rightly reiterates, and he reminds us that Stravinsky did not write atonal music before *Movements*, half a century later. On another level, the *Rite* is the archetype of Stravinsky's ritualized attitude to drama, the ballet "a strict 'liturgical' sequence . . . which, we understand, will always happen this way, with different participants but the same meaning."

Turning to a sketchbook for the *Rite*, Walsh notes that "Stravinsky's physical involvement in music like the 'Honoring of the Chosen One' is obvious from the sheer flamboyance of the penstrokes [and] is tantamount to a choreographic art in itself, almost a participation in the ritual"; Stravinsky, he adds, "certainly came to music as a dancer rather than a singer." The *Rite* reintroduces the ancient idea of rhythm as material, Walsh says, acknowledging later that "It is still something of a shock to experience music which treats rhythm as a vehicle for refined, intellectual, and subtle emotional utterance." One aspect of Stravinsky's modernism that emerges in *Renard* is the idea that the "new music need not be inhibited in scale and scope." Another, appearing within the next few years, is the acceptance of "stylistic plurality," the readiness to absorb a diversity of idioms.

For Walsh, *The Wedding*, Stravinsky's next work, is "conceivably [his] greatest," as well as, in many respects, "the most radical and original of his theater pieces." The action is ritualized, in Stravinsky's "almost ethnographic attitude to ritual," and the drama, as distinct from the particular occasion, is not unique but a prescribed ceremony. The parallels with *The Rite of Spring* are obvious—in the "inevitability of the cycle of birth, life and death," and in the rituals preparing the virgin for sacrifice in the presence of the tribal elders.

"Oddly enough," Walsh says, "the harmony in the first orchestral draft of *The Wedding* is essentially the same as in the final version." But in Stravinsky's music, harmonic emendations between orchestral drafts, unlike rhythmic and metrical ones, are not odd but non-existent, and they are extremely rare even from one sketch to another. "Harmony in Stravinsky's hands assumes a powerful symbolic role," Walsh continues, and in *The Wedding* "he achieves an emancipation of the dissonance more thoroughgoing than Schoenberg's, since, with Stravinsky, individual chords, whether consonant or dissonant, are endowed with an autonomy quite independent of contrapuntal or motivic considerations."

The Coda of *The Wedding* is one of "the profoundly solemn moments in 20th century music," Walsh asserts. Yet Stravinsky's performance instructions in the sketch score reveal that "At the very end a solo voice (tenor) sings in a saccharine or oily voice, drawing out the words." The mockery that this implies is consistent with the peasant bawdy that characterizes the whole of the last tableau, as well as with the distancing and depersonalizing that are part of the composer's psychological and artistic make-up. Perhaps Walsh too readily dismisses Stravinsky's criticisms of Boris Asafiev's ethnographic interpretation of *The Wedding*. After considering Stravinsky's angry disavowal of Asafiev's "fertility rite" explanation of the work, and of the composer's own description of it as a "*divertissement*," the Russian scholar William Harkins concluded that the original staging by the Diaghilev company must have contradicted Stravinsky's concepts, which, for practical reasons, had to be abandoned. Noting that the score nevertheless retains "a certain number of role indicators and stage directions," Harkins argues that "Stravinsky's artistic instinct was perhaps more correct than his theoretical aesthetics."

Walsh's discussion of *Mavra* contains nuggets of insight on every aspect of the piece and its unhappy history. But the suitability of Pushkin's story for translation to the operatic stage must still be questioned, and the joke about the servant problem is too thin and protracted—solo into duet into trio into quartet and on out in full retrograde order—to provide the centerpiece. Furthermore, the action, confined to the last two minutes, ends too abruptly, and the heavy, wind-band orchestration is a major miscalculation. Walsh resorts to special pleading: "carried through with such wit and invention, such variety of color and liveliness of tone," *Mavra* succeeds in turning "an apparent stylistic recidivism into a new kind of synthetic modernism."

The survey of Stravinsky's early neo-classical techniques is in agreement with prevalent views of them: "The use of classical form is referential rather than organic, and is best interpreted like his other classical devices, as symbolic." This recurring theme of symbolisms of classicism may be understood by comparison with Schoenberg, who

> refrains consciously from the use of commonplace tonal chords precisely because he wanted to avoid their familiar implications. It is just as clear that in retaining those shapes, Stravinsky accepted their inherited burden of meaning as part of their symbolism.

Choosing the Octet, Stravinsky's first neo-classical piece, for illustration, Walsh shows that the necessary length is achieved

> not by systematic tonal tension but by an elaboration of cellular motives [that allude] constantly to tonal phraseology. Nevertheless, by archly side-stepping on to the traditional dominant seventh at the end [of the Introduction], Stravinsky tricks us into hearing the whole as classical.

Walsh is apparently the first critic of *Oedipus Rex* to notice "Cocteau's omission of crucial facts of the plot (that Oedipus was the adopted son of Polybus [is] revealed only after Polybus' death)"; and the first to explain that the "opera-oratorio" subtitle means that the work cannot become either one or the other "at the convenience of its interpreters but that it is an opera on which certain aspects of the concert oratorio has [*sic*] exerted its [*sic*] influence." This leads to a speculation about Stravinsky's preoccupation with "frames." Is it possible, Walsh asks,

> to blame the growth of a new kind of sterile scholarly culture in which the artist and his audience, having lost their own potent feeling for art are reduced to a voyeuristic ogling at the performance rituals of earlier times?

With or without frames, Stravinsky "had been reinventing old rituals . . . as a mirror to modern consciousness," and in *Oedipus*, as in *The Rite of Spring*, "the survival of the people depends on the sacrifice of an individual." Looking back from *Threni*, composed three decades later, Walsh remarks that, like *Oedipus*, it "begins with a city in desolation, and ends with a ceremony of repayment."

The chapter on *The Rake's Progress* traces the different traditions that the opera combines, including the differences of approach between

Hogarth (social behavior) and Auden (moral law and the individual who breaks them), and between Auden and Stravinsky: the *Rake* is not Stravinsky's kind of opera, Walsh argues, since it is insufficiently ritualized, the only "ritual re-enactment" being "the cyclic idea of seasonal renewal." (Walsh refers to the "ritual solemnity of the moment in which time literally stands still as Shadow arrests the clock at the ninth stroke of midnight"; but in actuality the clock strikes one, whereupon Shadow turns it back to strike twelve.)

The longest part of the book is devoted to the post-*Rake* pieces (nearly a quarter, or 60 pages, as against 26 pages for *Petrushka* and *The Rite of Spring*), no doubt because, *Agon* excepted, this music is just becoming known. *Agon*, Walsh believes, is one of Stravinsky's

> greatest and most original works. What astonishing creative vitality to seize hold, at the age of nearly seventy-five, of an established and supposedly alien technique and convert it at a stroke into something that had been beyond the reach of its originators . . . one is inclined to feel that the particular achievement of *Agon* would not have been within the reach of any artist who had not already established Stravinsky's linguistic range, and the techniques to go with it.

In connection with *Agon* and the music that followed, Walsh restates some of the principal distinctions between Stravinsky and Schoenberg:

> Where for Schoenberg serialism was a way of sustaining the original forms of German classicism . . . it seems to have been the closed system itself that interested Stravinsky . . . [Stravinsky's] serial treatment typically makes capital out of the fact that twelve-note rows are in essence repetitive. . . . Where Schoenberg had usually preferred a method of combination which specifically avoided bringing out particular notes or note groups, Stravinsky takes the opposite course of designing and combining his series so as to bring out particular notes or particular harmonies.

Walsh's appreciation of *Threni* is the most sensitive in the thirty-year history of the work. He points out that to look at it next to *The Wedding* is "to see common ground even in detail, for all the forty-five years which separate their conception," and that this ground starts at the very beginning, with the same "semitone dissonance with octave spacing."

The *Canticum Sacrum* is no less sympathetically and illuminatingly dealt with, especially with regard to its ritualized, "quasi-liturgical" symbolism. Walsh rightly observes that since the piece was intended to be performed in a resonant basilica, Stravinsky

> used reverberation as a linking device at the end of the sections of the outer choruses. The long bass notes in the final choruses are meant to hold the music up, so to speak, while the more brilliant high sounds die away . . .

But those outer choruses are not, as claimed, marked by "much double-tonguing," the tempo being too slow for any but the single kind.

Glancing at the *Monumentum*, Walsh does not point to its principal achievement, the translation of purely vocal to purely instrumental music with no trace of any origins in the former—though earlier, in connection with *The Rite of Spring*, he had remarked on the phenomenon that music so intimately connected with one instrument, the piano, should eventually "live so vividly in terms of others." The attraction of Gesualdo's music for Stravinsky, Walsh believes, was its "harmonic obliquity," but its art of voice-leading was equally compelling.

Walsh's impressions of *A Sermon, A Narrative and a Prayer* suggest that he has never heard an adequate, let alone an inspiring, performance. (In one extended passage in Stravinsky's recording, chorus and orchestra are more than a beat apart.) Even so, one wonders how he can refer to the "muffled" drums in the last part (no drums at all in this work), to the "madrigalism" of the jagged double-reed double-canon, and to the "device of switching from speech (narrator) to singing (contralto soloist) . . . each time the name 'Stephen' is mentioned"—since the only switch is to the tenor, the other two mentions being rhythmically synchronized duets of speech and song. What, moreover, are we to make of the statement that Stravinsky keeps "silent" at the lapidation, when the first of the two references to it is answered by the cruellest brass chords he ever wrote. The coda, a beautiful threnody made to order for the ritual thesis, seems not to have been noticed.

Walsh's treatment of "the strange and idiosyncratic *Abraham and Isaac*" is regrettably perfunctory. To say that the piece is without "colorful imagery" is to overlook the episode of the ram caught in the thicket, the programmatic evocation of Abraham saddling the ass for the journey, and such literalisms as the two bassoons at "and they went both of them together." But he also fails to respond to the drama and lyricism in

Isaac's questioning of his father (the repeated melody in the upper instrumental part); in the voluptuous string chords at "I have learned that a fearer of God art thou"; in the passage, startlingly introduced by octave unisons, at the calling of "the angel of the Lord to Abraham a second time"; and, above all, in the quiet, profoundly moving conclusion, "and dwelt Abraham in Beersheba."

In other respects, too, the analysis of *Abraham and Isaac* does not inspire confidence. The baritone "is several times unaccompanied, or accompanied only by one or two instruments," Walsh writes, though this description fits much more than half of the vocal part. And on the technical side nothing is said about the greatly expanded rhythmic vocabulary, the varieties of rhythmic constructions, and the new uses of syncopation (in the canon at "On the day the third"). Finally, as if giving up on the piece, Walsh declares that it is "a move toward the esoteric which seems to be bound up with Hebrew, a language which for most listeners . . . is even more 'secret' than Latin . . . " But would this be true of the only American cities in which the little cantata is at all likely to be performed?

For Walsh, the masterpiece of the final decade is the *Requiem Canticles*, "The greatest (with *Agon*) of all those [works] composed with the serial method," and one that shows Stravinsky "at eighty-four still as modern-minded as he was at thirty." Here an ends-and-means attempt is made to distinguish serial procedure and musical purpose, though some readers might understand the argument as precisely that of the late Canadian prophet: the method *is* the music. What is meant, perhaps, was already conveyed in a statement about *The Rite of Spring* sketches to the effect that the technique can be seen responding to the musical images.

In conclusion, it must be said that Walsh is remarkably careless about matters of fact. This may be of little consequence in a statement that *Le Baiser de la fée* "copies Tchaikovsky's last ballet here and there" (not *that* ballet); that in *Petrushka* Stravinsky expanded "two short pieces into a 45-minute ballet" (slightly more than a half-hour one); that Stravinsky argued the merits of *Pierrot Lunaire* "on . . . Ravel and Debussy" (no evidence for Debussy); that the meeting with Dylan Thomas took place just after the "autumn of 1953," and that the poet died in December of that year; and that the *Japanese Lyrics* was not "scored with clarinets until after the *Pierrot* [*Lunaire*] concert" (a clarinet *is* indicated in Stravinsky's original, pre-*Pierrot* ensemble).

The musical errors are more important, the missing change of clef in the example from the *Serenada* [*sic*], and the examples from, respectively, *Histoire du Soldat* and the *Piano Rag Music*, juxtaposed to show derivation but chronologically the wrong way around and wrongly chosen as illustration: in melody, rhythm, and semitone intervals, the one from the *Soldat* resembles the *Rag* much less than it does a sketch in the aborted incidental music for Gide's translation of *Antony and Cleopatra*, composed months before the *Soldat* was conceived.

More puzzling than any of Walsh's mistakes are some of his questions. "Why should Persephone not be a singer?" he asks, though he cannot be unaware that Ida Rubinstein, not a singer, commissioned the score for her own use as narrator. And "Why," in 1947, did Stravinsky "suddenly discover the high bassoon timbre" that replaces the alto flute in a passage in the *Symphonies of Wind Instruments*, "when high-bassoon was already in 1920 an established Stravinskian color?" (Must composers avoid their "established colors"?) Walsh knows that Stravinsky's aims in 1947 were linear separation and contrast (versus blend), the elimination of the then comparatively rare alto flute, and, by this and other revisions, the securing of a copyright for a hitherto unprotected work.

Then, too, the reader is occasionally left wondering about what may have passed over his head in Stravinsky's music. Can it be true that "an air of the surreal hangs round [the] derisory folk-melody" (what is derisory about it?) of the tiny Andante from the *Five Easy Pieces*? And is the tacky *Tango* of 1940 "typical of the first American-period works at their best," as the *Circus Polka* ("ponderous vulgarity") is typical of them at their worst? De gustibus non disputandem.

Perhaps the paperback will encompass some revisions. As is, and shortcomings notwithstanding, Walsh's Stravinsky monograph is the most intelligent published to date.

* * *

A little more than two weeks before Stravinsky left Los Angeles for Venice and the premiere of *The Rake's Progress*, Arnold Schoenberg died.[1] Since Stravinsky did not know any of Schoenberg's music at that time, not much can be said about the *musical* meaning of this passing to the survivor, except that from the beginning of his professional life he had

---

[1] This brief informal talk on the subject of "Stravinsky After Schoenberg" was given in Boulder, Colorado, in July 1987, at the invitation of Giora Bernstein, Director of the Colorado Music Festival.

seen Schoenberg's name next to his in print—not to say *against* it. Stravinsky's development after the death of Schoenberg strikes us now as perhaps the most astonishing and certainly the least expected event in our century's musical history. One thinks of Eliot's line about exploring as a vocation for old men, but has any artist ever displayed powers of growth comparable to Stravinsky's between the ages of 70 and 85? The years of regression and retrenchment for practically everyone who lives that long were for him a time of passionate discovery.

Not much fuss was made about the *Rake* before the premiere, partly, no doubt, because in the spring of 1948 Stravinsky had cancelled a European concert tour that had been much publicized following an announcement that a festival of his music would take place in a Bayreuth still closed to Wagner. In 1951, Stravinsky had intended to leave Europe immediately after conducting his opera, but this was to change as soon as he arrived in Italy, where he was greeted as only film stars are in the Hollywood he had just left. In Milan, a large crowd met his train, and the streets around his hotel were cordoned off. During rehearsals at La Scala in the following week, his every move was reported in the European press, and by the time the *Rake* cast, chorus and orchestra entrained for Venice, he had contracted to conduct two months of concerts in Cologne, Baden-Baden, Munich, Lausanne, Geneva, Milan, Naples and Rome.

As a celebration of Stravinsky's first appearance in Europe in more than thirteen years, the *Rake* was a whale of a social-cultural occasion, whatever else—by which I mean that musically, and as an opera, no one quite knew what to make of it. Sir Donald Tovey had written that "Modern composers might as well attempt prehistoric Chinese as try to revive the convention of the secco-recitative." No one objected to Stravinsky's resuscitation of the convention either in Venice or in the dozen other European cities that mounted the opera during the winter season, but trouble lay ahead in New York for the Metropolitan Opera production, where those anachronistic harpsichord recitatives were the chief target of the *New York Times*-man. The opera failed at the Met for the first time anywhere and was dropped in its second year after only two token performances.

Shortly after Stravinsky's departure from Venice, a Schoenberg memorial concert took place there in the same theater that had presented the *Rake*. Since Stravinsky had not seen the advance publicity for this, he remained unaware of the celebration. It should also be said that none of his visitors—most of whom were old friends from Paris—talked to him about what was then widely known as the "dodecaphonic" movement.

(René Leibowitz's review of the *Rake* in a French newspaper, attacking Stravinsky as the anti-progressive, Brahms-like figure of his time, was received by the composer as a great compliment.)

Two weeks later, Stravinsky's views of the new music of his time were to change radically. In the Cologne radio studio he heard a tape of Hermann Scherchen's Darmstadt performance of *The Golden Calf* from *Moses and Aaron* but said nothing about it. A week after that, in Baden-Baden, he was stunned by Webern's Orchestra Variations, asking to hear the tape three times in succession and again the next day. No one here today younger than myself can appreciate the rarity, at that date, of a good performance of this music, and many of you will find it difficult to believe that before then Stravinsky had neither heard nor seen any music by Webern. As for Schoenberg, Stravinsky had said in his *Poetics of Music*, written in 1939, that "Schoenberg knows what he is doing," though Stravinsky himself, from all indications, did not at that time have the remotest notion of what Schoenberg was doing.

One paradox of Stravinsky's late American period is that an increasing portion of the main events in his musical life took place in Europe. Eight months after the Venice *Rake*, his music dominated a mammoth retrospective of twentieth-century music in Paris, as it was to do later in similar jamborees in Rome and Berlin. Moreover, commissions came from Europe in far greater numbers than from the United States, beginning with the String Concerto in 1946 and including the *Canticum Sacrum*, *Vom Himmel hoch* Variations, *Threni*, Movements, *A Sermon, A Narrative and A Prayer*, *Abraham and Isaac* ("Israel," to borrow Milan Kundera's phrase, is "the true heart of Europe—a peculiar heart located outside the body"), as well as such smaller pieces as *Epitaphium*, the Canon for String Quartet, and *The Dove Descending*.

On his return to Hollywood in January 1952, Stravinsky composed a Ricercar that, so I believe, would not have come from him had he not heard the Webern Variations in Baden-Baden. This cannot be proved, of course: he had always been interested in canonic devices, after all, and each new work of his had always diverged in unexpected ways. Furthermore, the static harmony of "Tomorrow Shall Be My Dancing Day" is even more than normally remote from Schoenberg and Webern. All the same, the introduction of pitch succession functioning as a series *is* indebted to the example of Schoenberg; and the Ricercar is the beginning of the parade of masterpieces culminating in the *Requiem Canticles*.

The Septet, following the Cantata, begins far away from Schoenberg, but Stravinsky's Gigue movement is indebted to the Gigue in

Schoenberg's *Septet-Suite*, which Stravinsky had heard in no fewer than 25 rehearsals for performances in more than one concert and for recording. Stravinsky's second movement Passacaglia may owe something to Webern, at least at the beginning, but when the piece was first performed, this movement became known as "Stravinsky's Brahms." I remember Stravinsky clearly during those rehearsals of the *Septet-Suite*. He followed the score and was constantly coaching the players. After attending a rehearsal of the work in Venice during the 1937 Biennale, he had dismissed it as cerebral experiment. Eric Simon, the bass-clarinettist in Venice, playing the part again in my New York performance in October 1950, told me that Stravinsky had expressed boundless admiration for the virtuosity of the musicians. In Hollywood, in February and March of 1952, Stravinsky was extolling the virtuosity of the composer.

What shall we call the late Stravinsky, always remembering that a different one must be distinguished at each stage? Though difficult to label, two or three generalities will stick. We *can* say that the music is predominantly vocal, that the texts are religious, that many of the pieces are musical memorials and that death is the principal subject—a *natural* subject in the sense that the *Requiem Canticles* was written by a man of 84. Contrast this period with the one from 1935 to 1947 in which Stravinsky produced instrumental music almost exclusively, partly, no doubt, because he did not yet feel at home in setting English, partly because his commissions specified orchestral and chamber works. As for purely musical differences between Stravinsky's compositions before and after the *Rake*, these are in his use of "tone rows," in his abandonment of references to triadic tonality, and in his radically re-ordered rhythmic language. But I leave the technical elaboration of these subjects for others, better informed.

Prokofiev and the Culture Curtain

Sergei Prokofiev died in Moscow, March 5, 1953, in the same hour and apparently from the same cause as Joseph Stalin. The coincidence extended the composer's tragic end to the grave, since his burial without due ceremony and before his death was even made public can only be attributed to the circumstance that Stalin lay in state. Indifferent to ideologies, Prokofiev spent the second half of his composing life in a society that was obsessed by them, and that subjected his art to the censorship of musically illiterate bureaucrats.

Harlow Robinson's biography of the composer[1] is the fullest account to date, a thoughtful study of a puzzling personality in and out of music, and a comprehensive history of the East-West culture curtain as it constrained the life and work of the only major artist who had been active on both of its sides. Prokofiev left Russia during the Revolution, returned in 1927 and became a Soviet citizen, shuttled back and forth in the early 1930s defending Soviet music in Paris and European music in Moscow, and settled there for good, or bad, in 1938. Robinson shows us the USSR as Prokofiev first saw it after nine years abroad, a homeland bestowing recognition, in contrast to a bickering clique-ridden Paris concerned only "with deciding what can be called modern."

Why did he go back? Robinson argues that Prokofiev lavished on Russia itself "the love, devotion and tenderness his friends and acquaintances found so oddly lacking in his relations with them." Russia, not the Soviet Union. But the deciding factor was a desire to compose in a more simple style. Robinson says that the simplification process in Prokofiev's music did not begin in the socialist paradise, nor with any intention of advertising the happy life there, but that it had been underway years before his return and was a natural stage in his artistic evolution.

---

[1] *Sergei Prokofiev*. A biography by Harlow Robinson. New York, 1987.

The biographer is fair-minded, generous to Prokofiev but no apologist. Drastically reducing the artistic size of his subject, Robinson says that Prokofiev's "greatest strength as a composer is in illustration," adding that if he had been a painter or a graphic artist "he would have done cartoons, not portraits." Prokofiev was a "born pragmatist" and a "natural ironist" who, at the same time, had "an instinctive understanding of the fairy tale world." The few critical judgments that beg to be differed with are of the late music. Whereas Robinson rightly sees *Romeo and Juliet* as a synthesis of Prokofiev's classical and primitive styles, and as richer in emotional variety than any of the earlier music, he wrongly proclaims the turgid Fifth Symphony one of Prokofiev's "greatest works"—this reviewer's "rightly" and "wrongly," of course.

What the book lacks is musical-level analysis of Prokofiev's harmonic language, his characteristic chords, especially in the "Scythian" pieces. The Second Symphony may be "an ungainly creation," at times "nearly unbearable . . . in pitch and volume," much of it "perversely complex in orchestration," and containing some "excessively clever variations." Not clever enough, surely, and the lack of a memorable theme may be the most serious shortcoming. But the Symphony's octatonic scale references and its successions of septachords and triadically-grouped hexachords would have made it a good choice for a musical anatomy lesson far beyond the mere naming of moods and key signatures.

Robinson understands Prokofiev's relationship to Stravinsky far better than any other biographer of either composer: Prokofiev "could not—or did not want to—appreciate fully [Stravinsky's] talent and significance." Less adroit at musical politics than Stravinsky, and unable to attract the aristocratic patrons and other support systems by which Stravinsky was sustained, Prokofiev, until he moved to the USSR, seemed to have been bluntly honest. Oddly, Robinson's description of the premiere of the First Violin Concerto does not say that Stravinsky's Octet was premiered on the same program, thereby leading the reader to conclude that Picasso, Pavlova, Nadia Boulanger and other artistic luminaries in the audience were present on Prokofiev's behalf rather than, as more likely, on Stravinsky's. The Concerto, a perfect composition with a quietly stunning idea—the quarter-note theme played by the solo violin pizzicato—delicate and refined in sentiment and limpidly orchestrated, was upstaged then and is neglected now.

The competitive figure in the late years was Shostakovitch. Mr. Robinson seems not to have seen the remarkable letter from Prokofiev to Diaghilev (September 21, 1928) published in a Sotheby May 1984 catalog.

Working on the *Prodigal Son* for the Ballet Russe, and evidently in good spirits, Prokofiev answers Diaghilev's inquiries about young composers in Russia with fairness and generosity: " . . . the most eminent is Shostakovitch." He goes on to say that the 22-year-old composer's first symphony was played by Bruno Walter and will be played in America by Stokowski, that his opera *The Nose* will be performed, that the "October" symphony is seen as a forward step by the best critics, but that he, Prokofiev, has heard only an early Sonata, which he found "vivid and definitely talented not without my influence." "But Shostakovitch's difficult character forces one to be careful when doing business with him."

Robinson astutely remarks that Shostakovitch's music and personal behavior became more private as a consequence of Party criticism, while Prokofiev's, for the same reason, became more public. The two lions of Soviet music were in no way compatible, and most of their statements about each other are frankly hostile. But some of Shostakovitch's early pieces are indebted to Prokofiev.

Prokofiev's criticisms of American musical life, found in correspondence to friends during several between-the-wars concert tours, are still valid today, especially his attacks on the conservatism of subscription concerts. The letters also acknowledge a measure of audience progress from the time when he was obliged to stand on a reception line somewhere in the Midwest, shake hands and say "very pleased to meet you" to three hundred people after one tiring concert and before catching a late-night train to another. The story of Cyrus McCormick's acquaintance with Prokofiev in Petrograd in 1917, eventually and indirectly leading to the premiere of *The Love for Three Oranges* in Chicago six years later, is one of the curiosities of American cultural history. Prokofiev's enthusiastic response to *Snow White* suggests that a collaboration between the creators of *Peter and the Wolf* and Donald Duck might have been more naturally favored than that of Prokofiev and Eisenstein.

Not many audiences are familiar with Prokofiev's large-scale late works, and those who have never seen his opera *War and Peace* might find Robinson's accounts of cuts and revisions difficult to follow. Add to this Prokofiev's positively bewildering personal life in the later years. In 1939, he fell in love with a woman half his age, left his wife and sons for her soon after but married her only in February 1948 and without having obtained a divorce. A few weeks later, and as if in some way connected, his first wife was arrested and sent to Siberia for eight years on an unreasonably vague allegation of spying.

Stalin Prizes, and, among foreign trophies, a *Time* cover story, mark Prokofiev's final period, together with such no less dubious musical achievements as the composition of *The Stone Flower*. "The Soviet system has never been comfortable with geniuses like Prokofiev, who disprove the socialist myth that all men are created equal." Or so Harlow Robinson concludes in one of the best-written biographies of a modern composer.

Maestro on the Market

Joseph Horowitz's new book ranges far beyond the limited expectations raised by its misleadingly specific title.[1] Three decades after Toscanini's death not many music lovers can be seriously concerned with "understanding" him. And if they were, in what sense, since neither he nor his music making is in any way enigmatic, and since this very absence of mystery constitutes part of Horowitz's criticism of him as an interpreter? The real subject of the book, we are told when well into it, "is less Toscanini than the manner in which he was perceived, procured, appreciated, marketed."

Understanding Toscanini is a history of the United States as consumer of European music and musicians; an analysis of the effects on the culture of assorted American entrepreneurial types from P.T. Barnum to the manager of Toscanini's New York Philharmonic, Arthur Judson; a socioeconomic study of the classical music industry and of the growth, through radio, recording, and television, of musical mass culture; and an indictment, intentional or otherwise, of the quality of music journalism in America during the first half of this century. On another level, the book exposes the promotional processes by which big business becomes the enlightened benefactor of high culture ("nearly all of the world's great music [is] Victor recorded"), "great music" and "Toscanini" become fused, and the conductor's name is equated with Beethoven's.

Horowitz's thesis is that America and Toscanini deserve each other, that by the time of his debut at the Metropolitan Opera in 1908, aged 41, the publicity machinery with its developed tradition of hyperbole was ready and lying in wait for just such a "genius" quarry— the legendary photographic memory, the awesome precisionist, the inspiring dictatorial leader—and that Toscanini's subsequent career at the New York

---

[1] *Understanding Toscanini. How He Became an American Culture-God and Helped Create a New Audience for Old Music*, by Joseph Horowitz. New York, 1987.

Philharmonic in the 1920s and 1930s, and, ultimately, as the godlike conductor of the NBC Symphony (1937–54), corresponds to the development of the broadcasting media for whose corporate interests he was both a comprehensible and a salable symbol of high culture. At this point, musical values were misled, and Toscanini's influence became corrupting.

The book criticizes in depth the values of the society as a whole as exemplified in the selling or, rather, selling out of its musical culture. *Understanding Toscanini* is intelligently argued and thoroughly documented—over-documented in some instances, and toward the end, when the case has already been won, run-on. The book, moreover, is also clumsily organized and repetitive, reaching all the way back to Tocqueville and devoting more time than needed en route to the Mark Twain syndrome of defensive Americans obsessively fascinated with Europe. Then, too, while the discussions of *Middletown*, Sinclair Lewis's novels, and the writings of C. Wright Mills and Richard Hofstadter are more immediately relevant to the growth of American mass culture and anti-intellectualism, general readers will find little that is new in these discourses, while the musically minded will very likely skip them as too remote from Toscanini.

The book's main shortcoming, however, is that Horowitz places too much responsibility on a person of Toscanini's limited intellectual, moral, and artistic stature. Not being a creative artist, the conductor does not have a historical position, and, so far from being a representative figure of his age, he was an anachronism. The book could be rewritten from the very different perspective of an old-fashioned prima donna conductor as the victim of his success, his press, his manipulators and exploiters. Nevertheless, and these reservations notwithstanding, no one concerned with the fate of the arts in our jingoist and dangerously confused society can afford to ignore Joseph Horowitz's courageous, necessary, and for the most part irrefutable cultural case history.

In considering Toscanini simply as a musician, as distinguished from the public totem of him, one must also say that he receives somewhat less than his due. If only as a corrective he merits the highest place, having established unsurpassed standards of ensemble playing. True, his repertory was limited—nonexistent as regards significant modern music—and he was unable to differentiate periods and styles, turning Mozart into Rossini. Yet during a brief spell in the late 1940s, not long enough to mitigate the criticisms, he did present important twentieth-century music through his guest conductors; or, at least, permitted them to present it. Thus Ernest Ansermet played works by Stravinsky (*Symphonies of Wind Instruments*) and Bartók (*Music for Strings, Percussion and Celesta*) that Toscanini did not understand and could not perform. It must be mentioned, too, that he was not the only conductor to vent his scorn on conspicuous colleagues ("I cannot look at [Stokowski's] *stupid* face without shuddering"), and that he deserves credit for having nominated Wilhelm Furtwängler, by far the most interesting of his 1930s rivals, to succeed him at the New York Philharmonic.

The Toscanini-Furtwängler polarity is the major musico-critical theme of Horowitz's book, a purplish one when the nemesis-hero's performances are under consideration: "[Furtwängler's] immersion in subjectivity and deep structure consummates his immersion in Wagnerian inner space"; the *Tristan* Prelude, conducted by him, "pulsates with tireless engines of desire." (For this reviewer, the marvel of Furtwängler's *Tristan* Prelude is its "chastity" and the complete absence of "pulsing.") Furtwängler, vacillator and self-doubter, awkward and unworldly, child of intellectual and artistic parents, educated by tutors and tours in Greece and Italy, was a contrast in every way to the decisive, sure-of-himself, down-to-earth, patchily educated child of poor parents, Toscanini. Furtwängler's beat was vague but his performances were "profound," while Toscanini's was precise and his performances were spit-and-polished and spectacular. The antipodal positions are further defined by Furtwängler's statement that "Beethoven's subjects develop in mutual interaction like the characters in a play. In every single subject of every Beethoven work, a destiny is unfolded." And by Toscanini's statement about the *Eroica*: "To some it is Napoleon . . . to some it is philosophical struggle; to me it is Allegro con brio."

What can be said of both conductors is that, for better or worse, their personal stamp is on every phrase of their music making. Horowitz dissects Toscanini's performance style in a long chapter on the discography that music lovers may want to read first. Let it be said that the tally of hard-driven, rushed-through, landscape-leveling readings—perhaps best represented by the hurried and feelingless *Pathétique* Symphony, which is not singled out—is near the total number, and that Furtwängler's Beethoven and Wagner, at least, are immeasurably greater.

Horowitz traces the roots of the Toscanini-Furtwängler rivalry to the beginnings of American symphony orchestras with their overwhelming predominance of German conductors and players, and, later in the nineteenth-century, with increasing Italian immigration, to the establishment of Italian opera in New York. The contest, ethnic and cultural, at the Metropolitan Opera between Mahler and Toscanini in the years between 1908 and 1911—"small excitable men whose ruthless idealism stirred achievement, turmoil and intrigue"—became the prototype for the Furtwängler-Toscanini feud. What should be said about this today is that although our sympathies are naturally with Mahler—the creative mind, the loser and in declining health—Toscanini, at that time, was no less highly esteemed as a Wagnerian (*Tristan, Götterdämmerung*) and as a reformer with progressive ideas about integrated theater.

World War I aggravated nationalist prejudices to the extent that Karl Muck, Furtwängler's fellow countryman and then conductor of the Boston Symphony, was incarcerated in Fort Oglethorpe, Georgia, as an enemy alien, partly on suspicion of plotting to blow up the birthplace of Henry Wadsworth Longfellow. After having been persecuted for not playing "The Star-Spangled Banner" in Providence, Rhode Island—on orders from the orchestra's founder—thereby provoking Theodore Roosevelt to a statement inviting him "to go back where he came from," the "Hun" did play it but only to be attacked for his "torpid rendition." Furtwängler's departure from New York in the 1930s was precipitated by some of the same sentiments.

The political conduct of Furtwängler and Toscanini during and before the Second World War cannot be placed in simple opposition, since the German's personal freedom and safety were in danger. His record of resistance to the Third Reich appears to be somewhat blemished, as is Toscanini's for having initially supported Mussolini in 1919. But no matter. In the 1930s, when it made a difference, Toscanini took sides, whether or not, as some believed, he was a political opportunist with his eye on the New York press. The anomaly is that the behavior in and out of music of this "law unto himself" was, by most definitions, fascist. New York critics, Horowitz writes, "thrilled to the spectacle of cowering players and smashed batons," and one of them, Olin Downes, actually lauded Toscanini's "glorious and despotic sway" as the proof of his *anti*-fascism. At this point, Horowitz might usefully have introduced Elias Canetti's discussion in *Crowds and Power* of the totalitarian relationship of conductor to orchestra.

In a reconsideration of the question of artists and politics, Harvey Sachs,[1] author of a book on Toscanini and one on music in Fascist Italy,

---

[1] See Sachs, "Salzburg, Hitler, and Toscanini" in *Grand Street* (Autumn 1986).

challenges a new and widespread attitude as expressed by Erich Leinsdorf in a talk to students in Cleveland. Artists who lend their prestige to exert influence in politics, the one-time Toscanini assistant and esteemed conductor said, are in effect endangering their seriousness in both areas. But Sachs's argument cannot be gainsaid: "When the issue is war, racism and blatant oppression, professionalism is no excuse for carrying on as usual." And Toscanini did speak out against Mussolini and Hitler, whatever one may think of his motives.

The David Sarnoff saga has long since entered into folklore,[1] but Horowitz's fresh account of how the ruler of the world's "first great communications empire" and "the world's greatest conductor" used each other is the best to date, above all in the reconstruction of the parallels between their rags-to-riches careers. As the man who returned the conductor to America, and who formed the NBC Symphony for him as his personal orchestra, primarily to broadcast great music to American homes, the RCA boss believed that he deserved as much credit as Toscanini, who became Sarnoff's alter ego.

The Sarnoff story is still astonishing. By 1938, 88 percent of the 25 million radios in American homes were supplied by RCA's child company, NBC. In the period 1933–38, RCA's sales rose 600 percent, and with symphonic rather than popular music on top. Whereas RCA produced only five thousand television sets in 1946, the figure jumped to seven million in 1950. By 1954, 20 million Toscanini recordings had been sold for a total of $33 million.

Almost as if to bring relief, Horowitz introduces an intelligent and musically sophisticated newcomer on the commercial music scene in the same period. Goddard Lieberson understood Toscanini long before *Understanding Toscanini*. And he supported new music by the simple expedient of making the popular pay for the unpopular. Oddly, one of Lieberson's most significant achievements is not mentioned: in 1940, though still in a subordinate position at Columbia Records, he managed to record *Le Sacre du printemps* and *Pierrot Lunaire* conducted by their respective composers, an event that changed the highest level of musical awareness in the United States.

Horowitz exposes the extremely poor quality of music criticism during the entire Toscanini period simply by quoting it. Only two exceptions need be mentioned. Here is Virgil Thomson's voice in the wilderness:

---

[1] See *RCA*, by David Sobel. New York, 1987.

> [In Toscanini's performance of Beethoven's Seventh Symphony] the second movement came out as a barcarole, the fourth rather in tarantella vein. In none of them was there any sense of mystery to make the Beethoven fury seem interiorly dramatic rather than merely of the stage.

The other, Theodor Adorno, is confined to his still-unpublished *Analytical Study of "The NBC Music Appreciation Hour,"* which attacks radio

> as an economic enterprise in an ownership culture . . . forced to promote, within the listener, a naively enthusiastic attitude toward any material it offers, and thus, indirectly, toward itself.

At least two of Adorno's observations have lost none of their pertinence: "Living room reproduction, extinguishable with the flick of a wrist, undermined the enveloping experience of symphonic space"; and, "[Thanks to the radio symphony concert] there exists today a tendency to listen to Beethoven's Fifth as if it were a set of quotations from Beethoven's Fifth." But Horowitz rightly scores Adorno's "bullying stridence," his "anger at commodity societies [which] seems mainly directed at its victims, whom he holds in contempt," and "his rejection of jazz [which] exposes his own Eurocentrism and ill will." As so often with Adorno, his editors' brackets beginning with "i.e." supply the word or words that make a statement intelligible.

Strangely, *Understanding Toscanini* does not offer a close-up examination of Toscanini's conducting technique. For this, one must turn to Norman F. Leyden's 1968 doctoral thesis.[1] Leyden's approach is uncritical, and he accepts the long superseded notion that "objective" performances and "textual fidelity" are attainable goals. The book is not verbal, however, but a collection of diagrams tracing Toscanini's beat as abstracted from his films with the NBC Symphony Orchestra, more importantly of diagrams placed above excerpts in music type connecting them to his movements. The beat, whether one or more to a measure, is always arc-shaped, fluid, and continuous—one reason why Toscanini could not have performed irregularly accented modern music—and it

---

[1] *A Study and Analysis of the Conducting Patterns of Arturo Toscanini as Demonstrated in Kinescope Films*, doctoral thesis, Columbia University. Reprinted in book form by University Microfilm International, Ann Arbor, 1984.

controls not only tempo but also articulation, phrasing, and various expressive nuances. The action is concentrated in the right hand and baton, with a minimum of motion in the axis of the right shoulder and elbow and only rare extensions of the arms to the vertical and lateral limits defined by the diagrams. The size of the beat corresponds to speed and dynamics, small for presto and pianissimo, larger for largo and loud. The bodily stance, with a spread of a few inches between the feet, remains steady, and the left hand participates only as an aid to balance, often merely holding the conductor's lapel.

Today's audience, accustomed to high jumping, bottom wiggling, artfully mussed hair and sprayed-on perspiration, eye mugging and the grimaces intended to convey the conductor's feelings about the music and how everyone else should feel, can scarcely imagine the focal force of Toscanini's Archimedean wrist. Not to have seen him, to know him exclusively from recordings, is an inestimable handicap to a full appreciation of the technical side of his art.

For a glimpse of a kind not found in the book, I beg leave to refer to my own experience when, during a misspent youth as a Juilliard conducting student, I often watched Toscanini rehearse through a peephole at the back of the orchestra shell on the stage of NBC's acoustically dead Studio 8H. The atmosphere was almost unbearably tense, the players never removing their eyes from Toscanini (orchestras today seldom glance at conductors), the quiet positively tomblike (most rehearsals today are characterized by a din of talk). By this date (1946), many of Toscanini's corrections were simply being repeated from past rehearsals. When he stopped the orchestra after the A major chord shortly before the Allegro in the finale of the Brahms First, and remarked that the second trombone's C sharp was too high, the musicians were aware that this was not true and that Toscanini was simply correcting a traditional fault.

Three years later, on November 21, 1949, during a rehearsal in Carnegie Hall for a concert that evening, I felt the power of Toscanini-RCA firsthand when my pickup orchestra and I were ejected without warning to make room for a suddenly called rehearsal of the NBC Symphony. This incident came to mind eight years later when I heard the news of Toscanini's death—from, of all people, the musical power broker Arthur Judson, during one of his business lunches with Stravinsky. The composer had always spoken disparagingly of Toscanini, though less contemptuously than Schoenberg, who dismissed him as "the Italian '*Trommelmajor.*'" But Stravinsky was moved by the death, partly because he had been gravely ill himself shortly before, partly because

Toscanini's performance of *Petrushka* in Rome in 1916, noisily acclaimed by Marinetti and the Futurists, had been a milestone in the composer's life. He recalled that in September 1939, both he and Toscanini happened to be on the same overcrowded boat from Bordeaux to New York, and that while he shared a small cabin with three other men, Marx Brothers style, Toscanini, with ill-concealed rage, preferred to pace the decks and sleep in the lounges.

The last two chapters, "Long-Term Legacies" and a personal "Conclusion," might have been saved for an even better book, neither being immediately relevant to Toscanini, who cannot really be blamed for the state of a culture in which "Pavarotti is depicted . . . hobnobbing with . . . Rona Barrett." American musical society, and not only musical, owes a great debt to Joseph Horowitz's incisive mind and humanist spirit.

Vive Kl'Empereur

Interpreters of music are not the most promising subjects for biographies, for the reasons that the intrinsic performance experience, and the underlying meaning of the life, are difficult to convey in words. Nor do studio recordings preserve the experience, particularly in a discography as old as Otto Klemperer's, where the technological barriers are considerable. To sustain interest throughout the chronicle of a conductor's concert and opera appearances, therefore, is no small achievement. But Peter Heyworth succeeds in this, and in much more. Those who have never heard Klemperer, or even of him, will enjoy and be enlightened by this book.[1]

American music-lovers are less aware than their British and European counterparts that Klemperer is one of the handful of great conductors. Unfortunately, his stints with the New York Philharmonic in the 1920s were overshadowed by those of Furtwängler and Toscanini, and with the exception of the years in Los Angeles, discussed in Heyworth's second volume, Klemperer's career did not unfold in the United States.

Exhaustively researched and smoothly written, the biography examines every issue with clarity and fairness. The portrait that emerges from the combination of the author's personal knowledge and insights, and his skillful piecing together of excerpts from letters, critical notices, documents and reminiscences, is of a man of high moral and artistic stature. And this must be said at the outset, since Klemperer's life was one of almost continuous scandal.

In addition to the story of the development of Klemperer the musician, the book can be read both as the case history of a manic-depressive and as a study of the Weimar Republic, from the first encroachments of National Socialism to eventual strangulation by it. Just as cyclothymia controlled

---

[1] *Otto Klemperer, His Life and Times* by Peter Heyworth. Vol. I (to 1933). London, 1983.

Klemperer's temperament and behavior, so the political and economic circumstances of the Weimar government determined the outward course of the conductor's professional life until 1933.

The effects of the most intense of Klemperer's manic and depressive phases were devastating to himself and to those around him. His elopement with the soprano Elisabeth Schumann, for one example, disgraced and nearly ruined both their lives, as well as her husband's. Like Jekyll and Hyde, Klemperer in his depressed state would reverse the decisions, undo the undertakings, and atone for or forget about the infatuations that had impelled him during the euphorias. While the pendulum was at one extreme, he composed music and arranged for its performance and publication; while at the other, he lost confidence in his creative efforts, withdrew, and even destroyed the manuscripts.

Naturally, Klemperer's colleagues, as well as the theater directors, impresarios, and concert agents with whom he dealt, were aware of his instabilities—more so of the "highs," the violent moods and aggressiveness, than of the "lows," with the attendant self-destructiveness. Yet no one seems to have realized that his condition was pathological. That a conductor with a reputation for terrorizing orchestra players, insulting singers, quarreling with any and everybody, should nevertheless be sought after by opera companies and concert organizations and venerated by his musicians and audiences, says much for his powers of music-making.

Heyworth never strays from the perspective of Klemperer's illness, nor does he evade its most unattractive manifestations. Not surprisingly, the conductor's personality embodied opposites on other levels as well. According to one collaborator, he was witty but quite without humor, "cynical and sarcastic" yet also "naive and childlike." He had "the driving power of a maniac," but was "a plaything in the hands of a bureaucrat," and he "combined sharp powers of understanding with the stubborn ignorance of someone who was unteachable." Other sources warrant that he was imperious, demanding, dogmatic (as a conductor must be in front of an orchestra), and far from conventionally polite. As one of his employers expressed it, "He had the mannerlessness of a genius." Moreover, Klemperer was a physical giant (he quite literally dwarfs Arnold Schoenberg in one of the book's photographs of them together), which doubtless made the worst of these characteristics still more frightening.

His rehearsals were unhappily tense and often marred by explosive incidents. He could be finicky beyond the point of profitable returns, expose individual players to ridicule, and even discharge violinists who failed to bow with the rest of the section, actions that today would have made him the respondent in law suits. In Russia in the 1920s, lacking the language in which to vent his fury at the failure of an instrumentalist to appear, "Klemperer threw down his baton, leapt into the stalls, and hurled the fur coat he had acquired for the journey to the ground." The most frequently recurring epithet in the narrative is "an alarming figure." But Klemperer could also move and even inspire his orchestras and audiences.

Heyworth's presentation of the life is strictly chronological: childhood, student years in Berlin, apprenticeship in Prague, a succession of posts in Hamburg (from which the affair with Elisabeth Schumann forced him to resign), Strasbourg, Cologne, Wiesbaden, and finally the Kroll Opera in Berlin. This last occupies the largest and most absorbing part of the book, but the Strasbourg chapter is the most entertaining. The Alsatian city's musical life remained almost as active during World War I as before, even though the front was close by. When Klemperer arrived at the Strasbourg Opera, its director was his former teacher, the cantankerous and conservative Hans Pfitzner. At least one anecdote from Heyworth's vignettes of both men is worth repeating:

> On one occasion when Pfitzner was conducting *Die Meistersinger* and the Beckmesser became hoarse, he handed over his baton to a deputy, had himself shaved, and sang the role in the third act with exemplary articulation and accuracy.

A glimpse of Klemperer in a manic state comes from a performance of *Tannhäuser*, which he

> conducted with his feet on the desk before him, so that the singers were confronted by the soles of his inordinately large shoes. He also shouted and beat time so noisily that the *Freie Presse* dryly asked whether he supposed himself to be without an audience.

In Heyworth's assessment, Klemperer's Berlin was a far greater musical metropolis than either Paris or Vienna. In the late 1920s, it supported three major opera houses, offering new as well as familiar works in astonishing abundance. There, more than fifty years ago, audiences at the Kroll heard Schoenberg's *Erwartung* and Janáček's *From the House of the Dead*, to name only two twentieth-century masterpieces not yet mounted on a professional stage in "The Big Apple." Concert life was equally full and diverse, with orchestras, chamber music organizations, choruses, recitalists, and early music ensembles. "Perhaps no city has ever enjoyed such a rich orchestral life as Berlin during the years of the Weimar Republic," Heyworth writes, and what with Furtwängler conducting the Berlin Philharmonic and Klemperer directing orchestra programs as well as operas at the Kroll, who can dispute it?

The other essential criteria for the measurement of a musical culture are the quality of its criticism and its audiences. To judge by Heyworth's copious quotations from the press, the former was not only intelligent and well-informed, but it also attained a degree of literacy. The musicologist Alfred Einstein (author of *The Italian Madrigal* and *Mozart*) was one of the regular reviewers, along with Theodor Adorno, whose notices, written from another side of the political and musical aisle, were mercifully free of the anfractuosities of his later writings. The audiences were discriminating, too, as well as representative of every stratum of society. Some of them glittered, for example the one on October 11, 1928, when Klemperer presented *Histoire du soldat* to a hall that included Albert Einstein (Alfred's cousin), Bertolt Brecht, Kurt Weill, Ernst Bloch, Walter Benjamin, and, well, Cardinal Pacelli (later Pius XII). Admittedly, a few days later an audience of workers received the same piece with eleven minutes of hissing and protest. Where else, however, would "lower-income" groups have had the opportunity to experience theater of this caliber? No matter how short-lived, the Weimar government's success in sponsoring the performing arts without lowering standards is enviable.

Most new music in the Berlin of the 1920s was aligned with one or the other of two ideologies, *die neue Sachlichkeit* (the new objectivity) and German Expressionism, the former personified by Stravinsky, the latter by Schoenberg, himself a Berlin resident during the last years of Klemperer's tenure there. Heyworth's explorations contribute substantially to the mythology of these composers, but especially to that of Stravinsky, who, for instance, was observed at a late party after the premiere of his *Oedipus Rex* at the Kroll (1928) "dancing a minuet with Ernst Bloch." (A few years earlier, Klemperer's approach to Stravinsky's Piano Concerto struck the composer as unduly romantic, whereupon he called out: "No! No! Think of Savonarola.")

Heyworth's thesis that Klemperer had firm footholds on both sides of this Berlin musical *Mauer* seems slightly tendentious, though the conductor himself, during a visit to the Soviet Union, had declared:

> I categorically reject the idea of an opposition between Schoenberg and Stravinsky. Both are geniuses, although representatives of different races. The difference between them lies more in the fact that they belong to different generations than in any explicit tendency of the one or the other.

But then, Heyworth says that Universal Edition, the Viennese publisher of predominantly Expressionist music, "had on its books most of the outstanding composers of the first half of the twentieth century." Perhaps, yet however formidable the array of Schoenberg, Berg, Webern, Bartók, Janáček, and Szymanowski, is it more so than that of the missing Debussy, Ravel, Puccini, Richard Strauss, Stravinsky, Varèse? Whatever the answer, Klemperer's performance tally of Universal Edition composers is poor. He conducted nothing by Berg, only one work by Webern, and by Schoenberg merely a single performance of *Pierrot* and not more than two or three of the *Begleitungsmusik*, *Die glückliche Hand*, *Pelleas*, *Verklärte Nacht*, and the Bach arrangements. Klemperer would not play music that he did not understand, a description that seems to have included most of the atonal kind.

This track record contrasts with the conductor's eagerness to program anything by Hindemith, directly from the factory. "Klemperer was to be one of Hindemith's most powerful champions," Heyworth states, and the facts support him, though the Hindemith pieces performed by Klemperer are too numerous to list here.

Notwithstanding, Stravinsky was incomparably the more important composer in Klemperer's life, and *Oedipus Rex* his and the Kroll Opera's greatest success. He repeatedly conducted *Pulcinella*, *Noces*, *Apollo*, *Le Baiser de la fée*, Capriccio, *Symphony of Psalms*, and the Symphony in Three Movements. And the two men were life-long friends. When the Kroll was about to be closed, they appeared on stage together after a performance of the *Soldat* and "were greeted by storms of applause." Three days later, in a newspaper interview, Stravinsky thanked Klemperer and the Kroll for the presentation of "almost my entire output." A day or so after that, Stravinsky "joined Thomas Mann, Weill, Hindemith, and others in an appeal for the preservation of the Kroll," which, as Mann wrote, "occupies a strong position on the intellectual left, because it stands at the crossroads of social and cultural interests and is a thorn in the eye of obscurantism . . ." He might have said National Socialism, which had recently been directing anti-Semitic abuse not only at Klemperer ("a Jew unable to enter Beethoven's world of feeling") but also at Stravinsky, referred to by the *Deutsche Zeitung* as "Isadore—sorry—Igor Stravinsky."

At a celebratory banquet in Berlin, shortly before the National Socialist shutdown, Artur Schnabel toasted his friend Klemperer:

> [An artist is confronted] by questions, not of personal advantage and security, but of truthfulness at any price, even at the price of lifelong insecurity . . . [Artists like] Klemperer are at once conservative, liberal *and* revolutionary; they are aristocrats and anarchists; they are for freedom and for discipline. Again like Klemperer, they have an inner independence that obliges them simultaneously to do justice both to what is timeless and to what is of their own time.

Glenn Gould

This memorial volume's[1] most revealing contributions about Glenn Gould, person and performer, are by John Beckwith ("Shattering a Few Myths"), who knew him as a fellow student, and John Roberts ("Reminiscences"), with whom he had a lengthy professional collaboration. For the rest, the late Curtis Davis's interview captures some of the originality and quickness of Gould's musical mind and displays his articulateness to advantage. Gould on his own, especially in the interview with himself but also in two of his other texts, is self-indulgent and, worse, cute. Some of his metaphors, moreover, are inapt: "A series of small islands overlap with one another like a crossword puzzle and protect Toronto Bay." Can islands overlap without becoming something else? With what does the crossword puzzle overlap?

The editor might have caught this and such other impossibilities as Yehudi Menuhin's statement "Schoenberg is not amongst the 20th-century composers for whose music I have an immediate and irresistible appeal." But Mr. McGreevy is not responsible for the book's chief shortcomings, the inevitable repetition in the descriptions of Gould's oddities of dress and deportment, and the absence of any reference to the woman with whom he had an intimate relationship in later years. The fact of the latter challenges the whole concept of his personality, as set forth, for example, in William Littler's "The Quest for Solitude" and in the essay by Richard Kostelanetz, who writes that "His major exclusion . . . appears to be intimate personal relationships; he lives with no one, never has . . . and probably never will."

Another, lesser shortcoming is that almost all the authors adopt Gould's own reasons in defense of his early retirement as a concertizing pianist. The exception, Judith Pearlman, a co-producer of one of Gould's

---

[1] *Glenn Gould: Variations* by Himself and His Friends, edited and with an introduction by John McGreevy. New York, 1983.

radio documentaries, believes that he "had robbed the world . . . of one of the rarest gifts any interpreter can offer, that of direct public communication at the highest level." Clearly Gould was temperamentally unsuited to the concert platform. Within a very short time of his sudden celebrityhood, the best-known quip about him was Goddard Lieberson's: "available for a limited number of cancellations."

John Beckwith, Gould's fellow pupil of the Chilean-Canadian pianist Alberto Guerrero, identifies Gould's world with his musical upbringing, in both the foundations and the props:

> Guerrero and Gould had an unusually close teacher-student relationship spanning the decade between Glenn's tenth and twentieth years . . . Guerrero . . . sat lower in relation to the keyboard and played with flatter fingers than most players; his performances [had] . . . exceptional clarity and separation of individual notes . . . Virtually no hand action was applied—the fingers did it all . . .
>
> Gould's physical appearance at the keyboard was in my view more like Guerrero's than was any other pupil's—the finger-angle very similar, the low-seated position similar too . . .
>
> The Bach keyboard repertoire was in many ways the core of Guerrero's work and must be accorded a similar centrality in Gould's . . . I myself was encouraged to learn the *Goldberg Variations* partly by Guerrero . . . [Gould's] decision to learn this piece [was] no doubt [influenced by Guerrero]. Guerrero himself knew the *Variations* intimately and had performed them in Toronto in the 1930s . . . Gould's enthusiasm for Schoenberg derived in part from Guerrero's. Guerrero had performed the Opus 11 and Opus 19 pieces on several occasions . . .
>
> It was . . . Guerrero who advocated soaking the hands in hot water before a performance . . .
>
> Gradually . . . they had a falling out . . . Guerrero disliked to watch the "platform antics," as he called them . . . [Later, Gould] found he could refer to Guerrero only anonymously, or else not at all . . .

Some of Beckwith's testimony is confirmed by the Turnabout recording of the 20-year-old Gould and Guerrero playing Mozart 4-hand pieces with no hint of Gould's later eccentricities, and by a Guerrero recording of Bach's Italian Concerto, which suggests that Gould's CBS performance of the Concerto was motivated to do the opposite of what Guerrero had done.

From John Robert's "Reminiscences," I—the first person is unavoidable—was flattered to learn that Gould had chosen me to conduct his recording of Schoenberg's Piano Concerto (January 1961). I will spare the reader my impressions of Gould at that time, but I am under obligation to amplify Roberts's Toronto-confined account of the relationship between Gould and Stravinsky. The pianist and the composer were introduced (yes, Gould shook hands) in January 1960 by Leonard Bernstein at the videotaping of a New York Philharmonic concert in which both of them were guest performers. Fourteen months before, Stravinsky had been invited to give an orchestral concert during a visit to Vienna to conduct his *Oedipus Rex* at the Vienna Staatsoper (November 1958). Subsequently he was told that Gould had already been engaged to play the Schoenberg Concerto with the same orchestra on the same date. After studying the score of the Schoenberg, Stravinsky decided that he could not conduct it and suggested his Capriccio instead, which Gould said he could not play. Eventually, Gould fell ill in Hamburg and cancelled.

Stravinsky did not hear Gould in California "years before" they met, as Roberts writes, but for the first time, apart from the telecast of the Bach D-minor Concerto with Bernstein, on April 25, 1961, in the Wilshire Ebell Theater, Los Angeles. The next time Stravinsky and Gould saw each other was at breakfast in the Park Plaza Hotel, Toronto, in January 1962. Thereafter, Gould attended many of Stravinsky's Toronto recording sessions and their meeting at one of them can be seen on film. Stravinsky liked Gould personally—thought him remarkably handsome—and admired both the technique and the intensity of his playing.

None of the other friends of Gould represented in this book can have looked after him with more devotion than John Roberts. Roberts recalls that at their last meeting Gould was "exhausted," and the book's late photographs confirm, disturbingly, to what extent this was true. Gould had apparently aged overnight, like Dorian Gray. On the occasion that Roberts specifies, he correctly divined that Gould was silently singing one of Strauss's *Four Last Songs*. Months later, Roberts remembered its last words, Eichendorf's

We sense the night's soft breath
Now we are tired, how tired!
Can this perhaps be death?

Pulling No Punches

No writer has contributed more toward the sophistication of musical life in the United States than Virgil Thomson, whose incumbency as music critic of the *New York Herald Tribune* between 1940 and 1954 defines the brief Age of Enlightenment in American music journalism. Though the whole of this anthology of his correspondence[1] adds cubits to his reputation as critic, moralist, and—no less substantially—entertaining gossip, the most valuable section is the long chapter representing his newspaperman years. While supporting such originals as Webern ("spun steel"), Varèse, and Carl Ruggles, and attacking the Beaux Arts provincialism, the managerial manipulation, and the misguided patronage systems controlling New York's musical institutions, Thomson generated an excitement difficult even to imagine in today's game of hit and run reviewing.

The first and regrettably the shortest part of the book opens with "Tommie" Thomson writing to his sister from army boot camp in Oklahoma in September 1917; and writing uncommonly well ("The mountains to the west are beautiful, just freckled with trees"). After the war, spent stateside, and two years as a music student at Harvard, he toured Europe with the college Glee Club in the summer of 1921, then stayed on in Paris for a year to continue his musical education with Nadia Boulanger.

Life in the French capital changed him, of course, for though he had brought his intelligence with him, the crucial artistic experiences of the time were not available in Boston and New York. *Ulysses*, which he described only two months after its publication as "*amazing*. Style and matter," would be banned there for eleven years, and *Pierrot Lunaire*,

---

[1] *The Selected Letters of Virgil Thomson*. Edited by Tim Page and Vanessa Weeks Page. New York, 1988.

the "real musical event, . . . Fascinating concurrence of noises," had still not been performed in America a decade after its premiere. Nor would Thomson's talents as critic have had much opportunity for exposure back home, whereas his reports on the Parisian musical scene for the *Boston Transcript*, singling out "a Russian conductor . . . who is giving magnificent concerts"—"Paris is full of Russian refugees . . . The French have finesse, but thank God for the Russians with the real ecstasy in their souls"—helped to bring Koussevitzky to the advertence of Back Bay and hence contributed in some measure to his engagement by the Boston Symphony Orchestra soon after. Returning to and matriculating at Harvard, then living for a time in New York, Thomson moved to Paris again in 1925, this time to remain there, apart from side-tripping (including four months in the United States in 1928–29), until June 6, 1940.

The letters of Part Two add a new feature to the landscape of American expatriate literature, a high and distinctively shaped hill if not an alp. Thomson keeps friends informed of each other's comings and goings ("Eugene consorts with princesses in Marseille and sailors in Toulon"), and of his own life à la mode, which included "dancing till two at Le Boeuf sur le toit" and perhaps longer than that at the Mardi Gras Bal des Tapettes. He also passes on the latest ratings of the artistic big guns—"Picasso, from lack of competition, has become a public monument . . . Music is carried on by me and George Antheil. (Stravinsky shares Picasso's fate, with Satie dead and Germany not a serious rival," but "*Oedipus Rex* turned out to be the mature masterwork one expected")—along with those of the lesser weaponry: Cocteau ("the Cocteau school are a harvest of leaves") is "at his usual work of ruining young artists." In an effort to distinguish his own artistic philosophy, Thomson says that while Joyce stands for "representation, depiction, emotion, the 'true to life' effect . . . Gertrude [Stein] and I represent play, construction, interest centered in the material, nonsense, magic, and automatic writing."

The most engaging letters of the period are the iconoclastic ones: a dissection for "Gertrude's" edification of Edith Wharton's *Glimpses of the Moon* ("a galaxy of prize examples to illustrate bad grammar, bad language, bad thinking, bad noise, and openly bad construction"), and an appraisal of Nadia Boulanger for Aaron Copland, provoked by a request for advice about her teaching from the young Paul Bowles, who nevertheless "prefers the life of a *poule de luxe*":

> If he wants Nadia's particular and special merchandise, namely, a motherly guidance to overcome American timidity about self-expression, then he had better go and get it and take the trimmings with it. Otherwise he had better buy his trimmings where they are cheaper and better.
>
> Nadia is not the same as when we were here [in 1922] . . . When I went back in 1926 . . . the main thing was all changed. The guidance wasn't worth a damn . . . Rarely is her advice practical, never disinterested . . . Her tastes are sentimental and *démodé* . . . She lives in a temple of adulation and knee-bending that is disgusting and her aged parent scents any heresy a mile off and begins putting the screws on to make you feel ashamed of eating her cakes and tea while you are secretly questioning the divine oracle . . . All this was to explain to Bowles that he might reflect a little before he puts his head into the noose.

Thomson hits just as hard writing to Copland himself about his book *What To Listen For In Music*:

> I read [it] through twice and I still find it a bore . . . [It] contains a lot of stuff I don't believe and that I am not at all convinced you believe . . . I find it a bit high-handed to assume the whole psychology [of analytical listening] . . . I don't think you are quite justified in discussing the sonata form as if it were one thing instead of two and as if no controversy existed about it. You know privately that it is the most controversial matter in all music, has been so since Beethoven. I find it a little dull of you and a little unctuous to smooth all that over with what I consider falsehoods . . . I'm not trying to rewrite your book for you. I'm just complaining that you didn't think it up for yourself.

Nor does Thomson pull any punches when confronting the formidable self-esteem of Gertrude Stein:

> If you knew the resistance I have encountered in connection with that text [of *Four Saints in Three Acts*] and overcome, the amount of reading it and singing it and praising it and commenting it I have done, the articles, the lectures, the private propaganda that has been necessary in Hartford and in New York to silence the

> opposition that thought it wasn't having any Gertrude Stein, you wouldn't talk to me about the commercial advantages of your name.

Thomson at the *Trib*, the core of the book and the author at his most buoyant, is a music critic's primer and a store of good sense for the laity. His abiding precept is that "whether or not [criticism] is of any service to the art, if one is to do it at all, one must tell the truth as one believes that to be." His own honesty and forthrightness stand out in a memorable line: "I am not sure that this is what I think, but I think it is what I think." Again and again he returns to the critic's obligations:

> It is important . . . to describe the event, so that your readers can imagine what it was like . . . Expression of opinion is incidental and will always come through, whether one states it formally or not. A critic does not have to be right about his opinion, because there is no right in such matters. He should, however, be correct in his analysis and description of works, styles, and artists' characteristics.

A newspaper is a "good place for controversy whenever there is a clear issue to state, . . . not a very good place for the exposing of irritation."

The best of Thomson's replies to letters from unidentified readers of his twice-weekly reviews and hebdomadal causeries are as good as the critical pieces themselves and might well, or better, have been published as addenda to them. This is true of his closing remark to a shocked reader of his review of a performance of the *Eroica*: "I assure you that I do not hold any controversial opinions about Beethoven. I do not think, even, that there is much possible controversy about Beethoven's musical works." And it is true, as well, of the following comments, in letters to two different correspondents, on Charles Ives, which do not appear in Thomson's well-known essay on the composer in *American Music Since 1910*:

> [Ives's] carelessness and volubility are sometimes hard to take. Your remark that his music does not have a characteristic sound I can agree with easily . . .
>
> Sometimes I am tempted to write the whole production off as a supreme case of Yankee ingenuity . . . His feelings about the Concord literary group do not interest me in any way. I think he was overimpressed.

Thomson seems to have been the first to notice the "Yankee ingenuity" that has recently been shown to have led Ives to Yankee-doodle with the dates of his manuscripts to make him appear to be further ahead of his time than he was.

Thomson's replies to readers loosely follow a formula that begins with an expression of gratitude for the "warmly indignant" letter, meaning an acrimonious impugning of his integrity and competence, and ends with the compliment that the intensity of the protester's feelings are proof of their sincerity. But his variant salutations are more diverting: "Are you sure you have written to the right man?" "Nothing would delight me more than to have my antipathies psychoanalyzed." He is equally prepared to clarify an obscure remark of his own—"By 'loyally composed' I mean that the author followed his own thought rather than somebody else's"—and to correct his correspondents' usage: "Aaron Copland is certainly the most famous living American composer, but he is not the dean of anything. That word means, I believe, the oldest member of a profession or the longest in business." Thomson regularly reminds his correspondents that what he wrote is "merely one man's opinion," without of course mentioning that his opinions, unlike theirs, are broadcast by a public address system.

On one occasion, in an apparent palliative gesture, Thomson tells an unknown someone that "I am really not at all such a horrid little guy when one gets used to me," not "a revolting 'smarty pants'," adding, what is surely disputable, that "people who really love music don't hate each other for very long." But his position is untenable only when transparently untrue: "It is easy to write a review of something that is very beautiful. When something is disappointing we have to use all our powers of self-control in order not to express our displeasure too extensively." From time to time the pretense that one or another of his unfavorable reviews was free of malice breaks down, and the piece in question is admitted to have been a "brickbat" or even a "little mean." And despite his claims of impartiality and his repeated expostulations to the effect that the *Tribune* pays him "to describe and appraise musical performances, not to do publicity work for any institution," he quite openly plugs the Philadelphia Orchestra, which was playing his music, and logrolls for performer friends, especially if French.

Censured for ignoring the music in New York's churches, Thomson seeks sanctuary in the argument that such music is "presumed to be presented in praise of God rather than in quest of public favor." (And the same God-praising music in concert halls?) But he goes on to say, with more justification, that his staff is too small to cover church performances, since "practically all of them take place on the same day and at the same time." He almost succeeds in extricating himself from the charge of dozing during an opera: "If Miss S—had committed grave misdemeanors about pitch, I am sure I should have waked up—at musical performances I sleep lightly, and only so long as nothing abnormal for good or ill takes place on the stage." His turning of the tables from defense to offense, after having confused a Vieuxtemps concerto with a Wieniawski—"Not that there is an enormous difference in either the style or the musical value of the works"—is dexterity of a consummate kind. But he is unable to worm out of the gaffe—blame the abdominal muscles of a five-star gourmet—of inadvertently omitting the name of Nathan Milstein as the soloist in an orchestra concert:

> I was chiefly interested in writing a little essay on Mozart performing style . . . I had never heard Mr. Milstein play before and I did not wish to make a superficial judgment about his work from last Sunday's performance.

A tenet of Thomson criticism is that a performer's "musical culture" is at least as important as his virtuosity. He serves notice at the beginning that he attends concerts to hear specific pieces of music rather than performers as such: "Whenever Mr. Horowitz plays in my vicinity a program of piano music that looks in advance even slightly interesting I shall go to it." Ernest Ansermet is among the musically cultured, Stokowski is not, yet when Thomson tells an objecting reader that "the musical world I know has mostly taken it for granted in the past fifteen years or so" that "Stokowski's technical mastery of the conductor's art is greater than his musical culture," his editors undercut him in a footnote: "*Pace* Thomson's qualms about Stokowski's 'musical culture,' the conductor was an avid champion of new works including several of Thomson's own," which is a non sequitur in any case, the more conspicuously so in this one in that Thomson's example is of Stokowski mistaking a motet by Nanino for one by Palestrina.

But Thomson is astute about conductors: "I find [Mitropoulos's] workmanship more interesting than the musical result"; Koussevitzky "mistakes Roy Harris for Borodin"; "Toscanini's reputed fidelity to the written notes is both a virtue and a fault. It protects him from interpretive bad taste, but it also blinds him to many expressive intentions on the composer's part that musical notation is incompetent to record."

Toscanini's "orchestras do not even have a characteristic sound, as the orchestras of Monteux, Reiner, and Ormandy do."

Thomson's unselfconsciously "natural" prose, extending from his natural, inborn pertinacity, is superior in its clarity and wit to most of the famous brands fashioned by America's full-time writers. True, he may force an aphorism: "The best work of our time, like the best work of any time, is that which least resembles the work of the other times" (which must refer to stylistic differences, since deep resemblances can obtain between the "best work" of different periods). And perhaps some of his homespun language sounds overly quaint ("lovey-dovey"; "shooing you out"; "even in Harvard English . . . the book would be a good plate of beans"; a "swell success"; "it sells swell"; *Rosenkavalier* is "a rather swell piece"). Still, his deliberate use of the demotic to treat "pretentious musical occasions" is always effective and has already outlived the "Augustan" of contemporary academe. And try the following for an alternative to the jargon of which this book contains not a single example: "The modern rhythmic concept [does not involve] any alteration in the basic tick-tock."

Some readers may be surprised to find that Thomson does not condone Americanizing pronunciation. After instructing a "radio-voice" narrator in Stravinsky's *Oedipus Rex* that " 'Oydipus' would have been consistent," that " 'Eedipus' is the classical Anglicization, since the long vowel preserves the original diphthong," and that " 'Eddipus' has . . . no precedent in any scholastic usage," he perorates, magisterially: "I cannot see that folksiness of any sort helps the dissemination of so distinguished a work . . . since . . . it is contrary to the basic stylistic conception that makes that work the kind of work it is."

The last part of the book, 1954–85, is chiefly concerned with Thomson's involvement in the promotion and performance of his own music, his film scores for *The Plow that Broke the Plains*, *The River*, and, above all, *Louisiana Story* having brought him fame and independence. But here, speaking as a composer, he seems less sure of himself than when speaking as a critic. He permits alterations in the vocal line of *The Mother of Us All* to accommodate a singer's range, and he tells a conductor that "Your tempo, which is more than twice as slow as the one I use, has convinced me completely." Yet precisely in these years Thomson's superabundant self-confidence becomes increasingly noticeable: "I appeared in one day as a speaker, composer and conductor and seem to have been pretty impressive too"; "the orch. boys are all crazy about [my] concerto. Everybody hates *Appalachian Spring*"; "I have been discovered here

[Chile] by press and faculty as the great American composer." Plaudits on his creations are paraded by, especially those from critics certifying them as masterpieces. Add to this the avatar's omniscience and *ex cathedra* manner, and new readers might be pardoned for imagining that he could be overbearing. Yet his humor and originality offset this egotism, and one's reservations are forgotten as he brings forth a major contribution to musicology:

> Regarding the tower scene with hair, in France we always supposed that Pelléas had an orgasm then and there . . . Regarding the second act of *Tristan*, one had been taught in former times that the lovers ejaculate simultaneously seven times.

He is outspoken: "I have not very much to say on the subject of Rudolf Bing. I do not find him very interesting, nor his management of the Metropolitan Opera very novel"; Philip Johnson's "NYU library looks like a jail courtyard. So does the promenade lobby of the [New York] State Theater." And he is not duplicitous. When he refers to Olin Downes, his opposite number on *The New York Times*, as among the "least distinguished intellectually" of a group of music critics, and gibes at him for having become "fond of cold-climate composers, like Sibelius and the Soviet Russians," surely he has said nothing that was not understood at the time. Nor does Thomson contradict himself in saluting Leonard Bernstein in a 1974 letter as "world master of the musical," and, a few years later, advising someone in a position to influence a prize award that the "world master" is "not an interesting enough composer, in my opinion, for this honor": different genres are under consideration. As in Part Three, the best letters are to anonymous correspondents:

> I follow no leader, lead no followers. As for being "American," I learned 50 years ago that all you had to do for that is to write music. National qualities follow. Similarly, of course, for being "modern." Once your apprentice years are over, only the discipline of spontaneity has value. And that, please realize, is the toughest of all the disciplines.

But enough of "reviewing." Virgil Thomson, now in his ninety-second year, deserves better. Instead, let us celebrate the man who could write with such cogency that "the important thing about a musical idea is not where it comes from but where it is going," then join the epigram to the instance: "Mendelssohn . . . was a reactionary figure with respect to the Romantic movement . . . because he was far more interested in where music came from than in where it was going." And who can match Thomson when he is writing really swell? "I did not notice the misprint 'Angus Dei.' Theologically the cow might as well have been adopted by the Deity as the lamb. Both are peaceful beasts."

BOOKS

Vidal in Venice[1]

The book of the television script is part pocket history, part waiting-room art, part tourist guide. But the best parts are those in which Vidal compares Venetian and American political systems and practices. Good, too, is the chapter on Thomas Coryate, the Jacobean "Innocent Abroad," England's first of the breed. And special mention should be made of the photographs, excellent in themselves, well-positioned as illustrations of the text, and comparatively successful in avoiding the over-familiar subjects and angles of postcard *veduti*.

Both republics, the Venetian and American, were equipped with "checks and balances" to prevent usurpation by doges and presidents. Each one "made sure that it would never become a monarchy—or a democracy," Vidal writes, adding that the heads of the two states were balanced and constrained by a Senate, as well as, in Venice, by a Great Council and a Council of Ten, and, in the United States, by a House of Representatives and a Supreme Court. These parallels are no more watertight than Venetian ground floors, of course, and Vidal is soon referring to the US "Acting President" as the "Emperor of the West," and to his Venetian counterpart of the past as a figurehead without "personal power" who was "not allowed to govern in Venice." But the similarity between the divisions of government does hold some water, and so do the further characterizations of both states as essentially mercantile—not religious or ideological—and as having "accepted as perfectly natural human greed." The Venetian desire for "a state in which it was possible for those of good family to do well in business" would also apply to America, that is if people of bad family were also included.

In view of the relative sizes of the two republics, the physical separation on the American side of the various branches and agencies is understandably at an opposite extreme from the Venetian, where the

[1] New York, 1985.

Doge's Palace, "a single, unfortified building," combined "White House, Pentagon, State Department and CIA." Radically different, too, are the levels of performance. As "directors of intelligence and counter-intelligence," the Venetians were incomparably more clever and economical than their American successors. The comparisons between the efficiency of Venice's Three Inquisitors, its three spies and secret codes, its agents and assassins, and the bungling CIA, with its mammoth apparatus, is vintage Vidal. So, less happily, is the claim, "There is one immutable law of government that the more money you spend on intelligence and counter-intelligence the less you know about what's going on in the world." There is of course no such law. Nor does Vidal explain that Venetian plots to remove political and other enemies were not always top secret, as when the Senate in open session voted to sponsor a scheme to poison the Duke of Milan (see Millard Meiss's *Mantegna as Illuminator*).

In the chapter "The Turning of the Tide," America's most mordant moralist seems to be in danger of becoming a merely conventional one, for Vidal follows his discussion of Venetian courtesans with the observation: "Moral fiber was plainly weakening in the early 1500s." We go on to read, with relief, that the reference is to bribery, scams, the sale of noble titles and privileges, the increase in corruption in both Church and State. Prostitutes were transformed into courtesans sometime after the closing of the zoned Castelletto, when, too, thanks to growing international notoriety, the ranks of the profession multiplied. Vidal's own visit to *Courtesans* (Carpaccio's, in the Museo Correr) is sheathed in prophylactic wit:

> A study of utter boredom . . . The young boy [is] their bell-hop . . . The elevated clogs are being aired prior to a promotional stroll through the Piazza.

If the weakest chapter is the one on the arts, it nevertheless diverts on the subject of correspondences between Renaissance painting and the movies:

> When a major painter revealed his latest work, it was like a film premiere. Carpaccio was one of the most splendid of proto movie-makers . . . [His] St. George is played by the Robert Redford of his day, while the dragon is handled by Steven Spielberg's special effects department . . .

> If Carpaccio [were], let us say, the William Wyler of Venetian painting, Tintoretto was the Cecil B. DeMille. Tintoretto, like DeMille, was at his best with crowd scenes and fires. In his portrayal of St. Mark, the saint, in the guise of whom else but the marvelous Charlton Heston, swoops down from heaven . . .
>
> Veronese, the Federico Fellini of his day . . . was asked to paint the Last Supper. But the Inquisition complained about the result. [The title was changed to] *The Feast in the House of Levi.* That is how the picture was finally released.

To say that the Colleoni monument is "considered to be the finest [equestrian statue] since antiquity," however, is to ignore the far larger body of opinion that rates the Gattamelata considerably higher. (Vidal tells us that Colleoni himself was said to have been over-endowed in genitalia, having as many testes as the balls on a pawnbroker's sign.) It is true that "Venice produced very little literature," and it may be technically true that Pasinetti is the city's only major novelist, though the Padovan Ippolito Nievo wrote a better Venetian novel, the *Castello di Fratta*, than Pasinetti's *Red Priest*, as well as one great book, a model, perhaps, for Svevo's *Memoirs of an Old Man.* And literature in Venice certainly flourished in the theater: Gozzi, Goldoni, and Lorenzo da Ponte merit mention. (A related omission is that of Venice as first world capital of printing.)

Vidal writes that "an age of religious music had begun, with Gabrieli [which one?] and Monteverdi"; but Monteverdi's importance in Venice is as a composer of operas. And finally, the art of Venetian mosaicists is alluded to only in passing, and perhaps should have been left out entirely: "As depicted in the mosaics of St. Mark's Church, the body of St. Mark was smuggled into Venice from Alexandria in 829." Yet "829" cannot be "depicted" and the furtiveness of the smugglers in the illustration indicates that the scene is the escape from Egypt, not the arrival in Italy.

Wee Willie Winkie

Only a few years ago, Graham Greene's notorious review of Shirley Temple in *Wee Willie Winkie* was deemed too explosive for inclusion in *The Pleasure Dome*, his collected cinema reviews. Reprinted at last in this anthology[1] from the short-lived (July-December 1937) weekly, *Night and Day*, Greene's notice might still shock people old enough to have grown up with, or soon after, Shirley Temple: "her well-shaped and desirable little body . . . dimpled depravity . . . In *Captain January* she wore trousers with the mature suggestiveness of a Dietrich: her neat and well-developed rump twisted in the tap-dance."

More than a year earlier, and without provoking any, well, rumpus, Greene had said much the same things about Miss Temple in *Captain January*: "a precocious body as voluptuous in grey flannel trousers as Miss Dietrich's . . . a little depraved with an appeal interestingly decadent." Twentieth Century-Fox sued *Night and Day*, claiming that the *Wee Willie Winkie* review accused the company of "procuring Shirley Temple for immoral purposes." The printers testified "that they recognized that the article was one which ought not to have been published," and the judge, pronouncing "the libel" a "gross outrage," awarded sizable damages. The reprint is accompanied by an "Important Notice" claiming "historical interest" and disclaiming any intention of "further maligning the good name of Mrs. Shirley Temple Black." *Further?*

Whether or not, in 1937, prepubescent children were acknowledged to have sexual instincts, Greene implies that Shirley Temple was consciously guilty of coquetry, to which "middle-aged men and clergymen" responded. So did he, obviously, not to put so strong a word as "projection" on it, or to suggest that whereas the dimples are undoubtedly Shirley's, the depravity could be Greene's. After all, he was one of the "discoverers" of *Lolita* and wrote the blurb for the original, unimportable Paris

[1] *Night and Day*, edited and with an introduction by Christopher Hawtree, preface by Graham Greene. London, 1985.

edition. Apart from all this, his review is as sharp—"The owners of a child star are leaseholders—their property diminishes in value every year"—as the well-known pieces he wrote as a young Marxist ("Groucho's lope") and Garbo groupie (producers treat her with "deathly reverence . . . like a Tudor mansion set up brick by numbered brick near Philadelphia").

Night and Day, which Greene coedited, was known as the London version of *The New Yorker*, and the derivation of the format—cartoons, departments, quotes of bloopers from newspapers, advertisements, even the typeface—is evident. The London offshoot could boast the better team of regular columnists, what with Greene as film critic, Evelyn Waugh as book reviewer, and Anthony Powell as Los Angeles correspondent. One of Powell's pieces describes a screening of *Spanish Earth*—"We continually cut back to one of those impassive peasant faces, the backbone of propaganda films all the world over"—followed by Hemingway himself reading an appeal for ambulances: "Two persons were taken to hospital, the rest were removed with shovels." Herbert Read's notices of detective fiction are a pleasant surprise: "The style is the best part of the intrigue. 'Maynard poured some more coffee and broke the narcissistic shell of another egg.' We have always found our eggs distinctly indifferent to their own appearance." The only regular contributor who disappoints is Elizabeth Bowen on the theater, though the Malcolm Muggeridge–Hugh Kingsmill dialogues creak with age, except for a few exchanges that sound like Waugh:

> H.K.: Brilliant at Eton, brilliant at Cambridge, [Arthur Hallam] wrote poems and essays.
> M.M.: What are they like?
> H.K.: Not brilliant.

Of the sixteen reviews by Waugh in this anthology, three were never published, and the one of *Eyeless in Gaza* appeared only in a dummy issue. Since Huxley's "thoughts tend to follow one another in classical sequence," Waugh legitimately asks why it has been left "to the binder . . . to sew up the chapters in their wrong order." His best review is the single paragraph on *Sally Bowles*, ending: "It conveys an odd sense that we may be reading a classic."

The most delectable writing in the book is in the restaurant ratings by A.J.A. Symons, Baron Corvo's biographer. Wine-learned, the most discriminating of ostreophiles, an aristologist *sans pareil*, he is equally reliable on Spanish cooking and Swiss–German *charcuterie*. Five stars.

"Silly Old Bugger"

If the letters to Juliet Duff,[1] the first of Maugham's correspondence to be published, are representative, his most entertaining book is yet to come. Here, for instance, is an excerpt from his explanation of the mechanics of the matriarchal system in the State of Travancore:

> Inheritance is through the female . . . The Maharajah . . . should he marry, would not produce an heir. His heir is his sister's child, and his children would not even belong to the royal family . . . The father of the future Maharajah . . . does not live with his wife the princess, but in a separate establishment; the princess sends for him when she wants a bit of nonsense . . .

Maugham spent World War II in the United States, and the book's most surprising letters were sent from Hollywood, New York, Oyster Bay, and a plantation near Charleston. Reminding Lady Juliet that "I am a writer and it is my instinct to put myself in other people's shoes," he sides with the Americans against the "many English people over here [who] seem to go out of their way to make themselves offensive," a statement provoked by the antics of Sir Thomas Beecham. Aldous Huxley, Gerald Heard, and Christopher Isherwood are the exceptions, their only real fault being that "they're all very busy with their soul's welfare and can't spare much time for social intercourse." But Maugham did not linger in Los Angeles, having already resolved in the late 1930s to do no more work with "pictures," though "gosh, I wish they would not offer me so much money."

Loren Rothschild provides candid notes—Rosamond Lehmann and C. Day Lewis are referred to as "lovers"—and a divertingly anecdotal account of the background. Lady Juliet, like her mother, the Marchioness

---

[1] *The Letters of William Somerset Maugham to Lady Juliet Duff*, edited with an introduction by Loren R. Rothschild. Berkeley, CA, 1983.

of Ripon, Diaghilev's London patroness, spoke fluent Russian. One might add that Lady Juliet's English did not exclude some of the expressions of a navvy. Thus, when walking with her in her garden, Maugham mistook Queen Olga of Wurtenburg roses for the Queen Hortense variety, she ridiculed him as a "silly old bugger."

Blue Suede Views

John Rockwell's survey[1] of the careers of twenty heterogeneous musicians in the United States from the 1950s to the present—*not* in "the late twentieth century" of the subtitle, obviously—reveals far more about the state of music reviewing in this country than about music. Publicity and promotion are Rockwell's fortes, not music criticism. To put it briefly and bluntly, *All American Music* reveals its author to be an amateur who does not understand music at either a professional or a technical level.

Most of the book is devoted to the postwar experimental movements and the musical populism that have arisen in reaction to serialism, identified here as "Northeast serialist rationalism." These movements include minimalism (Philip Glass); the recrudescence of a so-called tonality (David Del Tredici); mixed media (Robert Ashley); *musique concrète* (Walter Murch—but why not give us an Anglo-American term?); jazz, both traditional and free; rock, art rock, and folk rock; "composition beyond music"; and other goodies. Rockwell presents these genres evangelistically, stridently, and with a minimalism of argument that amounts to little more than the criterion "People *like* this music." If his "post-serialists" and "New Romantics" share a common attitude, perhaps it was best expressed by Philip Glass, the most famous of them, who declared, as Rockwell quotes him, that Boulez's Domaine Musical was "a wasteland, dominated by these maniacs, these creeps, who were trying to make everyone write this crazy creepy music."

Rockwell claims to be no more by "academic training [than] a cultural historian," adding, "and I hope it shows." It does, disastrously, and in other subjects than music. His introduction tells us that

---

[1] *All American Music: Composition in the Late Twentieth Century* by John Rockwell. New York, 1983.

> American intellectuals and artists of every sort have felt estranged from the mercantile and bellicose aspects of the culture as a whole since before the republic was born . . .

and, three paragraphs later, that

> the finest American artists and intellectuals have always been attuned to the breadth of American life as a whole.

Yet some very prominent pre-1776 "intellectuals," including Benjamin Franklin, managed remarkably well in mercantile America, and others, such as Tom Paine, throve on its bellicosity. Moreover, some great American artists, including Eliot and James, were remarkably ill-attuned to American life on every level. American society, Rockwell continues, overlooking a rich history of religious and racial intolerance, was "built upon the very ideals of ecumenicalism and catholicity." Other examples of his competence as a cultural historian are liberally distributed throughout the book. In Chapter 1, which could be the last one that demanding readers bear with, he claims that

> artists recoiling from the philistinism of democracy have been common in both Europe and America for centuries, from Molière's *Le Bourgeois Gentilhomme* . . .

But Molière's target is a parvenu, not democracy, which was not yet available to be recoiled from in 1670.

The book's New Right jingoism is still more marked in such cavalier pronouncements as "American intellectuals were crippled by an undue deference to Europe . . ." Why was the deference "undue" when *some* artistic and intellectual disciplines were practiced on a lower level in the United States than in Europe, until European refugees turned this around? We did not have a philologist to rank with Erich Auerbach, a philosopher of the stature of Cassirer, an historian of literature in the class of Wellek, an iconographer to compare with Erwin Panofsky, a composer deserving mention together with Arnold Schoenberg—to name only refugees.

Rockwell's showing as a music historian is equally poor, as examples both sweeping and specific demonstrate. For the first, he describes tonality as "the basic organizational principle of Western music" and characterizes it in part by "the modulation away from the home note or key . . . and back to it." For one thing, a culture historian should be aware that the beginnings of Western music and its florescence in the three centuries from Machaut to Monteverdi were not based on the as-yet-unknown key relationships and functional harmony by which tonality is defined. For another, and turning to cases, Rockwell dismisses Gesualdo as an "isolated eccentric"—the received opinion, long out of date, of those unable to follow perfect harmonic logic. Apart from this, a culture historian should know that the last three decades of musicological enlightening have populated Gesualdo's period with other chromatic-harmonic explorers, of whom the monodist and madrigalist Sigismondo D'India is the next most remarkable. (Compare D'India's fourth "Silvio" madrigal with the settings of the same text by Marenzio and Monteverdi.) And, since when has eccentricity been a stigma in an artist? Surely the word suits several of the more interesting figures described in *All American Music*.

Though "serialism" is Rockwell's bogey, he evidently understands little more about it than that it is "complex" and "cerebral"—deplorable attributes in his view—and has had a stifling effect on American music. Now, happily, he can announce that

> many of our brightest young composers have begun to question the basic assumptions of the European tradition—to doubt an automatic equation of artistic worth with complexity . . .

That that "European tradition" never "assumed" any such inane equation must be obvious, as well as that the abiding concern of the "brightest" artists everywhere is with exactly the opposite problem: to warn against condemning certain kinds of music simply *because* they are difficult. Rockwell seems to be unaware that the attraction of Schoenberg's music is not in its complexity but in the richness of its musical ideas.

Ernst Krenek, Austrian-born and exercising virtually no influence on music in this country, seems an unlikely choice to begin a volume entitled *All American Music*. (Many readers will wonder why this chapter, or a later one, was not devoted to Leonard Bernstein who, more than any other American musician, exemplifies the cross-fertilization between "classical" and "pop" that is Rockwell's *ignis fatuus*.) Apparently the justification for including Krenek is that he embraced the twelve-tone system "unreservedly" and that he represents

> Europe in the twenties and thirties, and . . . America in the fifties and early sixties, [when] serialism seemed a way out of the . . . tub-thumping of the American symphonists . . .

The exaggeration here borders on paranoia. In the 1920s and 1930s, Schoenberg did not share the twelve-tone principle with more than a handful of pupils, and the greatest of them, Alban Berg, applied it very differently. Furthermore, serialism was as little understood by musicians in pre-1960s America as it is today by John Rockwell.

In connection with Krenek, Rockwell attempts a definition:

> Schoenberg arranged the twelve notes of the chromatic scale in horizontal patterns, or "rows," and constructed his pieces from permutations of these patterns. This ensured a fashionable sonic abstraction . . .

What Schoenberg did, of course, was compose themes, motives, melodies, not arrange "horizontal patterns." (Surely Rockwell knows Schoenberg's "tonal" harmonization of the twelve-tone theme of his Variations, Opus 31.) To say that he "constructed his pieces from permutations of those patterns" is to omit the entire creative process, for the permuting—the inverting, reversing, and inverting of the reversing—is largely precompositional. It is also not peculiarly Schoenbergian, having been tried by composers 450 years before him. Finally, to charge Arnold Schoenberg with having done *anything* because it was "fashionable" is grotesque.

Rockwell is as innocent of the history of twentieth-century music as he is of its techniques. Could Schoenberg, he asks,

> still unsure of the principles of the twelve-tone system, have felt so free with the shifting "atonality" of *Erwartung* without a text as a compass?

"*Still* unsure" in 1909 of principles whose first inklings date from *Die Jakobsleiter* (1917)? Nor is this a trivial error, but one that exposes a fundamental ignorance. "Shifting atonality" is meaningless; and who but Schoenberg himself could say whether he felt more "free" in the atonality of *Erwartung* or more deeply constrained by inner laws of composition, to say nothing of such outer ones as avoiding octave doublings and the repetition of motives?

Rockwell provides an impressive variety and scope of misinformation. For instance, he likens the "working dynamics" between Stephen Sondheim and Harold Prince to those between Strauss and Hofmannsthal, though the Americans planned their pieces together, the Middle Europeans through the deliberations of correspondence. Moreover, while the "introverted" (Rockwell's word) partner in the Broadway team is the composer, it was the librettist in the Bavarian-Austrian one.

Back to his bugbear, Rockwell tells us that

> the arrival of so many distinguished composers from Europe in the late thirties . . . indeed, nearly every principal figure in twentieth-century Central European musical modernism . . . provided the catalyst for the post-war serialist reaction.

Hindemith, the only significant Central European arrival besides Krenek in the late 1930s, had no connection with serialism, while Schoenberg himself, who had come toward the beginning of the decade, was writing exclusively tonal music at the end of it. Two of the principal figures in Central European musical modernism, Alban Berg and Anton Webern, did not emigrate, and the other two, Szymanowski and Janâĉek, did not survive (Bartók did not come until 1940). Rockwell believes, incidentally, that Schoenberg "returned to religion—in his case, Judaism—in part as a reaction to the Holocaust . . ." In 1933?

Rockwell's misuse of language constitutes a considerable impediment. Subjects and verbs often disagree, pronouns are misrelated, contradictory words are juxtaposed ("these pieces purl rapidly past"), and jargon supplants clear and simple language, as when "musical Americanists" turns out to mean "American composers."

Rockwell taketh away more than he giveth. Thus Milton Babbitt, after being safely praised, is charged with having fathered a generation of "unthinking clones." The "achievement" of Elliott Carter is ultimately said to be "flawed by a lack of inner clarity and expressive directness." And Ralph Shapey, though ambiguously admired as a "loner," is far more strongly derided as "self-righteous." Shapey is credited with one of the book's few important opinions, "Great music is not for the masses," but this proposition does not receive the discussion that it warrants.

Give and take-back judgments are also meted out to Keith Jarrett, whose best solo improvisations are "wonderful" music but whose "scores sound not only received but dated"; and to Frederick Rzewski, Rockwell's representative "political composer" (*Attica*, Thirty-Six Variations on *The People United Will Never Be Defeated*), invidiously compared to Bob Dylan, whose music "says more about everyday life in this country than Frederick Rzewski will probably ever know. And says it more 'artistically' as well." David Del Tredici, who writes music "that players and the public genuinely like," is demolished with Erich Leinsdorf's verdict, after conducting *Final Alice*: "In my personal opinion [it is] totally without merit, parlaying the major-sixth chord into a fifty-eight minute work . . ." Clearly Maestro Leinsdorf's appetite for music of "unlimited" repetition in tandem with an extremely limited emotional range is in need of education.

Even John Cage receives less than his due, especially since the "site" composer Max Neuhaus, who has a chapter to himself, began doing "his thing" long after the master had tried it. (Neuhaus sets up "an electronic-music generating system in a public location and let[s] the audience come upon it," in, for example, a grate in the middle of Times Square, from which a "rich organ chord" mixes with the din of the city.) The feature of the Cage chapter is a digression on Henry Cowell that Rockwell should expand into a full study, since he believes that Cowell "will eventually take his place as one of the great American composers." Cage's "tapestries of boredom" are even more boring than the "abstractions" of Babbitt, Rockwell writes, but no matter, since Cage's greatest influence has been "through his prose." With less surprise than seems to have been intended, one reads that "Cage's attempts at a stream-of-conscious flow of word-plays and allusions hardly match the poetic clarity of Joyce."

Rockwell is said to be at his best with such jazz artists as Ornette Coleman and such rock stars as Neil Young. (Canadians might object to the inclusion of their native son as "All-American.") To Young, Rockwell even inspires what sounds like a confession:

> Rock critics . . . come most often from a literary background rather than a musical one, and hence feel uncomfortable with musical description and analysis.

Whether or not Rockwell meant this as an apologia, the passages on pop are as devoid of adequate musical exegesis as are those on serialism. Thus the folk-rock band, Crosby, Stills, Nash and Young, is said to have "specialized" in "innovative harmonies and song structures," but in what ways these harmonies and structures were innovative is not divulged.

For this reader, the book's only enjoyable moments occur in the chapter on the "performance artist" Laurie Anderson, whose lyrics "Walk the Dog" are quoted in full. Here is an excerpt:

I turned on the radio and I heard a song by Dolly Parton, And she was singing:
Oh! I feel so bad, I feel so sad, I left my Mom and I left my Dad.
And I just want to go home now.
I just want to go back to my Tennessee mountain home now.
Well, you *know she's not gonna go back home.*
And, she *knows she's never gonna go back there.*
And I just want to know who's gonna go and walk her *dog. (Her dog.)*

Waugh Zone

Shortly before his death, George Orwell made notes for a study of Evelyn Waugh:

> W.'s driving forces. Snobbery. Catholicism . . . even the early books . . . always centering round the idea of continuity/aristocracy/a country house . . . Waugh's loyalty is to a form of society no longer viable . . .
> . . . a Catholic writer does not have to be Conservative in a political sense. Differentiate G. Greene . . .
> Conclude. Waugh is abt as good a novelist as one can be (*i.e.*, as novelists go today) while holding untenable opinions.

Waugh's journalism[1] is limited to his opinions, and though some of these are prejudicial (preconceived, unreasonable), not all of them are indefensible. Nor has the judgment on his form of society been proven: viable or not, it still exists. But snobbery and the teachings of Catholicism *are* in contradiction, and one wonders how Waugh can be so unconscious of social injustice as to extoll Nancy Mitford for her good taste in living in a Paris street "so exclusively aristocratic that few taxi-drivers know its name." As for the Catholicism, the Church and the convert, with his love of the hierarchical, the paradoxical, and the dogmatic, had always been waiting for each other.

Catholicism, literary style, and the decline and fall of practically everything are the book's recurrent topics. The dust jacket emphasizes the importance of the second of these and quotes Waugh: "Literature is the right use of language irrespective of the subject or reason of the utterance."

---

[1] *The Essays, Articles and Reviews of Evelyn Waugh*. Edited by Donat Gallagher. New York, 1984.

But the statement exemplifies a wrong use (try "the making of literature is") and a too-circumscribed definition, for the continuation of literature depends as much on extending and renewing uses of language as on merely right ones. By what criteria would the use of language in *Ulysses* be considered right or wrong?

Waugh's meaning becomes clear with a glance at his shelf of preferred twentieth-century writers, most of them Catholic and none, with the possible exception of Henry Green, in any sense an innovator. Chesterton and Belloc (as a versifier "immeasurably Housman's superior") are high among the elect, along with Wodehouse, Beerbohm, H.H. Munro, Compton-Burnett, Edith and Osbert Sitwell, Alfred Duggan, Anthony Powell, and Graham Greene. Galsworthy's *Man of Property* is "tragedy in the Greek fashion," *The Forsyte Saga* "a great work," but to Msgr. Ronald Knox goes the palm for "the greatest work of literary art of the century." Despite the reviewer's narrow range—Péguy and Bernanos are the only foreign-language writers discussed at all—the book offers some surprises, including an equitable notice of John Osborne's *Luther* and a complimentary one of Peter Brook's staging of *Titus Andronicus*.

Waugh's Catholic *parti pris* is no less evident in his pronouncements on nineteenth-century literature. *Alice in Wonderland* is dismissed as an absurdity for the reason, it seems, that in all likelihood "Dodgson was tortured by religious scepticism." Even Waugh's deprecations of Dickens—a "thumping cad" who became "abject with self-pity in the smallest reverse" and who, "significantly, excelled in the portrayal of hypocrites"—evidently stem from the great "mesmerist's" anti-clericalism and because he "celebrated Christmas" while "proclaiming disbelief in the event which it commemorates."

Contrast this with Waugh's acuteness as a prescriptivist. He cites Orwell for misusing "intellectual," a word that should be reserved "to distinguish the analytical logical habit of mind from the romantic and the aesthetic." Answering Orwell's objection that Kipling's versions of proletarian speech are false, Waugh rightly says that "the stylization of the demotic is practically unavoidable," since real soldiers "swear continuously and monotonously." But Kipling's "When 'Omer struck 'is blooming lyre" is "ridiculous" because "the speaker would be ignorant both of Homer and of lyres." Malcolm Muggeridge is scored for "three painful conjunctival uses of 'like'," but welcomed "into that very small company of writers whose work would escape the red ink of the Victorian governess." Isherwood is another member: "Not only does he seldom use a cliché, he never seems consciously to avoid one [and] he never goes butterfly hunting for a fine phrase." V.S. Naipaul has "an exquisite mastery of the English language which should put to shame his British contemporaries."

Humor in Waugh's journalism, as in his fiction, depends on ironies and perversities, on "delicious incongruities," and on bizarreries (for the coronation of Haile Selassie, hotel bedrooms were equipped with "brand new enamel spitoons"). He can laugh at himself, as when a newspaper attacks his supposed sensitivity to his short stature:

> Has [the reporter] seen me tripping about Shoe Lane on stilts? Has he had an eye to the keyhole of the gymnasium where I was engaged in stretching exercises?

Whereas the bibliography of one book that Waugh reviews indicated that its author

> has been content to jot down what is apparently a list of most of the books she has ever read (whether or not they have any direct bearing on her subject),

another book displays a remarkable diversity of reading:

> Aubrey's *Miscellanies*, the *Vegetarian Messenger*, Dale Carnegie's *How to Win Friends*, *Near Home or Europe Described 1850* . . . the *Feudal Manuals*, Isaac Taylor's *Natural History of Enthusiasm* . . . are a few of the works casually referred to as though they were the normal currency of the literary market.

A set piece on the tipping crisis at the end of a Caribbean cruise reminds us of Waugh's early novels—

> Few except the very rich are actively parsimonious . . . the *maître d'hotel* in the last days . . . lighting flares of *crêpes* Suzette all over the dining saloon.

—as does the "process of Betjemanising":

> the undesired stop in a provincial English town, the "discovery" there of a rather peculiar police station, *circa* 1880, the enquiry and identification of its architect, [with] further research reveal[ing] that a Methodist chapel in another town is by the same hand.

As in *Scoop*, journalism itself generates amusement, the assignment to "run down to the zoo" and "write up a story about how the animals are preparing for Christmas," and the spoof on such "well-informed circles" as the postman ("a semi-official statement") and the stranger at a bar ("a source that has hitherto proved unimpeachable").

Most of Waugh's jeremiads have already been overtaken:

> In a few years' time the world will be divided into zones of insecurity which one can penetrate only at the risk of murder, and tourist routes along which one will fly to chain hotels, hygienic, costly and second-rate . . . All buildings will look the same . . . The whole country a speedway and a car-park . . . [People] stultifying and vulgarizing themselves before the television.

The decline in the art of painting—"A kind of cataract seems to seal the eyes of this half-century"—began with the failure to appreciate the Pre-Raphaelites. Whereas Holman Hunt's goal was "to record months of intense scrutiny, his contemporaries in France," whose works "are eagerly sought by the modern *nouveaux riches*," only tried "to record a glimpse." But do the extent of the artist's scrutiny and the social status of the collector have any bearing on the value of a painting?

Today's young people, too, are inferior to yesterday's. Waugh's gauge is the "sensual" and "brilliant young people" in *Antic Hay*:

> They do not come like that today. Today one knows quite certainly that a bachelor with a *penchant* for white satin sofas and *bibelots* would not be running after girls and, moreover, that though he might drop into idiomatic French, he would be quite incapable of writing grammatical English.

But too many of Waugh's own perfectly grammatical sentences begin with a variant of "In any gentleman's house, built in the civilized ages . . ."

Waugh's reputation as a controversialist suffers setbacks in the new volume. It is true that he easily demolishes Anthony Blunt's narrowly conceived argument that "Artists are men; men live in society and are in a large measure formed by the society in which they live. Therefore works of art cannot be considered historically except in human and social terms." Waugh: "It would be equally true . . . to say 'Men live on the earth, etc. Therefore works of art cannot be considered historically except in geographical and ultimately in meteorological terms'" (which is

Fernand Braudel's actual point of departure). But Waugh himself can be equally silly. He refers to "the revolution which destroyed France," disregarding the survival of French culture no matter how changed, the revolution having destroyed not France, but the power of the monarchy. And what can be the point of claiming that "for eleven centuries there were fewer notable suicides in Christian Europe than in a single year of the modern epoch," since the comparison is unverifiable? When Waugh declares that the view of the Renaissance as a "superstitious, sensual and romantic movement against the restrictions of Thomistic logic" and "a vindication of human reason against authority," he is forgetting that the "sensual and romantic" *Divina Commedia* is both a source of the Renaissance and an exposition of Thomistic philosophy.

Donat Gallagher's categories—political decade, Catholic epoch, etc. —overlap, and his adherence to a strict chronological order is an impediment. The articles on Abyssinia, for instance, would be easier to follow if they were not interrupted by a discussion of Edmund Campion. Similarly, the reviews of different books by the same author would gain in interest if placed side by side, irrespective of, partly because of, dates. And the book is mistitled. In addition to essays, articles, and reviews, it contains introductions and prefaces, open letters, cabled dispatches, autobiographical sketches, a lost-and-found advertisement, and a short story ("Consequences"). Moreover, "*The*" implies completeness, whereas a list of still unreprinted writings at the back of the book promises another volume of almost the same size.

* * *

The reissues of *When the Going Was Good*, which consists of excerpts from four of Waugh's travel books, and of *A Little Learning*, his autobiography (to his early twenties), are welcome, the earlier volume if only because not all the complete books are likely to be reprinted. Africa is the scene of almost a third of *When the Going Was Good*, and some of the same incidents and descriptions appear in the journalism. The first extract, a diary of a Mediterranean cruise in 1929, is callow and some of the effects misfire ("Etna at sunset . . . pink light fading gently into a grey pastel sky . . . was . . . revolting"), but the succession of simple declarative sentences would be ideal for foreigners learning to read English. *A Little Learning* is Waugh's most gracious book, unmarred by prejudices, snobberies, intemperancies, and distinguished by a mansuetude wholly new in his work.

By Any Other Name

When Umberto Eco's *Il nome della rosa* first appeared in English,[1] some reviewers avoided criticizing it, merely providing a resumé of the plot and describing the principal characters, the two monks, William of Baskerville, a fourteenth-century Holmes ("It seems elementary to me") and Adso of Melk, his Watson ("Once again I admired my master's erudition"), and the author of the novel within the novel. The reason for the sidestepping may have been that the mystery *in* Eco's story of medieval sleuthing is more easily solved than the one of the book's immense popularity.

How did the best-seller audience hang on during the interminable discussions of the Waldensian, Catharist and Albigensian heresies? How did it manage the Inquisition scene, in which action is constantly thwarted by the stuffing-in of information about the Fraticelli? Even more puzzling, how did Book-of-the-Month Clubbers cope with the paragraphs in Latin? And the forbidding English vocabulary? *viz.*, "The vibration of a climacus or a porrectus, a torculus or a slaicus . . . a resupine neuma." Musicologists are familiar with these words, as are zoologists and botanists with the terminology of medieval bestiaries and herbariums that similarly serves to fill long passages. But the general reader?

Whatever the answer, the attraction of the novel is in those long asides and historical footnotes. The film (1986) of the book—described in the credits as a palimpsest, presumably meaning a synopsis of the plot—which omits them, is pointless.

In the *Postscript*[2] to the novel, a book in the category if not the rank of Mann's *Doctor Faustus* diary, *The Story of a Novel*, Eco says that after the *Rose* was published, "I was trying to figure out why the book was being read by people who surely could not like such 'cultivated' books." If this

---

[1] *The Name of the Rose*. New York, 1983.

[2] New York, 1984.

"figuring out" produced any results, they are not shared with the reader. Instead, Eco goes on to say that "Adso's narrative style is based on that rhetorical device called preterition or paralepsis"—in simpler words, our way of saying "not to mention" what we then mention. Eco is, of course, well aware that his novel is a string of digressions, and that its popularity can only be attributed to the brilliance of his discourse and his ability, against his own obstacles, to sustain suspense.

The *Postscript* contains scraps of information about sources that will interest readers of the novel, particularly in the photographs of medieval sculpture, architecture and illumination. Six of these illustrate pages from the Book of Revelation that have direct bearing on *The Name of the Rose*, the last of the six from the Queen Eleonore manuscript at Trinity College Library, Cambridge, picturing St. John taking the book from the angel and swallowing it. The best pages in the *Postscript* raise questions, only generally related to the novel, concerning the meaning of "postmodernism."[1]

The *Postscript* condemns the technique of the omniscient author, the intruding novelist who interprets thoughts and motives and explains what his people say and do. But *The Name of the Rose* does not escape this criticism, for the reason that Baskerville is little more than a mouthpiece for his creator's real-life lectures. The reader quickly recognizes the voice of Umberto Eco, semiologist ("I have never doubted the truth of signs," William says, "they are the only things man has with which to orient himself in the world"), and as quickly forgets that William is the de facto speaker, Adso the de facto writer. William's glaring weaknesses as a fictional character are his Sherlockian infallibility, and his modern empiricism (and concomitant ignoring of First Principles), ostensibly derived from Roger Bacon. In short, he is too Reasonable and too Enlightened for the early fourteenth century. The same cannot be said of his anticlerical ironies, in the century of Boccaccio, but they are too predictable, as in his sermon on the virtues of worldly, as opposed to divine, love, and in such remarks as

> Fear prophets, Adso, and those prepared to die for the truth, for as a rule they make many others die with them.
> [The monks seemed] an assembly of gluttons, except that every sip or every morsel was accompanied by devotional readings.

---

[1] Also see Eco's *Sette anni di desiderio: Chronache 1977–1983*. Milan, 1984.

The accuracy of Eco's physical world picture of the year 1327 can be assumed from his *Picture History of Inventions*, written with the scientist G.B. Zorzoli. But the mental picture, compounded of everything that one person might possibly have known about the past and the present,[1] is not acceptable for the reason that no one could be acquainted with all the principal *trecento* philosophical movements, both because these had not been recognized as such at the time, and because instruments of communication to disseminate them did not exist. In any case, after Adso's wildly anachronistic reference to his "adolescent" mind, the reader no longer believes.

The Name of the Rose is heavily dependent on anachronism and disguised hindsight. The classic example of both is Dante's use (Canto XIX) of prolepsis to indicate that Pope Boniface VIII, though still alive during the journey of "Dante" and "Virgil" in the Inferno, is destined to be sent there: "Are you already standing there, Bonifazio?," Pope Nicholas III, himself among those buried headfirst, calls out. Similarly, William of Baskerville asks *his* contemporaries to "suppose we had a machine that tells us where North is."

Eco's set pieces, such as the description of Europe's vagrant populations with their diseased and maimed, their beggars and criminals, are highly accomplished, and many of the book's asides are memorable ("Young people need sleep more than the old, who have already slept so much, and are preparing to sleep for all eternity"). But the assumption of the plot, that Aristotle's *Poetics II*, on comedy, while officially lost,[2] is actually extant in the very abbey in which William is sleuthing, seems not to allow for a feasible dénouement.

The one monk aware of the existence of the text is determined to destroy it and, when others seem to be on the verge of discovering the secret, to destroy them. The clues and the suspects are examined in Holmesian fashion, but the culprit, Jorge of Burgos[3] is more an Agatha

---

[1] "The first year of work on my novel was devoted to the construction of the world. Long registers of all the books that could be found in a medieval library." (*Postscript*, p. 24)

[2] Richard Janko argues (*Aristotle on Comedy*, Berkeley, 1984) that the *Tractatus Coislinianus*, the tenth-century Byzantine manuscript in the Bibliothèque Nationale, is a précis of *Poetics II*. Unlikely though this is, some of the substance of the *Tractatus* clearly derives from Aristotle.

[3] In the *Postscript*, Eco says that the name came to him because Jorge Luis Borges was blind, Spanish-speaking, and a librarian. But Eco's monk is a homicidal fanatic who proves to be the Antichrist.

Christie than a Conan Doyle character, being both farfetched and obvious. Jorge is blind and well beyond the years of the physical strength that would enable him to perform the murders attributed to him. He gives the game away by expressing opposition to the idea of Christ ever having laughed, and in his response to William's assertion that "Laughter is proper to man, it is a sign of his rationality," Jorge says: "Not everything that is proper to man is necessarily good."

The final scene provokes proper laughter. When William learns that Jorge has the manuscript, Jorge poisons it. William has anticipated this, and escapes death. Jorge then rips the manuscript into pieces which he swallows in order to "seal that which was not to be said, in the grave I become." He goes on "tearing the pages and cramming them into his mouth," while William fears that "the old man will eat up all of Aristotle." Jorge is still tearing and eating when, after a chase, William finds him. At last sight "scraps of parchment" are "dripping from his mouth." But by this time, if not before, one wonders just how much poisoned parchment a toothless elder can devour while racing about.

The Real Thing

Professor Eco's title essay, much the longest in his collection,[1] describes a tour of American echoes of European works of art—reconstructions, copies, full-scale models, duplications, facsimiles, fakes. California is the most fruitful site, and Disneyland, Forest Lawn and San Simeon provide opportunities for comments long since familiar. Nor is any new territory introduced anywhere else, not the Nashville Parthenon, for instance, or the reenactments of historical events such as the battles of Lexington and Concord in full uniform and with actual musketry.

Professor Eco tells us that waxwork museums "spangle . . . the whole of the United States" and that between Los Angeles and San Francisco he saw seven wax versions of Leonardo's *Last Supper*. (He does not mention the discussion in Ursula Brumm's *American Thought and Religious Typology*[2] of the special significance for Americans of the Last Supper.) Europe has only four waxwork museums, he says, and these, in contrast to their American counterparts, are located in "subdued" and "diffident" settings. But surely the very thought of wax effigies is connected to their

---

[1] *Travels in Hyper Reality*. New York, 1986.

[2] Rutgers, 1970.

founding mother, Mme. Tussaud, who is not named. And since the Musée Grévin is the world's second most famous waxworks, perhaps the morbid fascination with wax images has claims to be French, like the realism exploited in David's painting of Marat dead in his bath that epitomizes the waxwork style.

America is "a country obsessed with realism," Professor Eco proclaims, referring to what he calls the American "past-izing process." But one might counterargue with as much justification that America is obsessed with fantasy. In fact, to some observers Disney World and the other exhibits in the Professor's itinerary of transplanted palaces and imitations of paintings and sculptures come under this heading first. And is this phenomenon peculiarly American? Whether realism or fantasy, the replicated Disney World near Tokyo is thriving, phoney gothic castles such as Neuschwanstein are found in Europe as well as in the Thousand Islands, and the sculptured fantasies in realist style in the Campo Santo in Genoa are more than a match for those in Forest Lawn.

Professor Eco has a just noticeable tendency to exaggerate. It is easier "to travel from Rome to New York than to Rome from Spoleto," he writes, forgetting the queues in holding patterns, at Immigration, Customs, Security, the baggage carousel, and in the trips to and from the airports. Manhattan is now "approaching the point where nearly all its inhabitants will be non-white." Nearly all?

After a visit to the San Diego Zoo, the Professor concludes that the "animals earn happiness by being humanized, the visitors by being animalized." But is anything known about animal "happiness"? According to the Professor, a certain American architect "deserves (in the sense that Eichmann does) to go down in history." Objectionable buildings compared to crimes of genocide?

The *Travels* contain two excellent short essays about films; or, rather, in the case of Antonioni's *The Difficulty of Being Marco Polo*, about the misunderstanding of a film owing to "unexorcised phantoms of ethnocentristic dogmatism"—meaning that the Chinese were offended by Antonioni's view of them and their country. The other, a deconstruction of *Casablanca*, is Professor Eco at his best. Read it again, Sam.

A Flood in a Time of Drought

Anthony Burgess tells us that the two hundred or so essays in *Homage to Qwert Yuiop*[1] represent only about a third of those that he wrote in the seven-year period 1978–85. A weekly average of two pieces of journalism, much of it good enough to reprint in hardback, sets a standard that few can match. In Burgess's case the mind reels. Book reviewing is a mere sideline of this novelist (he has published some thirty novels to date), author of a dozen literary studies including the best popular biography of Shakespeare, television and cinema scriptwriter, translator, editor (notably the guide and digest, *A Shorter Finnegans Wake*), prose anthologist (*The Grand Tour, Coaching Days of England*), composer of three symphonies and a quantity of other music. Burgess's prolificacy—a flood in a time of drought—his virtuosity and polymathy are among the wonders of the deutero-Elizabethan age.

The range and voracity of reading shown in *Qwert Yuiop* are of the same order. If Burgess got through the 1,267 pages of *Les Misérables* in a day and two nights, as he says, the speed and persistence suggest that he reads and drafts his reviews of most books in a single day—as some others do, albeit with short-cutting, or, like Auden, spot-checking. But when Burgess writes, "I, like most people, have read everything [Maugham] ever wrote," a tendency to inflate is exposed, since "most people" have not read any Maugham and very few have read all of him. Burgess's estimates of his *re*readings arouse some skepticism. Can he have finished Schulberg's *The Disenchanted* "about twenty times" and Hart-Davis's biography of Hugh Walpole "at least ten times?" One does not think of either book responding so repeatedly to Burgess's critical intelligence. Is it even likely that he has read Ellmann's *Joyce* "many times," instead of only three or four, no matter how frequently thereafter he has continued to refer to it? Estimates show that the music of Mozart and Schubert

[1] *Homage to Qwert Yuiop: Selected Journalism 1978–1985*. London, 1986.

probably cannot be copied in the known, or estimated amount of time in which it was composed, an indication that the creator can work faster than the drudge. And Burgess *is* a creator. The most fascinating chapter in *Qwert Yuiop*, an account of his conception of a television version of the "Synoptic Gospels," reveals some of the processes of his highly original imagining mind. Perhaps, like a migratory bird, Burgess does return annually to favorite habitats.

The inclination to exaggerate is of greater consequence in matters of literary judgment. Yet when Burgess confesses that "the greatest of all literary joys" is in "saying the dissentient thing in the guise of the harmless," he is probably speaking for himself and not for writers collectively. So too, such overstatements as "perhaps the greatest modern poet" is Hugh MacDiarmid, and that "one of the greatest fictional characters of all time" is Robertson Davies's Mamousia are obviously intended to promote little-known and underrated authors. Nor are all of these puffs out of proportion: many would endorse the claim that Richard Aldington's *Death of a Hero* is "far superior" to certain other British novels of the First World War, as well as to Remarque's German one. But moving to more familiar territory, we wonder if Scott Fitzgerald, however good a writer, is really a "great novelist," and whether an unnamed Irish playwright is really "the world's greatest . . . in the last hundred years." Not Chekhov, or Ibsen, or Pirandello? Since the word-quotas of the reviews seem not to have permitted argument of these cases, readers are left to agree or disagree according to their tastes and prejudices. One's guess is that Burgess persuades the majority of his audiences in the majority of such decisions.

Burgess's principal subject is the art of the novel, his main path the well-trodden one of the genre's modern classics. Good, as expected, on Joyce and Ford, he is still better on Wells and Nabokov, and his critical criteria are nowhere more sharply exposed than when he takes Nabokov's side in the row with Edmund Wilson, the side of the values of art as against those of art as social significance, of James (whom Nabokov detested) over Wells.

In an essay on Bely's *St. Petersburg*, Burgess characterizes Nabokov's literary judgments as "flighty" and acknowledges Wilson as "a person very dangerous to disagree with." But Burgess scores Wilson's "blindness to the excellence of Nabokov's prose" and his imperfect understanding of Russian—less reliable, Burgess suggests, than his own. Whether or not he has correctly diagnosed the origins of Wilson's Anglophobia, the writings of the American critic inspire *Qwert Yuiop*'s best analogy, the remark that anyone reading Wilson's *The Forties* after *Europe without Baedeker*, "must have the impression of a film running back from the dining room to the kitchen where the raw materials await the processing into a meal we have already eaten."

For readers not naturally disposed to stay to the end of very long new novels, Burgess's reviews of Vidal, Mailer (*Ancient Evenings* "certainly gives us a new look up the anus"), and other big best-sellers are particularly welcome. We want enlightened opinion-making, at least of the kind in which we think we can recognize and disregard a personal slant. If Burgess seems to be more candid and harder-hitting in his criticisms of his American, than of his British colleagues, the apparent reason is simply the distancing that he calls cisatlantic. This division does not appear in connection with writers of an older generation, Djuna Barnes, for one, on whom Burgess ultimately disappoints because he does not commit himself when citing the encomiums of Eliot, Dylan Thomas and Edwin Muir. (One wonders if Auden ever contemplated translating Dag Hammarskjöld's Swedish version of *The Antiphon* into English.)

Burgess excels at capsule summarizing, pinpointing strengths and prescribing weaknesses, and delivering short, sharp lessons for novelists. "The excruciating problem" of how "to show character in process of change" is avoided in *Ulysses*, he tells us, because the action takes place in less than twenty-four hours (which overlooks the changes wrought within the same time span in Greek tragedies). Stasis is the novel's major fault, Burgess admits, before going on to name the virtues outweighing it: "The epic vitality of the scheme, the candor of the presentation of human life as it really is, the awe-inspiring virtuosity of the language . . ." Impediments to movement and development are Burgess's concern again in reviewing a novel by Updike. With small adjustments of his own, Burgess sets up fifteen lines of Updike's prose in verse form, in order to show that a fine verbal gift can intrude to the extent of reversing priorities, "making the static examinations more important than the thrust of the plot."

Homage to Qwert Yuiop contains so many tidbits of autobiography that the reader, this one anyway, looks forward to the full repast that Burgess says he is not quite ready to prepare. We learn that he was "brought up in a lower middle class Catholic ambiance," had a "Lancashire bronchitic boyhood," soldiered in Gibraltar, was a civil servant in Malaysia for six years, returning to England in 1958. Embedded in critical writings, some of his personal glimpses sound slightly self-centred: "In the summer of 1940 the Luftwaffe was dropping bombs on Manchester and sidetracking me from typing my thesis on Christopher Marlowe." Relatives and friends of Mancunians who died in those raids may not feel sympathetic.

The last seventeen essays, the lagniappe as Burgess might say, are devoted to music. Though no less competent than the pieces on fiction, they do not come from inside the subject in quite the same way, and their primary importance seems to lie in disparaging bad writing on music, or "why so much musicology has a bad name." From time to time he trips: Richard Wagner did not, as Burgess says, coin "for his own works the term 'music-drama,'" and to refer to "the uneasy Jewish atonalists of the Austro-Hungarian Empire," is to exclude—unintentionally, no doubt—Anton Webern and Alban Berg. From Burgess's remark dated October 1, 1984, "I still write orchestral scores," we infer that he composes regularly. Though some of his music has been performed, it remains an all but unknown quantity. Perhaps an enterprising recording firm could be induced to release the sound track of his musical *Will!* (Shakespeare). The unelaborated statement that he has "devised" an "operatic version of *Ulysses*" only begs questions, more of them when he adds that "nobody wants my *Singspiel*. Opera houses are not yet ready, despite Peter Hall's production of *Moses and Aaron*, for the stage prancings of the id." Did the qualities of the music enter into the decisions of those "opera houses"?

Moments of breast-beating are faintly audible in Burgess's references to his philological knowledge and linguistic attainments. He knows Greek, Latin, Italian, French, German, and some Russian, of course, and it is not greatly surprising to be told that he understands Cymric, reads, writes and speaks Malay, and that he is able to hold conversations in Anglo-Saxon—as he did with the other Borges in the Argentine Embassy in Washington, to the wonderment of bystanders. He also says that Arabic script is not difficult to learn, or was not for him, and from a travel piece on Barcelona we discover that he reads Catalan, along with "the lisping tongue of Madrid," in which language, as well as twice in English, he has read Thervanteth's masterpiece.

The Burgess vocabulary can get in the way, not only with "thetatismus" and "alamdakismic" but also with ugly and difficult-to-pronounce everyday words, such as "rawer," "surlily," "scholarly." His fondness for Greek words does not guarantee that he always uses them aptly. Why would anyone bring in a "stomatological authority" instead of an ordinary dentist when no more is involved than two kinds of teeth? The story of discovering the meaning of the pink marzipan pig, the feminist booby prize, "in an old *Punch* in a thanatologist's waiting room" also fails to convince. Thanatologists—doctors of somatic death—if they exist (none is listed in the Yellow Pages), would not seem likely to have waiting rooms. Finally, the term "cacotopia," encountered several times, is not wholly successful when used with reference to present societies, since the meaning of "remote" seems to cling to it from "utopia." These are odd instances, of course, but Burgess is sometimes pedantic (read sesquipedalian).

So much for the mandatory fault-finding part of a formula that in most instances Burgess himself manages to vary or disguise. *Qwert Yuiop* contains an embarrassment of riches and a plenitude of wit, ingenuity, moral discernment, and humane intelligence. We can say of it, as he does of D.H. Lawrence's *Mr. Noon*, and of Lawrence's remark therein that books are leaves on the tree of life to be blown away and forgotten and that life is what matters: "This book is full of it."

Burgess and Music

Anthony Burgess's chapter, "Let's Write a Symphony," and important points throughout his *This Man and Music*[1] depend on some sixty-five examples in music type. The book will make little sense to musical dyslexics, therefore, but is well worth reading, nevertheless, for the essays on Hopkins, a helpful guide to "The Wreck of the Deutschland" and "The Windhover"; on Joyce (containing some new discoveries in *Finnegans Wake*); and on Eliot, which includes a perceptive digression on Lorenz Hart.

The transcription of the rhythms of poetry and prose into music notation is the unifying subject of the book, and Burgess's ability to fit individual lines to notes, with or without pitches, is remarkable. His setting of Pope's "the proper study of mankind" couplet, for example, would be difficult to improve upon both in rhythm and in melodic style. So, too, the rewriting in note-values of the jazz rhythm of "Some men don't and some men do" ("Sweeney Agonistes") is an astute illustration of Burgess's theory that "an honest musical setting of speech . . . fights against regularity of accent." In the discussion of "The Windhover"—which includes a convincing explication of the word "buckle" (Empson's seventh type)—Burgess observes that

> The meaning does not yield itself until we fully understand the distribution of stress and pause, and the variations in tempo enforced by the syllabic patterning. Ultimately the poem cannot be appreciated at all without a skilled performance . . . or a mode of notation which . . . indicates precisely what sonic patterns we are meant to hear.

Burgess bravely offers his interpretation in musical notation of the rhythms of the sestet in "The Windhover," and the result, though stiff

---

[1] New York, 1983.

and foursquare, must be applauded for ingenuity in relating rhythmic patterns, as well as for the imaginative application of the musical sign for an appoggiatura to indicate Hopkins's slack syllables. The weakness of Burgess's version is that the stresses, particularly in the rhymed endings, are too long.

To turn from his discussions of verbal music in the latter part of the book to his account of writing a symphony near the beginning is to experience a jolt. For all his protestations to the contrary, and his definition of music as "a non-referent" language, he thinks in programmatic terms, describing one passage in his symphony as "an attempt to avoid a serious meditation on death in battle." What would be the difficulty in attempting to *avoid* writing anything? The statement is followed by a music example in which the reader's attention is called to "the tendency to avoid the major third." Yet this interval is the melodic peak of the excerpt, and, though used only there, it confirms that "the theme is in, as it seems to be, E flat major."

Burgess goes on: "We do not want, these days, the unambiguous blatancy of such modal assertion: the major third seems vulgar." The theme might have been composed by a first-year conservatory student forty years ago. And almost all the music in the examples is characterized by simple diatonic tunes, rhythmic poverty, flat-footed parallel chords, and numbing sequences, while one of the musical quotations, described as "a bitonal canon," is neither canonic nor tonal, let alone a combination of two tonalities.

In the chapter "Music and Meaning," Burgess asserts that "Behind all music of an instrumental nature lies the dance." But Mozart's concertos and serenades are well stocked with arias for instruments. And what kind of dance is behind the *Tristan* Prelude? The oboe solo in the first movement of Beethoven's Fifth "must have a private significance," Burgess contends, because it breaks "the consistent rhythm of a public utterance." But surely the oboe cadenza, as public a part of the symphony as any other, is a calculated, necessary interruption of the rhythmic overdrive.

Burgess employs so many obscure words that one suspects he may experience his greatest satisfaction when introducing a term that absolutely nobody understands. "I never learned to sound a note . . . that was not, as they say, vaccicidal," he writes. *Who*, may we ask, says "vaccicidal"?

As Though to Some End

Life Supports, William Bronk's collected poetry, received the 1982 American Book Award for Poetry. That his *Vectors and Smoothable Curves*[1] was not a contender in the following year for the Essays Award must be attributed to the "fault" of his too quiet voice.

The poet-essayist's distancing from the marketplace, at any rate, is apparent in the accuracy of observation and economy of description in a passage near the beginning of the first essay, "An Algebra Among Cats." In Machu Picchu,

> stone surfaces have been worked and smoothed to a degree just this side of that line where texture would be lost. Where one stone meets another the surfaces recede slightly forming a small indentation at all the joints. And no doubt it is the joints more than any other one factor which makes the perfection. Since no mortar was used[2] it was necessary for each stone to match perfectly all other stones that it touched and these are not like bricks or building blocks that are regular, interchangeable units. Probably no stone was cut quite like another. In many cases they are roughly rectangular, but each one has its variations in size and shape. An inner angle of one is perfectly reflected by an outer angle of the one adjoining, and even after all the intervening time, there is no space at all between. The correspondence, moreover, was not merely of the surface but extended as deep as the stone.

As if in imitation of the Inca masonry, the writing forbids interstitial comment.

---

[1] *Vectors and Smoothable Curves.* Collected Essays by William Bronk. San Francisco, 1983.

[2] According to the chronicler, Pedro de Cienza de Leon, who was in Cuzco when the city was being rebuilt after the siege of the 1540s, pitch was used instead of mortar. (R.C.)

Bronk's point of departure may have been a fellow visitor's dismissal of Machu Picchu as "an interesting ride, but there's nothing there." The world of the Incas is quite gone, of course, but Bronk believes that "we can a little way, with their aid, feel into it." He demonstrates this by defining an Intihuatana as "The post to which the priests tied the sun at solstices to force it back again when it had reached its furthest decline," and by remarking that while today's traveler easily loses his nerve on a certain high path, "the old inhabitants moved undoubtedly with ease and composure." (In the newly rediscovered city of Gran Pajaten, about 400 miles north of Lima, the burial towers can be reached only by a narrow pathway skirting the edge of a 1,000-foot cliff.)

Only once does Bronk "feel" too far. After considering our "assumption" that "given time enough and good will and energy, we can evolve a world subject to our reason and wisdom," he goes on to say: "one supposes that whoever may have lived at Copan may have thought this way." Obviously we can suppose the existence of reasoning faculties in Copan. But the same is not true of concepts of evolving—which we say, remembering that the Chinese were adept at deduction (*viz.* their discovery of the theory of inoculation), but could not, if only because of barriers in linguistic structure, develop an Aristotelian logic.

The first part of *Vectors and Smoothable Curves* consists of meditations on reality, time, space, and historicity in Pre-Columbian cities. Thus at Tikal (Guatemala),

> Time was invented and refined quite independently of any similar process elsewhere. [Here] time was perceived in the circular patterns of recurrence . . . before any coupling of time with the apparent movement north and south of the sun.

The unit of the cycle, the day, was determined by reference to the sun, yet the 260-day Mayan year was not related to the agricultural seasons. And without external reference, one culture's ordering of the experience of time—the Mayans counted by twenties, the Babylonians by sixties, the modern world by tens—is as valid as another's. Nor was the Mayan calendar devised for religious reasons, since "the relation between time and worship [was so close] as to suggest that time itself was the object of that worship." Bronk's question is that since time has no logical beginning or end, how do *we* feel it? He answers: "as though from some beginning, as though to some end."

Palenque and Copan provoke thoughts on space and historicity, or, more exactly, on the shaping and defining of space and on the absurdity of *our* historicity. The Mayan occupation of space, though it humanized the landscape, imposing on it "a kind of form in human terms," was no less abstract than the Mayan response to time. The great constructions were not houses and not in any other way utilitarian—the Mayans lived in thatched huts much as the Indians do today—but "ceremonial, even symbolic." Symbolic first of all, as Mesoamerican archeology has discovered since Bronk wrote, and extending to color, red signifying the human world, and blue the divine.

Contemplating the ruins of Copan, Bronk considers the subject of our own disappearance:

> Whatever we are, we are not historical. The world we make and ourselves . . . in the particularities of time and space . . . all this can be destroyed and make no matter. We are happy at Copan to witness our own destruction and how we survive it . . . to be delivered from our continuous failures and frustrations . . . from our self-limited successes, [and] the awful banalities of the good life.

This leads to the question of duality, which Bronk wants both ways:

> Whatever there is, if there is something, we, if we are, are part of it. There are not two realities, man and his medium, of which one is the subject and one the object. [At the same time] what there is—we are part of what there is—is what it is regardless of us. It has real being without our help.

(Bronk returns to the subject of "are we one or are we two?" in a late prose poem:[1] ". . . Something about one seems to think two necessary as perhaps it is . . . It is in the dualism of either and or that oneness discovers itself, that the indefinite is defined, that duality makes unities.")

Two brief essays in the same vein, "Costume or Metaphor" and "Desire or Denial," resist excerpting and summarizing. They are followed by long ones on Melville, Whitman, and Thoreau, written in the 1940s and now familiar as both argument and exegesis. The first part of the one on Melville traces his progress in understanding Evil from the conviction that "white civilized man is the most ferocious animal on the face of the earth" to the belief that some men are not entirely vicious. The

---

[1] *Manifest; And Furthermore.* San Francisco, 1987.

part devoted to *The Encantadas* skilfully conveys the Sisyphean feeling of the dragging giant tortoises' "infinite endurance and hopeless, toiling persistence."

Bronk's Whitman essay fastens on the poet's "maintenance of a state of constant emotional excitement"—auto-erotic excitement one sometimes thinks during those enumerations of the character attributes that he had created for himself, and when, too democratically, he was writing pseudonymous reviews of his own poems. But the range of Whitman's stimuli and the diversity of his transferences are always impressive, whether imagining himself as a mother or a dangerous pyromaniac.

O the fireman's joys!
I hear the alarm at dead of night,
I hear bells, shouts! I pass the crowd, I run!
The sigh of the flames maddens me with pleasure

The Thoreau essay centers on concepts of friendship and comity, the dignity of persons in social relations. Bronk allows Thoreau to speak for himself much of the time, which inadvertently exposes Thoreau's tendency to slip into verse:

> Constantly, as it were through a remote skylight, I have glimpses of a serene friendship land, and know the better why brooks murmur and violets grow.

Always excepting such insights as "the heart is forever inexperienced," Thoreau, as seen by Bronk, is at his best when most indignant, denouncing those aggressive doers of good who "rubbed you continually with the greasy cheeks of their kindness," fulminating against a "charity that disperses the crumbs that fall from its overloaded table," and defending John Brown against the pusillanimity of those who asked, "Yankee-like, 'What will he gain by it?' as if he expected to fill his pockets by this enterprise."

99 and 44/100% Ivory Tower

Robert Fitzgerald's death immediately after the publication of *Enlarging the Change*[1] has inspired memoirs amplifying the impression that this esteemed translator of Homer, Virgil, and St. John Perse was a tactful and considerate as well as a learned man. Few of the seminarists in his chronicle of the 1950 Princeton symposia on literature display even a touch of the first two qualities: Ernst Robert Curtius "stirred testily and spoke in a manner that made his former pupil turn momentarily a little pale"; "Erich Auerbach went on to say, even more cantankerously . . ."; Gauss "severely interposed." But then, as another observer said to Fitzgerald, "A man making a study of Dante could be appointed [to the Institute for Advanced Study] but Dante could not."

Fitzgerald sets the scene of the symposia:

> There were about thirty people in four rows of folding chairs with tubular metal frames. The speaker sat on the other side of a big table . . . a portable blackboard at his back . . .
>
> Friends greet arriving friends, coats are plunged in a corner, conversations begin, smoke rises, people fetch atrocious ash trays . . . The man with the briefcase or typescript arrays himself behind the table . . . At five minutes past the hour the last dinner party comes in . . .

In the final series, the reality of the Korean War ("the shock of the quilted Chinese") momentarily ruffles placid, feudal Princeton ("Ancient black waiters moved softly in the Nassau Club dining room"). One of the scheduled speakers is called to active duty, and for the second time in a decade the brains of Robert Oppenheimer, the Director, are

---

[1] *Enlarging the Change*. The Princeton Seminars in Literary Criticism 1949–1951. Chicago, 1985.

requisitioned by the U.S. Government. But soon the talk, which is of the ivory tower variety, continues as before.

Since the most substantial of the lectures were subsequently expanded into now classic books—Auerbach's *Mimesis*, Wellek's *A History of Modern Criticism*, Maritain's *Creative Intuition in Art and Poetry*—readers will be less interested in Fitzgerald's summaries of them than in his versions of the often acrimonious post-lecture exchanges, and in his concluding critical remarks. He does not conceal his Maritainist bias:

> the interest in poetry-making as a process had moved, with Maritain, into the forefront of things . . . The level of discourse was now rising toward something superior, some revelatory largeness and accuracy . . . The essential emotion, he said, was not an emotion to be expressed by the emotion *which causes to express* . . . The emphasis that [Baudelaire and Eliot] put on the words itself was an emphasis that Maritain wanted to keep; the poet's intuition, the creative intuition, is an obscure grasping of his own Self and of Things of knowledge . . . virtually contained in a small lucid cloud . . .

Do the last two words form an oxymoron? These remarks might be compared to a passage in an unpublished letter from Maritain to Stravinsky sixteen years earlier (July 23, 1934), apropos the composer's single most quoted remark, "Music is powerless to express anything at all." After praising Stravinsky for his concept of "the victorious power of the creative effort and the effacement of the individual by his achievements," Maritain adds:

> as philosophy—and Thomist philosophy—I agree with you on music and the expression of emotion. But I myself believe that there also exists something absolutely different which I would describe as that creative emotion or creative intuition through which the artist unknowingly expresses himself in his works.

Fitzgerald's own lectures on Sophocles and Aristotle have survived the intervening years as well as any except Auerbach's, whose philological range and power to vivify seem to have been less than fully appreciated at the time. Mann's *Doctor Faustus* is brilliantly exposed, in two senses, by the 26-year-old Joseph Kerman, but the chapter as a whole has worn least well, like the novel itself. One wonders why, both as a representative of contemporary literature and in view of the quality of learning to hand, it was chosen in preference to, say, Musil's *Man Without Qualities*.

In the subsequent three and a half decades of the "change" indicated by the title, the inclusion of the Russian poets is the most important development; in 1950, Osip Mandelstamm and Anna Akhmatova were not even mentioned. At that time, too, German-shaped niches were found in the disproportionately French-populated pantheon only for Lessing and Schiller, and then only as aesthetic theorists. Auerbach discoursed on Pascal, Flaubert, and Baudelaire, and Maritain's texts are from Rimbaud, Mallarmé, Valéry, and the Breton manifestos ("surrealist poetry was required to provide man with deceptive and flashy substitutes"). By contrast, the Ivy League ratings of novelists have remained the same at the top (Joyce, Henry James), no matter how drastically the ups and downs at the levels of Hardy, Conrad, Lawrence and George Eliot (the preeminence of *Middlemarch* was just beginning). For Fitzgerald, the other Eliot was still the supreme poet and critic.

Too Innocent Eye?

The present selection of essays,[1] representing a quarter of a century, affirms that Surrealism remains the central event in Roger Shattuck's view of modernism. This is puzzling, if only because his critical perspectives have been broadened with social history and other disciplines, while Surrealism, both as doctrine and achievement, has shrunk. Or, at any rate, its political, religious, psychoanalytical, and sexual (anti-homosexual) biases, and its stereotyped imagery, have become increasingly apparent, while André Breton's manifestos, not to mention *Nadja* and the *Ode to Fourier*, are not merely dated but dead.

Breton, nevertheless, is the hero of "Having Congress," an account of the 1935 Paris International Congress of Writers for the Defence of Culture, and the most immediately engaging essay in the book. Pieced together from newspaper files and the testimony of survivors, the story is suspensefully told, and Shattuck's summaries of the positions taken by the most prominent participants—Gide, Malraux, Aragon, Breton, Ehrenberg, Salvemini—form an important chapter of politico-literary history. Not everyone will agree that *Man's Hope* is a "magnificent novel," Malraux himself "one of the last great prophets of high humanistic culture," but the book is worth acquiring for the descriptions of him in action at the Paris jamboree.

Even so, Breton's performance, compared to Malraux's, was like that of "an old walrus of intractable political sagacity," whose "political naïveté" (a contradiction?) "took the form of an uncompromisingly principled idealism." Breton rejected any kind of political control of literature and courageously distanced himself from his totally Soviet-directed colleagues.

In the title essay, Shattuck asserts that "It is possible, and sometimes advisable and rewarding, to start by looking at individual works with as

---

[1] *The Innocent Eye* by Roger Shattuck. New York, 1984.

innocent an eye as one can attain." (Why only "sometimes"?) But he continually contradicts this recommendation and approaches works of art, individual or otherwise, through glasses tinted with classroom precepts. We read *Madame Bovary*, he says, to "learn about nineteenth-century provincial life, to take account of Flaubert's mastery of French prose, to examine the novel form at its peak of perfection . . ." But surely most people do not come to the story of Emma Bovary seeking knowledge about life in another period, to "take account of" (instead of simply to savor) Flaubert's prose, and to examine the novel as a supreme specimen of the genre (rather than to follow the fates of the characters)? As Robert Fitzgerald wrote, "*Madame Bovary* does not belong to critics, scholars, and writers only but to the unknown people."

Shattuck is incorrigibly academic. One section of his book is called "In the Professor's Den." Another is an *à la mode* lit-crit dialogue between a teacher and an ex-student on a Christmas night (!) train ride. He even confesses that while driving on Texas "loop roads"—which circuit from main highways to hinterland habitations and, without connecting with other roads, rejoin the principal ones further along—he "had sensed" that they "would later furnish a compact analogy I could not yet identify." When identified, the analogy is that a work of art diverts us "from the regular path of our life," a platitude that does not accord with the view of "life as the theater of art" espoused elsewhere in the book.

Still, Shattuck the rural philosopher may attract more readers than Shattuck the cosmopolitan intellectual. *This* reader, at any rate, is wholly unable to keep up with the apodeictic statement that:

> . . . certain forms of presumably rational thought such as the implications of quantum and relativity theory, or theories about time and entropy bear a close resemblance to their decreed opposites, dream and fantasy . . .

Confidence is less seriously threatened in these rarefied atmospheres, nevertheless, than in regions much nearer, if not quite down to, earth. For example, when Shattuck writes that "Valéry falls back on the sexual metaphor, or rather, on erotic ritual with which man, more than any other animal, has sanctified the act of mere coupling," the reader wonders which other-than-human animal has ever sanctified anything. And when Shattuck quotes an out-of-context remark by George Balanchine—"Only the new concerns me; I am not interested in the past"—and says that "Behind the bad faith and professional irresponsibility of this statement lies an unwillingness to acknowledge dependence of the new on the old," the reader is puzzled how anyone concerned with the arts in the present age can be unaware that Balanchine's genius is precisely in his renewal of the past.

"Critics who debate the qualities and merits of individual works attract me more strongly than those who debate theories and processes," Shattuck writes. But his book belies him, revealing a far greater concern with movements and corporate voices than with individual artists and their works, and more interest in what artists have in common than in their *differentia*. In the first place, most of the artists whose names appear in the titles of the essays serve as representatives of modes and attitudes. In the second, Shattuck habitually refers to artists in the plural, asking, for example, whether they are "subliminally aware of the predictive flattening of the curve of invention" (as if De Kooning, Balthus, and Frank Stella are likely to share an opinion about the, in any case unascertainable, answer). He remarks, typically, that Dada and Surrealism "explore the possibilities of collective endeavor in psychic experiments, in political action and in artistic creation," and he claims "greatness" for the figures who loom largest, Breton and Duchamp, though this would have to be found in some area other than artistic creation, which is significantly last in Shattuck's enumeration. Ironically, where collective endeavors have succeeded in the arts—in Giorgione's, Bellini's and Titian's *Feast of the Gods*, in the writings of the Goncourts—the first job of the critic is to separate the individual contributions.

An essay on Apollinaire—with Valéry one of the "two major poets of the era"—provides still another example of Shattuck's attraction to movements, as well as to the futile exercise of parallel-making among the arts. Troubled by the absence of a literary work to stand beside the revolutionary *Sacre du printemps* and *Les Demoiselles d'Avignon*, he proposes to fill the gap with Apollinaire's calligram, "*Lettre-Océan*." This, Shattuck says, unintelligibly to this reader, "represents the mind raised to the level of omniscience, ubiquity, self-transcendence in the complete instance: a form of self-divinization." Study of this "major exhibit and achievement of modernism," as reproduced in the text, suggests that he, like Kruchenikh and Ilya Zdanevich, has mistaken a typographical revolution for a literary one. Whereas the *Sacre* provoked public violence—while incidentally proving Bakunin's dictum that "The passion for destruction is also a creative passion"—the explosiveness of the calligram is imperceptible. Picasso's *Demoiselles* marks a stage in the evolution of Cubism, not the overthrow of the government of painting.

For this reader, Roger Shattuck's most valuable observations occur in connection with the "take-over of literary criticism by linguistic science," which is to say by critics in white coats, and with the "complacently alienated, demythologized, self-referential" scene of "post-modernism." Like most things "post," including post-nasal drip and post-coitus, "post-modernism" lacks appeal. But many of us would be grateful to Professor Shattuck for a full-scale study of the subject.

Beachhead into Broch

One reason that the English-speaking world has not yet taken the measure of either Hermann Broch or Hugo von Hofmannsthal is that both are extremely difficult to translate. Another is that in the United States, at least, German literature is still so much more remote than French that the novels of Theodor Fontane are probably known to no more than a fraction of the readers of the novels of Emile Zola. The new book,[1] far more digestible than *The Spell*, *Sleepwalkers*, and *The Death of Virgil*—Mr. Steinberg describes this last as a "500-page trance"—provides a beachhead into Broch, as well as historical and other perspectives for an approach to Hofmannsthal.

Not all the barriers have been swept away. Broch is oracular, the opposite of economical, and notoriously dense. Instead of developing a statement, he makes new ones containing new themes, and he only rarely resists the inclination to digress. The vocabulary, moreover, is jaw-breaking: "patheticizations," "evolutionistically," "Renaissance-ish." Still another impediment is his habit of focusing on an irrelevant point of communality while ignoring far more significant differences. Thus he notes that Franz Kafka and Henri Rousseau were "almost entirely free of tradition," adding that "at the time" of these two strange bedfellows "a no man's land beyond the bounds of tradition" no longer existed. One wonders in what sense the Douanier and Kafka, born forty years apart, share a "time."

Broch's principal subjects are the "decline of the convention of a universally valid value system," and the epoch, defined by Hofmannsthal's lifetime (1874–1929), of "non-style," or "style-vacuum," the "void of eclecticism" where "personal style is all there is." The spirit of an epoch in any country is represented in architectural forms, Broch

[1] *Hugo von Hofmannsthal and His Time* by Hermann Broch. Translated and edited, and with an introduction by Michael P. Steinberg. Chicago, 1984.

observes, but these did not exist in the Vienna of Hofmannsthal, the Vienna of "poverty masked by wealth," of "the overadornment of the ugly," of, in a word, the "caryatid-crammed hall of the Musikverein." Broch on Vienna, "the metropolis of kitsch," the "capital of a dying monarchy [that] had every connection with dying but not the slightest with death," is scarcely distinguishable from Karl Kraus.

All of this is presented as part of the ethical and cultural background for a study of the life and work of Hugo von Hofmannsthal. Yet it is evident that Broch's primary interest is in his historical analyses, and that he chose Hofmannsthal simply as a prototypical figure. Hofmannsthal's avoidance of the new exasperated Broch, even though he takes into consideration that the new "was not available to him because the epoch in which he lived did not form a whole." Hofmannsthal "knew less than anyone else how to come to terms with the twentieth century . . . He writes on D'Annunzio and Barrès but not on Mallarmé." Broch's "malevolent" (his word) dissection of a poem by Hofmannsthal removes several rays from the halo.

Hofmannsthal's libretti, the main attraction of the book for many readers, receive short shrift. They "become pure conservatism," Broch writes, and he dismisses *Ariadne auf Naxos* as "an experiment conducted against the new direction." *Die Frau ohne Schatten* is lauded as the pinnacle of Hofmannsthal's "voyage of discovery into the primal forest of symbols," and as "a high technical accomplishment," but condemned as an "artificial fairy tale grounded in no kind of popular myth." Only in *Arabella* is the "symbol principle, merely hinted at in *Der Rosenkavalier*, carried to its perhaps most theatrically felicitous resolution."

Broch's discussions of early twentieth-century art and music are dated, but then, the revival of interest in Jugendstil and the rediscovery of Mahler were not easily foreseeable when the book was written (1947–50). It remains to be said that Broch's best aperçus occur when he is at his least polemical: "Wagner is perfectly humorless and perhaps in *Die Meistersinger* more than ever"; "Music is uninterpretable through words, and yet . . . it informs the word of its meaning."

New Letters from Joyce and Lawrence

The publication of some 200 items of correspondence by James Joyce[1] is a literary event, but Melissa Banta's claim that "these letters give witness to the unguarded moments" is true of only a few of them. The large majority testify to Joyce's unrelaxed punctiliousness in even the briefest statement ("Transition sent me the enclosed outburst which please return when marveled at"), to the inventiveness of his humor ("A clause should be added that the sum . . . shall be paid over a certain date say 32 December 1999 if the book is not published . . ."), the inimitable richness of his vocabulary (a "tarry pigtail, a hamfrill beard"), and the accuracy of his ear (in, for example, imitating Léon-Paul Fargue's accent in "*angliche*").

This said, it must be admitted that Joyce's importuning pervades the book and that, for all her admiration and dedication, Beach must quickly have come to dread the sight of his handwriting in her mail. Not many of the letters are without requests for money ("Can you loan me 1000 fr for a day or two, please?" "If cheques arrive for me please [send] them. The possession of these makes all the difference in the world to hotelkeepers"). In addition to her duties as Joyce's banker, Beach becomes his telephone exchange and answering service, his social and business secretary, public relations director, delivery and errand girl, and post office ("The form is then to be [sent] registered"). Many of his letters contain lists of changes (one of them with no fewer than 60) that his factotum is instructed to insert in his proofs. Moreover, Joyce's wants ("I shall be obliged if you ask Mrs. Puard to send me also a bottle of lotion") are to be attended to "the sooner the better." Even the message of thanks on the publication of *Ulysses*, the day of Joyce's laureation, ends with a nuisance assignment for her.

The inclusion of a few letters from Beach's side would have provided a

---

[1] *James Joyce's Letters to Sylvia Beach*, 1921–1940. Edited by Melissa Banta and Oscar A. Silverman. Forward by A. Walton Litz. Bloomington and Indianapolis, 1987.

helpful angle of perspective. Banta remarks that the Joyce family withheld access to some of these, but she does not quote from a revealing, as she says, unsent letter dated April 1927, now in Buffalo and apparently available. Nor does Richard Ellmann's biography give any portion of the "angry letter" that Beach sent Joyce in the spring of 1923, a period marked by a gap on Joyce's side. The most evident source of friction in the letters printed here is in Joyce's occasionally over-zealous promotion of *Ulysses*, as when he asks Beach to "take a copy to [Natalie] Barney . . . as this is her reception [salon] day and it would arrive at a good moment."

Joyce's relentless work of correcting the French and German translations of his books is a principal subject of the letters. Another, related, one is his failing eyesight. "I am very disappointed indeed at the (so far) result of this operation," he wrote in 1924. "My sight in that eye seems to be slowly nearing extinction. I have the other (with 1/3 of vision) but how long can I continue to overwork it?" ("I shall mention you in my prayers, if you do not consider that an impertinence," T.S. Eliot wrote, and Joyce responded: "I need all the prayers that were ever breathed.") The quantity of his reading remains prodigious, however, and the subscriptions to magazines and the books that Joyce orders from Beach's Shakespeare and Company make an astonishing library: all 8 volumes of *The Complete Peerage*, Bury's *The Life of St. Patrick*, a monograph on César Franck, Joseph Clouston's *The Lunatic at Large*, and much more.

In Ostende, in 1926, Joyce was pleased to be able to talk to a small girl in Flemish ("I have now taken 43 lessons in it!"). He was equally fluent in Dutch. In the Hague a few years later, he was amused on Bloomsday (June 16) when a waiter told him that a certain wine was "Een bloem. (pron. ane bloom). 'It is a flower (of wine).'" No doubt Joyce would have been delighted to know that this collection of his letters was published in Bloomington (Indiana).

* * *

Aldous Huxley's edition of D.H. Lawrence's letters does not include any of his correspondence with Amy Lowell, while the *Collected Letters* (1962) publishes only four of them, and the Cambridge University Press edition has not yet reached the end of the Lowell period. Thus the present volume[1] offers the only complete text of the diverting exchanges between

---

[1] *The Letters of D.H. Lawrence & Amy Lowell 1914–1925*. Edited by E. Claire Healey & Keith Cushman. Santa Barbara, 1985.

the oddly assorted Back Bay Brahmin who smoked Manila cigars and dared to live with a woman (and seven dogs), and the author of *Women in Love*, still in his twenties when they met.

Amy and D.H.L. saw each other only three times (summer of 1914), and as the personal encounters recede, the strain to perpetuate the friendship becomes increasingly difficult to hide. Yet Amy, not Lawrence, falls behind, despite her accounting responsibilities to him for his royalties from American poetry magazines and the *Imagist Poets* anthology. Her letters are conventional in style and critical judgment ("*Spoon River Anthology* [is] a very great book"), but their comparative lack of spontaneity is more glaring than might have been the case with a different correspondent.

Lawrence's bouts of preaching—"Do write from your *real* self, Amy, don't make up things from the outside"—do not seem to offend her, and from time to time she even stands up to him. One of his main themes is that "your classic American Literature"—he rates his *Studies* in the subject as "very keen essays in criticism"—is "*older* than our English. The tree did not become new, which was transplanted. It only ran more swiftly into age. . ." She challenges this at the level of poetry: "It does not seem to me that you have quite got [Walt Whitman]," and goes on to say: "In prose, you [English] are miles ahead of us; in poetry, I am not so sure that, taking it by and large, the American output is not better than the English just now."

Lawrence is refreshingly unliterary—"writing is for when there is nothing nicer to be done"—and, as would be expected, never at a loss for an image. Critics walk around him in "trepidation, like dogs round a mongoose." Among the wartime annoyances are "those indecent search-lights fingering the sky." As always, he prefers animals to men—"I want some little place in the country, with a goat and a bit of a garden"—at any rate men such as Lloyd George, a "clever little Welsh *rat*, absolutely dead at the core, sterile, barren, mechanical." But exceptions must be allowed for: "I'd like to know Coleridge when Charron has rowed me over." Scarcely a letter does not mention flowers: "the little white & yellow narcissus are out"; "There are myriad primroses . . . and bluebells"; "the last poppy falling"; "The honeysuckle smells so sweet tonight."

One letter describes the encounter between Frieda Lawrence and her quondam husband two years after her elopement with the new one. "He did it in the thorough music-hall fashion," Lawrence writes, setting "it" up as vaudeville dialogue:

Q.H.: . . . isn't the commonest prostitute better than you?
Frieda: Oh no.
Q.H.: If you had to go away, why didn't you go away with a *gentleman*?

Most of Lawrence's letters were written on the wing, Cuernavaca and Capri, Florence and San Francisco, Sicily and Ceylon, Taos and Taormina. Or on the seas. He answers one of Amy's, received in Perth in May 1922, on a P & O barque, in this case *not* worse than the Bight—the Great Australian, that is, "swelling from the Antarctic."

Required Reading

The late Philip Larkin, poet, critic, novelist, jazz buff, while scarcely "visible" for two decades, was the most sought-after reviewer on the literary labor market at the moment of his untimely death (1985). With the exceptions of his best-known line of verse, "They fuck you up, your mum and dad," his scathing essay on Auden, and *the* unmentionable anthology,[1] the ascent was quiet: "I have never read any poems in public, never lectured on poetry, never taught anyone how to write it." The "required" in the title of the new book[2] means "produced on request," and Larkin boasts of never having proposed an article or review to an editor, and of merely developing "someone else's idea" ("He liked to have his mind made up for him," Larkin wrote of his hero Louis Armstrong). Larkin's output is small, and the miscellaneous articles are neither numerous nor long. They are pieces to be read and reread, whatever the occasion.

For someone so intensely private ("I don't like plays. They happen in public"; "I find the idea of other people reading my favorite books rather annoying"; "I find it very sensible not to let people know what you're like"), Larkin, in these interviews and in asides, is remarkably forthright about his life and background. When told that "not getting married" was one of his themes, he says that "the idea of always being in company" oppresses him, and he quotes from his poem "Love":

The difficult part of love
Is being selfish enough
Is having the blind persistence
To upset someone's existence

---

[1] *The Oxford Book of Twentieth-Century English Verse* (1973), which provoked "scandalized disbelief," in the words of John Gross, who also described Donald Davie as "recoiling aghast from page after page." See *Larkin at Sixty*, edited by Anthony Thwaite. London, 1982.

[2] *Required Reading: Miscellaneous Pieces 1955–1982* by Philip Larkin. New York, 1984.

Just for your own sake—
What cheek it must take.

Then take the unselfish side—
Who can be satisfied
Putting someone else first,
So that you come off worse?
My life is for me:
As well deny gravity.

Lucky the never-to-be-born next generation of Larkins! "Children are very horrible . . . Selfish, noisy, cruel, vulgar little brutes," says the won't-be-papa, who attributes the early "waning of my Christian sympathies" to the bit about small hominids being inheritors of the Kingdom of Heaven. In the remark, "Personal relations were not, in the last analysis, as important to him as doing what he wanted and thought was right," Larkin is obviously speaking as much for himself as for Rupert Brooke.

Home is Hull—"the hermit of Hull," a London *Times* profile (February 16, 1984) called him—and Larkin said that he liked living there because it was "so far from everywhere else," and because he wanted to be "on the periphery of things." He was a stay-at-home, too, and had been outside Britain only two or three times ("Nothing, like something, happens anywhere"). He did not believe in enduring happiness (because you grow old and are pushed to the side of your own life, and "because you know that you are going to die and the people you love are going to die") but in what he called the right-wing virtues of "thrift, hard work, reverence, desire to preserve," in contrast with "idleness, greed, and treason," all associated with the left.

His modesty (on being bibliographed: "as long as no one thinks I thought all these things worth exhuming") was a visor ("One gets more dividends from keeping out of sight"), for he invariably gave the impression that he was in the superior position. But his admiration for simplicity was genuine, and one can believe that he read no "philosophy, . . . sociology, . . . anything to do with technology," "almost no poetry," or "anything hard." He was addicted to novels, from Dickens to Trollope ("about three novels running"), to Ian Fleming, Waugh, Anthony Powell, Peter de Vries, Michael Innes, Gladys Mitchell, Barbara Pym. "I like to read about people who . . . aren't beautiful and lucky . . . who can see, in little autumnal moments of vision, that the so-called 'big' experiences of life are going to miss them . . . In all [Pym's] writing . . . [there is a] courageous acceptance of things which I think more relevant to life as most of us have to live it, than spies coming in from the cold." Since Larkin regarded classical references as "a liability nowadays," no one can be surprised to learn that his unreadables were Spenser, Milton, and Pound. Larkin was a nearly impeccable writer (only one wince in the book: "when it came to the crunch").

As poet and critic, Larkin is most handily defined by his likes and dislikes. "Many times over the best body of poetic work this century so far has to show is Hardy's." In each poem "there is a little spinal cord of thought and each has a little tune of its own." Hardy is "not a transcendental writer, he's not a Yeats, he's not an Eliot; his subjects are men, the life of men . . ." Since writing this, Larkin must have been pleased to find in E.M. Forster's letters the conclusion that Hardy is the writer "one trusts," the writer who does not have that "allround intelligence . . . a lack that is often a sign of creative power." But not everyone will agree with Larkin's claim that Wilfred Owen is "the only twentieth-century poet who can be read after Hardy without a sense of bathos," or applaud his Yeats-bashing. Yeats's remark that "passive suffering is not a theme for poetry" is "fatuous," Larkin says, moreover, Yeats's verbal music is as "pervasive as garlic."[1]

Hardy's heir is John Betjeman, whose *Collected Poems* "make up the most extraordinary poetic output of our time." It is not unlikely that "as Eliot dominated the first half of the twentieth century, the second half will derive from Betjeman," for whom there has been "no symbolism . . . no reinvestment in myth, no casting of language as gesture, no *Seven Types* or *Some Versions*, no works of criticism with titles such as . . . *Implicit and Explicit Image Obliquity in Sir Lewis Morris*." Deploring "the emergence of English literature as an academic subject," and denouncing "the culture-mongering activities of the Americans Eliot and Pound," Larkin suggests that "Betjeman was the writer who knocked over the 'No Road Through to Real Life' signs that this new tradition had erected."

"Americans" may seem gratuitous, but except for jazz, Larkin always kept things Stateside at a distance. Pretending to know very little about American poetry, he told an interviewer, in an embarrassing lapse, that if he were in America and somebody had asked him about Ashbery, "I'd say, I'd prefer strawberry."

---

[1] In the Introduction to the second edition of *The North Ship*, Larkin recalled an occasion when he was reciting Yeats's "When such as I cast out remorse" and a friend remarked: "It's not his job to cast off remorse, but to earn forgiveness."

But clearly Larkin did know American poetry, from Dickinson (whose work appears to posterity "as perpetually unfinished and wilfully eccentric") to Plath (her last poems "are to the highest degree original and scarcely less effective"), and from Cole Porter ("he was Gilbert as well as Sullivan") to Ogden Nash (who makes you laugh at things "not because they are funny but because laughing at them makes it easier to stand them"). When Edmund Blunden defeated Robert Lowell for the Chair of Poetry at Oxford, Larkin compared the proceedings to the election of "a cow to a chair at an institute of dairying."

The most notorious piece in the book, the one by which Larkin's name as a critic is still best known, is "What's Become of Wystan?" (1960). According to Larkin, almost everything of value in Auden's work belongs to his first decade as a poet, and the loss of "his key subject and emotion," by going to America in 1939, has been "irreparable." To dramatize the loss, Larkin compares "the disrespectful reference" in 1937 to "Daunty, Gouty, Shopkeeper, the three Supreme Old Masters," with "the eulogistic invocation in the *New Year Letter* of 1941: 'Great masters who have shown mankind . . .'." But "disrespectful" betrays a misunderstanding not of Auden's, but of Joyce's, phrase. Can the bard of Humberside have put *Finnegans Wake* on his Modernist Index before reading the book?

One of the shortcomings of the American Auden is that "literature was replacing experience as material for his verse." And of course it was, but isn't this a common effect of age with writers everywhere? Larkin allows that Auden recovered to a degree in the 1950s with the return to the shorter poem as his proper medium; the long poems of the 1940s are described as a "rambling intellectual stew" (*New Year Letter*), an "unsuccessful piece of literary inbreeding" (*The Sea and the Mirror*), and as simply unreadable (*The Age of Anxiety*: "I never finished it and I never met anyone who has"). In the 1950s, Auden "recovered a dialect," but one that "sets the teeth on edge."

Larkin gives himself away by admitting that the Auden he wanted would be a "*New Yorker* Walt Whitman viewing the American scene through lenses coated with a European irony." But surely Auden was always a C. of E. parishioner, never a European. Moreover, the *New Yorker* pieces are precisely those that have not worn well. The "Metalogue," for instance, with its up-to-date references—a weakness in much of Auden's verse—is stale beyond reprintability. "Auden was happier when his work had an extraneous social function," Larkin concludes, but unless he means simply that for him the poetic results were happier, who could agree? Auden's condemnation of his 1930s social and political attitudes as dishonest made him a happier man, whatever it did for his poetry, and he became progressively less interested in these attitudes with age.

The piece on Marvell is the prize of the collection. On the phrase "vegetable love," which Eliot had singled out, Larkin quotes some critical jargon ("*Vegetable* is no vegetable but an abstract and philosophical term . . . the doctrine of the three souls"), and remarks that "another reader might simply think that 'vegetable' was a good adjective for something that grows slowly." Empson is quoted on "To a green thought in a green shade" (". . . the seventh Buddhist state of enlightenment") and is similarly punctured by the comment that "another reader might simply think the lines a good description of the mind of someone half-asleep under the summer trees in a garden." On the other hand, Larkin observes that Marvell is the poet of enigma and ambiguity, the poet about whom the reader is never "quite sure how serious he is." This would account for exegeses of the sort at which Larkin likes to poke fun. For him, the "witty, tender elegance" in some of the best-known pieces remains Marvell's greatest accomplishment. Larkin concludes that "every poet's reputation fades in so far as his language becomes unfamiliar, his assumptions outmoded, and his subject-matter historical, and despite the iron lung of academic English teaching, Marvell is no exception."

Larkin loses his cool only once, in the "Introduction to *All What Jazz*?" The book itself contains some of the best-written music criticism of its time. (On the Beatles: "Like certain sweets, they seem wonderful until you are suddenly sick.") Nor is the "Introduction" less good about jazz, and its demise, or murder, in about 1947. But the anti-modernist philosophy is specious and unworthy of so fastidious a critic. The title derives from *Serious Music—And All That Jazz* by Henry Pleasants, author of *The Agony of Modern Music*, an attack on Schoenberg, Berg and others, too feeble to be taken seriously. Larkin does not comment on this, but he is recklessly contemptuous of all "modern art," and to link, as he does, Picasso and Joyce (the latter declined "from talent to absurdity"), is to expose an imperceptiveness of these very different artists. Nor are "mystification and outrage" the "two principal themes of modernism," as Larkin contends. The modern artist has indeed "painted portraits with both eyes on the same side of the nose," written "a play in which the characters sit in dustbins." But he has also expanded and intensified experience in new and marvelous music, painting, and, as a few of Larkin's own best poems exemplify, literature.

Anglo-Indian Masterpiece

As Vicereine of India (1899–1905), Lady Curzon, the Chicago-born daughter of Levi Leiter, co-founder of Marshall Field's, attained the highest position ever held by an American in the British Empire. Her letters and Hyderabad diary[1] provide from an extreme angle the contrasting background to David Rubin's survey of English fiction[2] set in India in the last years of the Raj.

In the India of the Curzons, Indians are all but invisible. The Viceroy stands when speaking to English people, but sits "if the body is a Native one." The Vicereine complains about "a park—which, alas! is open to the public who pour into it and destroy all privacy . . ." Dinners are served for a hundred "with a waiter for every person at table . . . the waiting is admirably done—and they all glide about in red livery & bare feet." *They*. Famines and droughts, if not regarded by the English with Malthusian complacency, are said by them to have been offset by the stopping of such barbarities as infanticide and the ritual burning of widows.

Some of Chicago Mary's snobbery can be excused as typical of the period and class:

> some *awful* people *insisted* on being asked to the ball at Gov. House last Thursday, a Mr & Mrs Jack *Latta* of Chicago . . . They appeared, Mrs Latta wearing an immense Scotch plaid *day* dress *turned* in at the neck. I had seen her at Polo with the same dress in the afternoon.

But some of it is cruel. On her second voyage out from England, she writes with approval about how Princess De Shimay, in disgrace because of her

---

[1] *Lady Curzon's India*. Letters of a Vicereine. Edited by John Bradley with a foreword by Nigel Nicolson. New York, 1986.

[2] *After the Raj*. British Novels of India Since 1947. Hanover, New Hampshire, and London, 1986.

elopement with "a bandman," was "so stared at and laughed at that she retired to her cabin." On reappearing, she was "removed by the head steward!" at the demand of the other people at her table.

In a 1901 letter to his wife, the Viceroy describes a tiger hunt in which 220 elephants ringed the target in a field of tall grass. His Lordship, safe in his howdah, took aim, pulled a trigger and, "As the brute was still convulsively struggling and roaring [I] put a second bullet into him." The beast "showed no pluck." Contrast this with an account of the same sport some fifty years later, as narrated by the principal male character in Paul Scott's *Birds of Paradise*: "The tiger stood quite in the open now but I made no move to bring the gun to bear on him . . . awestruck . . . by the realization that it had a right to be where it was, as much right as I . . ."

More than half of David Rubin's *After the Raj* and nearly all its sympathies are devoted to Scott, to whom the book brings intelligent interpretation and overdue recognition as the most accomplished of the novelists inspired by the subcontinent. Rubin maintains that the only other fictions worth taking into consideration, Kipling's *Kim* and Forster's *A Passage to India*, are far from faithful pictures of Indian life. *A Passage* is examined in detail, nevertheless, and Rubin's approach to Scott's *Raj Quartet* is through the parallel between the rape of a less than beautiful European woman by a handsome Indian that did not take place in Forster's novel, and the gang rape that did in Scott's, following the consummation of a love between a man and a woman of similar attributes and racial mix.

Forster's failure, Rubin says, is in his Indian characters. They are few in number and "superficially glimpsed," while the most important of them, Aziz, "is childish, sentimental, vindictive, and given to fantasies and lies." Aziz, like his creator, lacks political awareness, which would not have mattered in 1912, when the book was begun, but which, a dozen years later, when it was finished, is improbable. Where *A Passage* succeeds is in communicating "how it *feels*, emotionally and physically, to be in India," and in its historically important assault on British prejudice.

The discussion of Scott's pre-*Quartet* novels, all eight of them in some degree connected with India, will interest new readers in search of a guide to the writer's earlier work. Exploring prefigurations of the *Quartet* in the relationships of the English to India and Indians, Rubin concentrates on *The Alien Sky*, a pivotal novel in that after it Scott abandoned the Eurasian question for the far deeper one of the conflict of cultures. "A genetic mixture is a much too facile embodiment of this conflict," Rubin writes, and he reminds us that Hari Kumar, the Indian falsely accused of the Bibighar Gardens rape, "is *not* a mixture of anything but actually *entirely* Engish in culture and outlook."

Scott's artistic creed—"Creative writing is showing . . . not telling"—and his social and moral convictions are exposed in direct, non-fictional form in the recent selection of his critical writings.[1] If the editor had included some of the novelist's book reviews, especially of Masani's *Indira Gandhi*, Chaudhuri's *Clive of India*, and Turnbull's *Warren Hastings*, the reader would have had a clearer notion of Scott's politics as well. Still, *My Appointment with the Muse* contains illuminating statements on the subject. "The lasting monument to the perfidy of Albion," Scott says, "is, to me, the way we pointed British India towards democracy, but preserved through thick and thin the autocracy of the Princes." And, in another essay: "I see [India] as the place where the British came to the end of themselves as they were. It was, even more than England was, the scene of the victory of Liberal Humanism over dying paternal imperialism."

Against the received view that the *Quartet* should be understood as essentially a historical novel, Rubin rightly holds that history provides the background and structuring to the fictional events, but is secondary. "Man is explicable by nothing less than all his history," Emerson wrote, but Scott's character Barbara Batchelor comes to understand that this should be the other way around: "It's our history that gets in the way of a lucid explanation of us." And in one of his essays, Scott himself puts "history" in its place, saying that in August 1942, when the *Quartet* begins, "it was no longer possible for Britain and India locked in their imperial embrace to know whether they hated or loved one another."

Scott's story, unfolded in four long novels, cannot be summarized in a critical notice, but it is known, at least in outline, through the television series that has been and is still being seen by millions. Nor can Rubin's synopsis be recommended as a crib, since it omits important episodes and stops short of a full account of the crucial one, in which Ronald Merrick, the police chief, attracted to Kumar but thinking he is in love with Daphne Manners, has Kumar "stripped, bound to a trestle, and sexually abused." This avoids the specifics without which the reader will not realize that Merrick is homosexual and a sadist.

[1] *My Appointment with the Muse*: Paul Scott, Essays and Lectures. Selected by Shelley C. Reese. London, 1986.

The main plot, which develops from the Bibighar Gardens affair—"Bibighar" recalls the house[1] in Kanpur where English women and children were massacred in the 1857 Mutiny—is pieced together from the testimony of a large variety of characters. The same can be said of the skillfully-woven subplots—"interchangings of identities," Rubin calls them, though, being successive, "reincarnations" seems more apt—of Edwina Crane in Barbie Batchelor and Daphne Manners in Sarah Layton.

Scott's greatest achievement is not in plot construction, however, but in the exploration of character. In exposing the effects of India on people representing widely different British social backgrounds, he shows how the military and professional classes stuck together, isolating themselves and upholding racial barriers the more stubbornly as the war threatened to usurp their power. On the other side, the schoolteacher, the missionary, the governess, and the student-historian become increasingly pro-Indian—one reason that the upper-class liberal Daphne Manners is more convincing than Sarah Layton, daughter of an army officer, in the role of spokesperson-indicter of the British failure, after a two-hundred-year rule, to prevent Hindu-Muslim bloodshed.

Each of the four novels is dominated by a single figure: Daphne Manners, Sarah Layton, Barbie Batchelor, and Guy Perron, respectively. These "good characters" are known through interior monologues, conversations and actions. In contrast, the thoughts and feelings of Ronald Merrick, the "bad character" and the only major figure to appear in all four books, are known exclusively through dialogues and deeds. Scott "seems to have stacked the cards against" Merrick, Rubin remarks. But the real case against him is simply that he is too unsympathetic to occupy so large a part of the canvas. (One wonders why Scott thought that the reader had to be told that Daphne and Sarah do not like Merrick, this being abundantly evident from the outset; and Rubin, as if taking a cue from Scott, says that Daphne finds Merrick "unaccountably distasteful," even though her feelings are perfectly accountable.)

Rubin ignores inconsistencies in Merrick's career and character. In a scene not mentioned in *After the Raj*, Merrick briefs an assembly of army officers on the progress of the war in Burma. But this is a highly improbable assignment for a latecomer to the army from the civil police, where, moreover, his reputation was under a cloud. So too, when Merrick

---

[1] Actually Bibgarh. See Raleigh Trevelyan's *The Golden Oriole, Childhood, Family and Friends in India*. London, 1987.

recounts his version of the Bibighar Gardens rape to Count Bronowsky, most readers are bound to object that the confessional mode is wholly out of character for the policeman.

Bronowsky could draw anyone out, it is true, and he is the only person in the book to whom Merrick would conceivably talk; after all, Bronowsky, a homosexual, is able to explain Merrick's death as a consequence of Merrick's homosexuality, or, rather, of his recognition of it. But this last-act revelation is not altogether plausible. Merrick is too self-aware to have been able to hide his inclinations from himself. The revelation, moreover, is lacking in suspense. The reader has had a sense of it from the beginning, in Sister Ludmilla's observation of the way Merrick watches Kumar bathe—"the way later I saw Kumar watched on other occasions" (*i.e.*, European women found him desirable)—and in her realization that Merrick love-hates Kumar because he is good looking and has a perfect upper-class English accent.

Scott's finest character studies are inspired by his older generation of Englishwomen, Edwina, Barbie, and Sarah's aunt Mabel, all of whom are endowed with large powers of sympathy and understanding. Of the three, Edwina Crane, the spinster schoolteacher with 35 years of service in India, wins our highest admiration. When her Indian friend Mr Chaudhuri is killed in an attempt to protect her during an outbreak of anti-English violence, she puts on a sari and burns herself to death, the act of suttee for the Indian who was not even her husband. But Scott's women in general have greater dimension than his men, and while "English" fairness, trust, bravery, and considerateness are virtues in the women, the same qualities in some of the men—in Teddy Bingham, for one—are made to seem ridiculous.

None of the Englishmen is a match in intelligence and reasonableness for the elder Mohammed Ali Kasim. But, as Rubin rightly remarks, the *Quartet*, like Forster's *Passage*, does not have a major Indian character as richly conceived as the English characters. The Kasim family, "noble bores," simply fill out the political background. Rubin might have added that Scott does not conceal a pro-Muslim bias, indeed, openly displays it in the chapter about the savagery of the supposedly nonviolent Hindus in August 1947.

Of the *Quartet*'s several loose ends, Hari Kumar, the largest and most vexing, is adrift throughout. The whole story revolves around him, yet the reader is never vouchsafed a glimpse of his mind, and this from a novelist ready to tour the thought interiors of even his most minor characters. The longest of the many flashbacks, the interrogation of Kumar for the enlightenment of Lady Manners—Daphne's mother—can be said to counter this in that it tells as much as need be known about Kumar. This episode strains credulity, however, and a full picture of Kumar himself does not emerge, but only his version of Bibighar and its aftermath. Perron's attempt to visit him at the end of the *Quartet* seems to have been intended as a *deus ex machina*. But Kumar *could* not have been reintroduced at this final stage if only because he and Perron would have either too much or too little to say to each other.

No less troublesome is the absence, at the end, of any connection between Kumar and his four-year-old daughter. Not bringing parent and child together is true to life, but not true to a fictional genre that brims with not-always-probable link-ups and crossings-of-paths, as in the case of the three old-boy Chillingburians, Kumar, Perron and Captain Rowan. Even so, the reader may be less deeply bothered by the fates of the girl and her father—these could change—than by that of her mother, Daphne Manners, whom we would like to have known better, and whose death in childbirth so early on almost discourages us from continuing.

As Rubin says, the final novel, *A Division of the Spoils*, is more diffuse than its predecessors. But it is weak in other ways as well. Whether or not the contrast between Guy Perron's winning personality and Merrick's losing one is "loaded," Perron's philosophical overviews are neatly worked out beyond likelihood, even for a future history professor. The reader who has lived with Scott through the first three novels begins to think of Perron in the fourth as the author's mouthpiece. Perron's statement "I have come to suspect that the aim of creation is not ethical at all" even sounds like non-fiction Scott.

Staying On, the postscript novel tying up some of the loose ends and satisfying the reader's wish for the good Guy to marry Sarah, the right girl, cannot make complete sense to anyone who has not read the *Quartet*. Besides, Scott falls short of his aim even with these two lovers, partly for the same reasons that Falstaff's death in *Henry V* does not counterbalance the shock of his rejection in *Henry IV, Part Two*: in each case the new contexts are factitious and the tone is jarringly different. The high-comedy scenes in *Staying On* are unlike anything in the *Quartet*, where, for example, Mrs. Fosdick's gossip is more an essay in caricature than an attempt to supply comic relief, Teddy Bingham's wedding night more a vignette of middle-class behavior than a set-piece farce.

Staying On is a neatly accomplished novel, and the Smalleys, minor characters in the *Quartet*, inspire Scott's most moving scene, that of Lucy's monologue after the death of Tusker, her husband:

> But now, until the end, I shall be alone, whatever I am doing . . . Alone for ever and ever and I cannot bear it, but mustn't cry and must . . . get over it but don't for the moment see how, so with my eyes shut Tusker, I hold out my hand and beg you, Tusker, beg you, to take it and . . . take me with you . . ., Oh, Tusker, Tusker, Tusker, how can you make me stay here by myself while you yourself go home.

Rubin does not comment on stylistic questions in the *Quartet*, but he might have mentioned that the language of the dialogues and interior monologues is much the same in the mouths and thoughts of most of the principal characters, and that much of it, realistically speaking, is too intelligent. Sarah is mature and sensible beyond all probability for a girl in her early twenties, and Merrick, only a few years older, is articulate far beyond what could be expected of a police officer in rural India. Count Bronowsky, the subtle, perceptive intellectual in the service of an autocratic Indian prince, might be an exception, but he is too worldly-wise and up-to-date for an elderly White Russian, no matter how well educated.

The more individualized language of Major Clark, Sarah's seducer, whom Rubin dismisses as "cynical" and "coarse and brutally hedonistic," brings a welcome change of pace. As the only character with an appreciation of Indian culture (sitar playing and dancing, at any rate) and the only one who straightforwardly expresses left-wing political views—"British India is British self-interest"—Clark is too engaging not to have been allowed a reappearance; but, then, he is another loose end. Such instances apart, one doubts that the Raj's administrative personnel and commissioned army spoke English anywhere near the level to which Scott raises it, since nowhere do bureaucrats and soldiers command resourceful, tip-of-the-tongue vocabularies and form perfect sentences in long and well-structured paragraphs.

Not that verbal realism, in the sense of associating characters with idiosyncratic tags of speech, is desirable or necessary. But near the beginning, Scott does experiment with the idea, poking gentle fun at the Indian abuse of gerunds, planting colloquialisms in Lady Chatterjee's English, and copying the cockney of those "other ranks" who play such an insignificant part in the novel. One of the main attractions in *Staying On* is the speech of the Bhoolaboys, brilliantly capturing the idiom of the new post-Raj Indians of the commercial class.

Paul Scott is the most elegant writer of his generation. What fine distinctions he makes: "an attitude more of self-control than of self-possession." And what nimble analogies: "She could feel the prayers falling flat, little rejects from a devotional machine she once worked to perfection." How nicely understated, too, is his irony: In the allegorical painting *The Jewel in the Crown*, an Indian prince offers "a gem to Queen Victoria while Disraeli flourishes the map of India and all the subcontinent joyfully looks on—princes, merchants, and remarkably clean and tidy beggars."

CODA

A Poet between Two Worlds

In March 1980, Joseph Brodsky told *The New York Times* that, despite an occasional opus in English, he continues to write his poetry in Russian. He went on to speculate whether he would not be a better poet if he were still in the Soviet Union, thereby reminding us that he was not a refusenik awaiting permission to emigrate, but a reluctant refugee who, when expelled from the USSR in 1972, feared the consequences of separation from the land of his native language. By October 1987, and after winning the Nobel Prize, he revealed to the London *Observer* that he was then composing four out of five of his poems in English.

How, then, are the English poems to be classified? Clearly they cannot be described as extending from any Anglo-American tradition. Nor is the parallel exact with Eliot's quip about the increase of Chinese characters in late Pound: "He is becoming the best Chinese poet in English." Language apart, Brodsky's voice, his role as poet, and his poetic roots are still Russian. And unlike other bilingual poets—Petrarch, George Herbert, Rilke—whose different languages served different purposes, but in each case those of a single culture, Brodsky has had to encompass a linguistic dichotomy. Even Joseph Conrad, with whom Brodsky can be compared at least to the extent of their both having mastered English in mature years, did not write under the burden of this split.

A poet in one language does not become a poet in another one merely by learning the second language. No matter how we categorize Brodsky's poems in English, he is trying to fulfill in America the infinitely larger moral and social function of the poet in Russia. Which American versifier—academic, rock star, beatnik ("Granted my lungs all sounds except the howl," Brodsky wrote)—speaks for more than a segment of the population or an age group? Perhaps Robert Frost, at the Kennedy inauguration, did have a broader audience, but hardly one with the dimensions and directness of communication of a Yevtushenko, whose conveniently impossible "I would like to fight on all your barricades, humanity," is unthinkable in the mouth of Brodsky. In his quiet way, and partly by restoring words like *dusha* (soul) and *sovest* (conscience) that had disappeared under Stalinism, Brodsky is a far more profound global spokesman than his Soviet counterpart. We can say of him, as he says of Lermontov, that his "feverishly burning lines are aimed at the world order itself."

A perennial Brodsky theme is the acceleration of history—the "terrifying acceleration" of the 1930s ending in Osip Mandelstam's final "psychic acceleration." The danger in the process has never been more eloquently expressed than in the new collection, *In Urania:*[1]

> . . . *shouldn't cruelty be termed a form of speeding matters up,*
> *accelerating the common fate of things?* . . .

So, too, in a foreword to an anthology by one of his translators,[2] Brodsky defends the human scale of reality in the nineteenth century, when much less stood between man and his thoughts about himself than today, the "last century of seeing, not glimpsing; of responsibility, not the incoherence of guilt."

In Urania is distinguished by a finer focus of feeling and greater technical powers than ever before. Brodsky remains an elegist without equal, and not only in the "Roman Elegies"

> . . . *midsummer*
> *Clouds feel like angels, thanks to*
> *their cooling shadows,*

though, as was early evident, Italy inspired him as it had Goethe. And Brodsky's genius as an observer of common experience is as acute as ever. "The daytime is a deceiver;" he writes, "Are the lights out already? Or not yet on?" And, "There are places in which things don't change . . . Meanwhile soldiers keep growing younger."

Brodsky is his own best translator, whether alone or with collaborators. To judge from *An Age Ago*, Alan Myers is less successful on his own. His vocabulary can be ill-chosen. A "geriatric ward" is distractingly anachronistic for the Russia of 1840, and is it possible in the 1830s that tartans replaced rags?:

---

1 *In Urania* by Joseph Brodsky. New York, 1988.

2 *An Age Ago: A Selection of Nineteenth-Century Russian Poetry*, selected and translated by Alan Myers with a Foreword and Biographical Notes by Joseph Brodsky. New York, 1988.

let me not go mad
far better beggar's staff and plaid.

Surely "hiss" is too menacing for the sound of, as Evgeny Baratynsky affectionately calls it, "friend champagne." Nor are all of Myers' rhythmic roads free of potholes, as in the Kiplingesque couplet,

It's love, love, love, I long for
and that is what I've not got!

Premonition pervades the poems of *An Age Ago*, both national—

The Russian mind is still in chains, . . .
whole centuries will grimly flow—
Before our Russia starts to waken!

—and personal, as in Lermontov's "my time on earth is nearly gone," which was true, and Pushkin's

Every season, each day's dawning
I follow with anxiety,
attempting to predict the morning
my coming death will choose for me.

He had eight more years.

Brodsky begins his biographical notes with the statement that the dates in them refer to the Old Russian calendar "which differs by 12 and 13 days from its modern counterpart"; but he means 11 (in the eighteenth century) and 12 (in the nineteenth—no twentieth-century date is given) and neglects to say in which direction. But never mind. His evaluations of his poet ancestors in these thumbnail portraits reveal some of his own artistic beliefs. He asks us to read "the Russian poetry of the nineteenth century—of its first half especially"—the period of nine-tenths of the book—"if only because it gives you an idea of what gave birth to that century's Russian psychological novel."

But whereas we readily relate to what we no doubt stereotypically think of as peculiarly "Russian" qualities of mind and character in those novels, we must take Brodsky on faith when he ascribes the "ringing" and "vigorous verse" of Nikolai Yazykov to "the precision of his vocabulary . . . and the buoyancy of his rhythms," and informs us that Nikolai Nekrasov's diction "gravitates toward the vernacular." The English-only reader cannot discover these attributes for him- or herself in this or any other poetry in translation.

We would like to readdress the ending of one of *In Urania*'s most beautiful poems to Joseph Brodsky himself:

> *Yet until brown clay has been crammed down my larynx,*
> *only gratitude will be gushed from it.*

Jews and Geniuses

Two music-related essays of broad general and complementary interest have recently appeared in periodicals, the more important of them, on the connection between Schoenberg and Einstein in relation to Zionism, in an esoteric journal with limited readership,[1] the other, on the politics of Schoenberg, Stravinsky, and selected colleagues, in a more widely circulated but primarily political weekly.[2]

Completing research for a book on Stravinsky, Richard Taruskin, the esteemed musicologist, and by no one more than this writer, has uncovered documents that animadvert on the Russian composer's political and ethnic prejudices. Some of these findings Taruskin has set forth in an article enthusiastically glossed by the critic John Rockwell ("Reactionary Musical Modernists," *The New York Times*, September 9, 1988).

Rockwell describes Taruskin's paper, "The Dark Side of Modern Music," as "Ostensibly a review of Harvey Sachs's book *Music in Fascist Italy*, [which] lays out biographical evidence indicating Fascist, or at least authoritarian, tendencies of Stravinsky, Schoenberg and Webern."[3] In fact, Toscanini occupies a larger share of Taruskin's space than do the composers. But the more disturbing misrepresentation is in the added interchange of "authoritarian" equalling "Fascist" (Rockwell's, not Taruskin's, upper case). Though the three composers were obviously authoritarian, like, one supposes, the major masters of the past, to associate Schoenberg with Fascism is plainly preposterous.

---

1 E. Randol Schoenberg, "Arnold Schoenberg and Albert Einstein: Their Relationship and Views on Zionism," *The Journal of the Arnold Schoenberg Institute*, Vol. X, No. 2 (November, 1987).

2 Richard Taruskin, "The Dark Side of Modern Music: The Sins of Toscanini, Stravinsky, Schoenberg," *The New Republic* (September 5, 1988).

3 New York, 1988.

"Mr. Taruskin," Rockwell goes on, "cites two letters not included in Robert Craft's collection of [Stravinsky's] correspondence." Rockwell then quotes Stravinsky on Mussolini, not from correspondence but from an interview with a newspaperman in Rome in 1930. But no matter: the Stravinsky-Mussolini conjunction has not been news for a long time, and my books are the duly acknowledged source for nearly all of Sachs's discussion of the question.

Turning to the "second" letter, Rockwell writes that ". . . shortly after Hitler took power in 1933, Stravinsky queries his German publisher: 'I am surprised to have received no proposals from Germany for next season, since my negative attitude toward communism and Judaism—not to put it in stronger terms—is a matter of common knowledge.' "

The letter, however, is not to Stravinsky's German but to his Russian publisher, the director of Koussevitzky's Russische Musik Verlag, and the difference is significant: anti-Semitic remarks between White Russians, like anti-*goy* remarks between Jews, are not invariably, or even usually—so one must believe—expressions of deep hatreds.

Stravinsky's statement is all the more shocking, however, because a cultured cosmopolitan of artistic genius is simplistically identifying Jews with Bolsheviks, and, at the same time, revealing his willingness to perform anywhere for money. But it puzzles on other counts as well. Stravinsky was perfectly aware that the Third Reich had classified him as a Jew. And if his "negative attitude" toward Judaism had ever been "common knowledge," Taruskin would not have to be digging it up now.

Russian anti-Semitism, imbibed with mother's milk, promoted by official decree, the Orthodox Church, and even university philosophy courses—Stravinsky's background in this sense can only be understood from his undergraduate notes on Nesmelov's *The Science of Man*—has been the subject of many studies. The most recent that I have read, encouraged by a blurb from Sir Isaiah Berlin, is David Goldstein's *Dostoevsky and the Jews*; and though Dostoevsky's case is that of an extreme paranoid, many if not most of his fellow countrymen whose biographies have been made public shared some of the same prejudices. Gogol's stereotype "Yankel" is an example. (Leon Bakst once complained to Diaghilev about "the Yankel Shtravinsky"—the Yiddish pronunciation.) Tchaikovsky's diaries, for another, expose an anti-Semitic bias, as do Diaghilev's letters, including one that scolds Stravinsky for "trusting your Jewish friends," though Diaghilev's own closest artistic intimates, Benois and Bakst, were Jews.

Rockwell is soon portentously referring to Stravinsky's "fervent pro-

Fascism and anti-Semitism," and sermonizing that "those for whom political and moral correctness is inseparable from art, and consider themselves staunch defenders of democracy and the Jewish tradition"—democracy and *which* Jewish tradition?—"and have heretofore loved Stravinsky's music but were unaware of his beliefs, may have a problem." (Inferentially the problem does not exist with Schoenberg's and Webern's music because it is unlovable.) "Political and moral correctness," indeed—as if great artists have not been delinquent in both and great art has not flourished in undemocratic societies, as if artistic genius were somehow an assurance of personal integrity. Rockwell belongs on a Wheaties box.

Taruskin mentions two other anti-Semitic references in Stravinsky's correspondence, and quotes a third, also from the spring of 1933: "Is it politically wise vis-à-vis Germany to identify myself with Jews like Klemperer and Walter?" Here one hangs one's head in shame for the composer's selfishness and callous indifference to the fate of friends, Semitic or otherwise. By my count, five more anti-Semitic remarks, none of them after 1933, occur in Stravinsky's *Nachlass*. To judge from this and other criteria, Taruskin's speculation that if the composer had not come to America in 1939, "he might very well have ended like Pound" betrays an alarming misunderstanding of Stravinsky's character—as well as the limitations of scholarship based entirely on the almighty document. But in the first place, an American citizen committing traitorous acts, and a French citizen who could at worst have collaborated, are not comparable cases, and, in the second, while Pound was rabidly and increasingly anti-Semitic, Stravinsky developed in the opposite direction.

Taruskin damages his exposé by falling into factual errors. He says that "Stravinsky performed . . . in Germany right up to the beginning of the war." No; he performed there only once after the Nazi accession, in 1936, against his will and under pressure from his German publisher, though by choosing to play the piano rather than to conduct he managed to avoid all personal encounters and to confine his trip to a single day. (Taruskin mentions a recording made in Germany, but recordings are not public performances.) In the mid-1920s, Taruskin goes on, the word "modernism" had become a "code" for Stravinsky "exemplified by the expressionistic atonal works of Schoenberg." No; at that date Stravinsky did not know *any* "expressionistic atonal" music except *Pierrot Lunaire*, which, in 1912, he was the first to herald as a masterpiece.

Taruskin grants nothing to the other side of the story: Stravinsky's defense of Vittorio Rieti against the Fascisti after the enactment of racial laws in Italy; Stravinsky's presidency of the Martin Buber Society; Stravinsky's gift to Israel, *Abraham and Isaac*. Nor is mention made of the Nazi persecution of Stravinsky's "*entartete*" (degenerate) art in the 1938 Düsseldorf exhibition, and of the Nazi murder of his Jewish son-in-law in a concentration camp. In fairness to Webern, too, why does Taruskin make an exception of Berg, who was petitioning for an official Austrian declaration of his pure Aryan descent while Schoenberg, in Paris, was formally returning to Judaism? At the same time, when Hindemith invited Berg to join the faculty of the Hochschule für Musik, Berg wrote to his wife: "It would be more feasible now than before as S[choenberg] is no longer in Berlin: it would be a colossal triumph for me." (Taruskin *does* mention the production of *Wozzeck* in Italy in 1942, but wrongly locates it at La Scala rather than at the Rome Opera.)

The most glaring weakness in Taruskin's arguments, nevertheless, is his failure to mention the biblical beliefs behind, and so much more important than, the shallow politics of this century's two greatest composers of religious music. Admittedly, Stravinsky's denominational connections are not always clear, the Russian Orthodox musician confounding everyone by composing both Russian and Latin liturgical music, an anthem for the Anglican hymnal, and a sacred cantata in Hebrew.

The Jewish world began to fascinate Stravinsky in St. Petersburg in early childhood, in the religious observances of the family in the apartment below and the mysteries of the synagogue across the canal from his home. Later, during ten summers in the Ukraine (both of his parents were born there, within the Jewish Pale of Settlement), he lived next to a *shtetl* and was on affectionate terms with his neighbors. In France, between the wars, his closest associates, Arthur Lourie, musical secretary and spokesman, Samuel Dushkin, with whom he logged tens of thousands of miles on concert tours, and Roland-Manuel Lévy, to whom he entrusted the expression of his artistic philosophy in *Poétique Musical*, were Jews. In America, Stravinsky's "inner musical circle"—Sol Babitz, Ingolf (Marcus) Dahl, Claudio Spies, Lawrence Morton—was almost entirely Jewish. This obviously, is not the "philo-Semitism" that many Jews see as the simple inversion of the non-Jew who prefers the society, traditions, and culture of Jews and is therefore an anti-Semite in disguise unknown to him- or herself.

To turn to the other, more permanently valuable article, "Arnold Schoenberg and Albert Einstein: Their Relationship and Views on Zionism," E. Randol Schoenberg, the composer's grandson, has recorded in engrossing detail the different paths by which the two men reached the decision that their dedication to Jewish affairs would take second place only to their scientific and musical work. But while Einstein's role is part of contemporary history, Schoenberg's involvement was hitherto unknown. Told from Schoenberg's side, this new version subjects Einstein's changing political positions to bitter criticism, notably in a polemic, "Einstein's Mistaken Politics," published here for the first time.

In 1914 the political views of the two men could hardly have been further apart. Einstein, antimilitarist, virtually alone among German scientists in opposing the war, signed a "Manifesto to Europeans" advocating "internationalism, pacifism and socialism." Schoenberg, prowar and serving in the Austrian army for part of it, claimed to be a monarchist as late as 1950. He soon discovered that the war "was being waged not only against foreign enemies, however, but at least as heavily against inner ones. And to the latter belonged . . . the Jews" (letter to Dr. Stephen Wise, New York, May 12, 1934). So, too, in 1929 Einstein recalled that "when I came to Germany [from Zurich] fifteen years ago, I discovered for the first time that I was a Jew. I owe this discovery more to gentiles than to Jews."

By 1921 Einstein's experience of anti-Semitism had attracted him to the Zionist movement. Early in the year he predicted that he would "be forced to leave Germany within 10 years." In late March, in company with Chaim Weizmann, he departed on a two-month tour in America, where "I first discovered the Jewish people," and where he was to become Zionism's most famous advocate. But Einstein's subsequent political career, beginning with his flight to Holland after the 1923 Beer Hall *Putsch*, is as well known as Schoenberg's has been obscure.

At the beginning of 1925, Schoenberg, who had also suffered his share of anti-Semitism, wrote to Einstein requesting a meeting to discuss Zionism. The letter was not answered. Understandably. Schoenberg began with a protracted account of his "position in German artistic life," including the complaint that a Berlin musicologist listed him not in order of importance but alphabetically.

"Though I am considered, at least abroad, to be the leading German composer," Schoenberg wrote, the Germans were ready to relinquish predominance in music if they could avoid linking him to it, and "in their hatred of me, the Jews and the Swastika bearers are of one mind." He then digresses on an unexplained connection between the musical art of the Netherlands and the Talmud and cabala until, in the next-to-last paragraph, Zionism is mentioned only in order to say that he "deviates" from its "propaganda." Einstein must have thought his correspondent deranged. Schoenberg, greatly offended by the snub, wrote to a friend: "I had to swallow a very terrestrial treatment from this astronomer who sees far too distantly but overlooks what is close at hand."

Whereas Einstein rejected all forms of aggression and of nationalism—for him, Jewish internationality was its nationality—Schoenberg approached "the Jewish problem" militantly: "The re-establishment of a Jewish state can come about only in the manner that has characterized similar events throughout history: not through words but through the success of arms"; and Schoenberg feared that in the Diaspora the Jews had lost their "fighting spirit." Einstein, it is important to remember, warned against "the establishment of a Jewish state without the agreement of the Arabs."

Schoenberg wrote again in 1930, seeking Einstein's support for a testimonial honoring the architect Adolf Loos, and without referring to the "Jewish problem." This time Einstein responded but did not comply, on grounds that he was insufficiently acquainted with Loos's work and felt too distant from it to make a judgment. Schoenberg drafted an irate answer, but wrote instead to Loos's wife: "Loos has in his field at least the same importance as I do in mine. And you know perhaps that I pride myself in having shown mankind the way for musical creativity for at least the next hundred years."

Both Schoenberg and Einstein avoided Berlin as much as possible in 1931–32, and in the latter year Einstein decided to leave Germany permanently. By this time his every word on the political situation was receiving world publicity and, of course, total distortion in the German press. The imprudence of his criticisms of Germany greatly disturbed Schoenberg—"he must surely . . . have learned that they have given occasion for far-reaching revenge action against innocent people"—"hostages at risk," Stefan Zweig called them in a letter to Romain Rolland, refusing to join a protest—and the anti-German boycott of 1932 horrified the composer. The Zionists admit that they cannot help the German Jews, he wrote, but "Mr. Einstein is endangering the lives of the Jews who have had to remain. Does he not consider what consequences the Boycott-decision can have for the Jews in Germany?"

In mid-summer 1933, Schoenberg confided in a letter to Anton Webern that "Zionist affairs are more important for me than my art. . . . I am decided . . . to work in the future solely for the national state of Jewry." The resolve was carried out, without the sacrifice of his art, until the creation of the state of Israel. But while Schoenberg thought that Jewish unity could be achieved only through "devotion to a single, abstract idea," the idea of the one God, Einstein felt no ties at all with the faith of his fathers. Years before, when his wife and children had "turned Catholic," he wrote to a friend: "It's all the same to me."

One of Schoenberg's main tenets was that anti-Semitism should not be opposed, and his grandson emphasizes that "the fight against anti-Semitism rather than for Judaism" was always the main disagreement between Schoenberg and other Zionists. "To oppose anti-Semitism is nonsense," one of the composer's notes reads,

> and the only Jews who could want to do this seriously are those who want to stabilize the conditions of Diaspora into infinity. . . . Anti-Semitism is the natural and necessary answer for the claim "chosen people." To fight anti-Semitism is . . . like fighting envy. Mr. Einstein does not have the courage to see anti-Semitism as a given reality, to put up with it . . . something which it was not possible to eliminate in the whole history of mankind.

In 1920 Einstein had expressed some of the same opinion: "It may be thanks to anti-Semitism that we are able to preserve our existence as a race." But by the early 1930s he had understood the necessity of fighting Germany—an about-face from his pacifism that momentarily undermined his credibility. Schoenberg quickly seized on this: "Mr. Einstein is a kind of Janus face. . . . He is against war in general, but for one against Germany." But when Schoenberg eventually understood that the survival of civilization was at stake, he supported Einstein's call for preparation against German rearmament.

On October 7, 1933, Einstein sailed for the United States to take up the position that he was to hold for the rest of his life at Princeton's Institute for Advanced Study, and it was at Princeton, when Einstein and his wife attended Schoenberg's "Twelve Tone Lecture," March 6, 1934, that the two men finally met. A few weeks later, on April 1, the composer and the physicist were photographed together after a Carnegie Hall concert to raise money for the Settlement of German-Jewish Children in Palestine and the New York Zionist Region, and honoring Einstein—a "Tribute of Music to Science."

One more exchange of letters took place, with results similar to the appeal on behalf of Loos. In August 1938, Schoenberg sent a rambling letter seeking a recommendation for a professorship in astrology (to *Einstein*?!) for his friend Oskar Adler, violinist, physician, and professional astrologer. Einstein answered briefly that he had read Adler's book and considered it "so well written that it presents a real danger for immature intellects," suggested that Schoenberg and his friends should "try to find means of support for him as a musician," yet offered to write on Adler's behalf "if in so doing I don't have to indirectly support astrology." The great composer's grandson does not tell us what happened.

The essay's most arresting remark is one of Einstein's, dated 1936: "The intellectual decline brought on by a shallow materialism is a far greater menace to the survival of Jewry than numerous external foes who threaten its existence with violence."

Update on Klimt

With the exhibition "Emilie Flöge and Gustav Klimt" in the Hermesvilla,[1] the Empress Elisabeth's summer home in the Vienna suburb of Lainz, following so soon after the installation of the restored Beethoven Frieze in the Secession Building, the Klimt craze has reached a new apogee. Loden-wrapped art lovers have walked the two miles through the Lainzer Tiergarten to this former Imperial Palace, undergone the "stress test" of Vienna's museum staircases, and, in the Kärntnerstrasse, bought Klimt books, calendars, "life-size" reproductions, prints, postcards and even T-shirts.

The dispersal of the Hermesvilla show is unfortunate: the creaky gothic-revival relic would have been a fitting permanent home for the richly varied contextual displays of Art Nouveau clothes, jewelry, tableware, boudoir and other furniture, and the likelihood of reassembly on such a scale seems remote. The recently released *Nachlass* of Emilie Flöge, Klimt's model (*The Kiss*), mistress and creator of haute couture—in the "Casa Piccola" salon that she and her two sisters directed in Mariahilfestrasse—reveals the considerable extent of her influence on the painter. Klimt's 1902 portrait of her, his first use of the ornamental style in a picture of this kind, on loan at the Hermesvilla, was alone worth the trek.

Anyone interested in the development of female high fashion in turn-of-the-century Vienna—and not only there: Emilie frequented the centers of mode in Paris and London—would have been fascinated by the exhibits of the Flöge Damenmodesalon "reform style" *c*. 1904, more than a dozen years after Klimt's portrait of Emilie aged 17 had marked the

---

[1] *Emilie Flöge und Gustav Klimt, Doppelporträt Ideallandschaft*. Hermesvilla, 30 April 1988–28 February 1989. Catalog of the exhibition published by the Historischen Museums der Stadt Wien. See also *The Reluctant Empress* by Brigitte Hamann, New York, 1984, for an account of the young Klimt's *Midsummer Night's Dream* frescoes in the Royal bedroom.

beginning of a collaboration that would include contributions by him in pattern and design to Flöge dresses. Briefly, the sisters replaced the bustle, high-bosom and tight-waisted Empire-style outfit of the in-other-ways "comfortable classes" with one-piece, figure-concealing, floor-length and trailing gowns. Sleeves were ample at the elbow and generally long, covering the wrists, and collars tall, as if to support the bouffant coiffures. The most striking example of Emilie's own wardrobe, seen in a 1907 profile photo of her by Klimt, conceals the contours of the body but sets in motion a flow of folds from back to side. Klimt himself of course wore a blue smock with surplice neckline, long and loose enough to hide . . . well, the hooves, for something about his head as well as a great deal about his art suggest that he was part satyr.

The products of the Wiener Werkstätte (Viennese Workshops) shown at the Hermesvilla are of an elegance unsurpassed in the Western Europe and America of the period—Karl Kraus, Adolf Loos, Hermann Broch and other distinguished enemies of ornament notwithstanding. To judge from this presentation, Josef Hoffmann[1] is the artist who consistently achieved the most satisfying forms—in a silver chain-necklace, silver étui, square silver-backed hand mirror, silver tulip cup with acanthus motif midway up the tall slender stem. The furniture is no less attractive, especially the monochrome panels of the Flöge salon's trying-on rooms, which anticipate the Mondrian of thirty years later, and the Charles Rennie Mackintosh chairs, one of them apparently from Klimt's last studio.

Of the new books, Wolfgang Fischer's,[2] published in conjunction with the Hermesvilla exhibition, adds the most to Klimt biography. Fischer catalogs 400 items of Klimt-to-Flöge correspondence, but more important is the new trove of photographs, from which we learn that Klimt collected not only Chinese scroll paintings, Japanese woodcuts and Samurai robes, but also wood figurines from the Congo. The photos of Emilie herself enable us to see how Klimt's portrait glamorizes her naturally attractive but somewhat heavy face, rounding it, enlarging the eyes, much increasing the fullness of the lips, refining the nose, rougeing the skin. Similarly, photos of the Flöge model Friederike Beer, compared with the paintings of her by both Schiele and Klimt, show that the artists

---

[1] See *A Design For Living* by Lillian Langseth-Christiansen (New York, 1987), a still-active New Yorker who had studied with him at the age of fourteen and through him met Klimt.

[2] *Gustav Klimt und Emilie Flöge, Genie und Talent, Freundschaft und Besessenheit* by Wolfgang Georg Fischer. Wien, 1988.

slenderized the body and remodeled the everted-lip face. No doubt Klimt cosmeticized the women in all his portraits.

Johannes Dobai's essay on the landscapes[1] is distinguished by some color reproductions that are closer to the originals than the versions in any other books. About a fourth of all Klimt's oils *are* landscapes, a large proportion, considering that he began to paint them relatively late in life (*c.* 1898), and that the primary world of his painting at the beginning of this same period was the remote one of allegory. Of the total of 222 paintings in Dobai's catalogue raisonné,[2] 16, including five landscapes, were destroyed in the 1945 fire in Schloss Immendorf, where they had been stored for safety. The whereabouts of 39 others,[3] two of them landscapes, have not been traced. This means that as many as a fifth of the total, including the famous ceiling-panel allegories *Philosophy, Medicine, Jurisprudence* for the University of Vienna, are known only from preliminary studies or old photographs.

The landscapes are unique in Klimt's own work in two ways, first in that he continued to paint them to the end of his life with no radical variation of approach—in contrast to the stylistic diversities and fusions in his other work—and only one major submission to new influence (Van Gogh's, after the 1906 Vienna exhibition of the Dutch master); and, second, he did not make sketches, as against the 300 or so for a single painting of another kind, though in a picture such as *Poppy Field*, the underlying charcoal outlines are so transparent that they catch the eye even before the impasto clouds. The viewer is always *in* a Klimt landscape, *in* the meadow, forest, garden (in which, botanically speaking, the genus of a flower may not be identifiable and is less important than its color), *under* the pear tree, *out* on the lake with no shore in sight behind. (Like Monet, Klimt painted in a boat.) This feeling is created in part by the absence of a natural frame *within* the picture, which seems to be a detail of a larger one—indeed, may have been, in the sense that Klimt apparently used binoculars and a view-finder to choose the patch of landscape he wished to paint. The whole of the woods or the field is never shown, and limbs and blossoms are arbitrarily cut off at the end of the no

---

[1] *Gustav Klimt: Landscapes* by Johannes Dobai, translated by Ewald Osers. Boston, 1988.

[2] In *Gustav Klimt* by Fritz Novotny and Johannes Dobai. London, 1968.

[3] Dobai's figure has been slightly reduced by a few recent rediscoveries, one of them *The Golden Knight*, originally owned by Ludwig Wittgenstein's father.

less arbitrarily quadrilateral picture space. The horizon, moreover, is with few exceptions reduced to the smallest chinks of sky, thereby giving the picture the sense of an upward, bottom-to-top slant.

To intensify this claustrophobic effect, Klimt blurs perspectival boundaries, if not wholly flattening the picture into two dimensions, then at least obliging the observer to look very closely for the third. This calculated geometrical confusion is exploited to extremes in pictures of lakeside buildings (the deliberately off-kilter relationship between the two turrets in the 1908 *Schloss Kammer*), and of background mountains that seem closer than, as well as about to topple into, foregrounds. Further aspects of Klimt's scheme of dislocation are that light does not come from a particular direction—the whole picture is lighted equally—and that less may be shown of objects themselves, shrubbery, houses, an island, than of their shadows or reflections in water.

Klimt's landscapes are terrestrial, as opposed to celestial, in that the sun, moon and stars are absent from them. This is in accord with what might be deduced about the artist's philosophical cosmos in other regards. The only Christian symbols in any of his pictures are the black crosses on the robe of the skeleton in *Death and Life*, and the crucifix, clearly no more than a part of the scenery, in *Country Garden* (1911–12). But Klimt's world of Nature is also empty of human beings—a haunted emptiness, in which blank windows stare, woods (tree barks with eyes) are all-seeing, and the silence of ever-growing vegetal life deafens.

* * *

Angelica Bäumer's feminist account of Klimt[1] and the origins of "the Modern Movement" is extravagantly odd. "The first steps towards [it]," she writes, "were taken [in 1810 by] the Nazarenes [who] had outlived themselves by the middle of the century . . . Any [sic] revolution was not brought about by them." (What they attempted to do is not explained.) "A more important move was that made by Theodore Rousseau . . . In search of light . . . in 1848 [he] exchanged the gloomy studios of Paris . . . to paint in the open air." (This had been done before.) "The next step . . . was in 1874, when Cézanne, Monet and others exhibited . . . [Then] Oriental

---

[1] *Gustav Klimt Women* by Angelica Bäumer, translated from the German by Ewald Osers. New York, 1986.

and African works of art [were brought] to Europe [and] eyes were opened. [Finally, Munch] paved the way for expressionism." (Irrelevant, since Klimt was never an expressionist.)

This omits rather a lot. Nothing is said, for instance, about the Gestalt perception psychology, developed in nearby Graz in the 1890s, to which Klimt was certainly indebted:[1] the transposition of such forms as the rounded "K" (the right portion of the letter) in his personal colophon to paintings such as *Goldfish* show that he was aware of Ernst Mach's theory that "Geometrically similar constructions oriented in the same way" are immediately recognizable. And Bäumer makes no reference to Baudelaire, Seurat, Nietzsche, or even Wagner, whose attack on conventional forms in the 1870 essay on Beethoven's Ninth Symphony not only sets forth the main principles of Art Nouveau intent but is also the key to Klimt's *Beethoven Frieze*. Bäumer's title, moreover, *Gustav Klimt Women*, is redundant in the sense that a monograph on Klimt's men is unthinkable. After the academic portraits of the mid-1890s, his only men are Franz Schubert in profile, the comic-strip hero of the *Beethoven Frieze*, and a few faceless, partly faceless, or disembodied lovers. Women, no one could deny, are Klimt's obsessive, perhaps dementedly obsessive, subject, incomparably more important than men.

Bäumer's thesis is that Klimt was fearful of women: "While woman has liberated herself from the constraints of society, no longer being man's appendage, she has instilled fear in man . . . Klimt has expressed this insuperable fear in his allegorical paintings." Women clearly dominate in these paintings, of course, yet the meaning of the University allegories—that Philosophy will not spread enlightenment, Medicine not bring an end to suffering, Jurisprudence not implement the rule of justice—applies to mankind and womankind alike.

The "fear" thesis depends on Klimt's portrayals of woman as the serpent of seduction, as Judith, and as Salome. She might have added "The Forces of Evil" which, in the *Beethoven Frieze*, are female: "The unveiled woman is the frightening revelation of a completely feminized universe," Jean-Paul Bouillon writes in relation to the *Frieze*.[2] But this is

---

[1] See *Gustav Klimt* by Werner Hofmann. London, 1972. Hofmann's analysis of Klimt in his social, political and intellectual Viennese setting is still the major essay on the subject—as it was in the judgment of Carl E. Schorske published in *The New York Review of Books* as long ago as December 11, 1975.

[2] *Klimt's: Beethoven. The Frieze for the Ninth Symphony* by Jean-Paul Bouillon. New York, 1988.

to overlook Klimt's irony in presenting the famous female decapitators of the Bible as Viennese contemporaries, two more portraits in his gallery of bejeweled high society women to go with his Zuckerkandls and Bloch-Bauers.

The serpent symbol—phallus, surely, as well as seductress—is sufficiently pervasive in Klimt's painting to warrant a study in itself. Dobai tells us that the spirals in Klimt's Tree of Life mural for the Stoclet Palace in Brussels are "motifs from Byzantine mosaics." In fact the motif is that of the far older Vitruvian scroll, possibly brought to Klimt's notice by Josef Maria Olbrich, the architect of the Secession Building, who introduced it in his own work.[1] It became a kind of artistic monogram for Klimt from as early as the 1884 *Portrait of a Woman*, and in 1908 was adopted by many of the Wiener Werkstätte artists.[2] Klimt sometimes uses the scroll as a purely abstract decoration, but most conspicuously, and recurrently, as the coil of a serpent's tail, which he associates—it is the union of life and death, health and disease in classical symbolism—with naked truth (naked woman). But whatever Klimt's water snakes may signify, shimmering with color as they slither among his naiads, they neither repel nor threaten. (They suggest the Ancient Mariner:

> *I watch'd the water snakes:*
> *they moved in tracks of shining white, . . .*
> *I watch'd their rich attire:*
> *Blue, glossy green, and velvet black.*)

The main shortcoming of Bäumer's argument is that she has based it exclusively on the paintings, ignoring the 3,000 drawings in which women are presented as purely sexual objects. Whereas the paintings of women include backgrounds, the women in the drawings, nude, semi-nude, fully dressed, are themselves the whole of each picture. The painted portraits, moreover, idealize, though likenesses are preserved even when figures are replaced or disguised by decoration. Apart from the formal portraits, women in the paintings are associated with symbols—the female principle and flowing water, brilliant colors and eros (the jackpot of gold

---

[1] See *Josef Maria Olbrich Architecture, Complete Reprint of the Original Plates of 1901–1914*. New York, 1988.

[2] *Mail Art Anno Klimt. Die Postkarten der Wiener Werkstätte* by Otto Breicha. Graz, 1987.

pieces between Danae's spread legs). The women of the paintings, moreover, are for all the world to see.

The drawings, on the contrary, free of settings and of symbols, are private, intimate, simple, classical in line, natural, spontaneous and unornamented. Klimt drew them for himself. His friend Ludwig Hevesi, chronicler of the Secession, reported that during the exhibition of *Goldfish*, Klimt took the painting home with him each night "to fantasize a bit more on it." This Pygmalion as painter, in love with his creations, no doubt "fantasized" as well on his drawings of nudes. A substantial number of them, especially from the years 1913 to 1917, can only be described as pornographic, in the sense of intending to stimulate,[1] which does not contradict Alice Ströbl's observation that "Klimt succeeded in spiritualizing his female nudes to the extent that they seem transparent, consumed by their passion; the ecstasy becomes more and more an integral part of the representation."

In the domain of the erotic, no discussion of either Klimt or Schiele manages to avoid comparisons with the other, though their birthdates are three decades apart and their temperaments antithetical. Both artists feature pairs of female lovers, more apparently lesbian in Schiele's case. Both exploit semi-nudity, the stockings rolled just above the knee, the raised or lowered clothing, the half-opened blouse. Both exploit the same writhing postures, open legs, the head resting on the raised arm or arms, parted lips and half-closed eyes. And both betray a predilection for pubic hair. Klimt is the originator, though not the more original, Schiele the follower, and not only here but in numerous particulars in the paintings: compare Klimt's *The Kiss* and Schiele's "steal" from it, *Cardinal and Nun*, as well as the color mosaic in Schiele's *Self-Portrait With Black Vase*, borrowed from Klimt's *Portrait of Fritza Riedler*, though this was derived in turn, as Hevesi was the first to notice, from the arc of color behind the head of Velasquez's Infanta Maria Teresa.

The drawings are still the under-appreciated category of Klimt's oeuvre, and the two new samplings by Serge Sabarsky will not change the rating. The better book is the catalog in French and Flemish for the exhibition at the Musées Royaux des Beaux Arts in Brussels in September–December 1987,[2] which offers 14 color drawings as against

[1] For superior reproductions of some of these, see *Gustav Klimt Die Goldene Pforte* edited by Otto Breicha. Salzburg, 1985, and *Vienne 1880–1938 L'Apocalypse Joyeuse*, Paris, 1986.

[2] *Gustav Klimt. Europalia 87 Österreich.* Selected and organized by Serge Sabarsky.

only one in color of the 12 pastels in the selection of 100 drawings[1] for the American buyer. Preliminary drawings for paintings are not represented in either volume (though surely the pregnant nudes of 1902 are related to the *Beethoven Frieze*), but only those that are ends in themselves. These include examples of the teenager's academic work, of which it can be said that his erotic sensibilites are no less precociously evident than his natural artistic gifts. To judge from Sabarsky's selection, a change seemed likely to occur *c.* 1897 when the character of a seated woman is the picture's main interest, but faces are not endowed with much psychological animation again until the last years. An English edition of Ströbl's three-volume *Zeichnungen* is long overdue.

From the beginning, Klimt's friends regarded the *Beethoven Frieze* (1902) as his masterpiece (most others looked on it as an insult), partly because it is his most ambitious, largest-scale—145 feet of painted surface in length—most "meaningful" creation. This was Hevesi's verdict, but the opinion was perpetuated by generations of critics who had not seen it, since it had been removed from public view after Klimt's death in 1918 until 1985, and returned to the Secession Building after restoration only in 1986—not in its original position, as Professor Bouillon writes, but in a replica of the original room in a newly excavated basement. Meanwhile, the Secession Building, "the Golden Cabbage," as it was popularly known, because of the open gilded bronze cupola of laurel leaves and berries, had also been restored.

At the fourteenth Secession exhibition, April 15, 1902, Max Klinger's life-size statue of Beethoven enthroned occupied the center room, Klimt's allegorical mural an anteroom. The occasion included a performance of an arrangement for wind instruments of part of the Finale of the Ninth Symphony conducted by Gustav Mahler. Klinger's Beethoven is nude (white marble), young, handsome, slender, smooth-skinned (no pock marks). Bent slightly forward and with legs crossed, the lower body, except for the composer's white sandals, is draped with a pleated garment rendered in polished gold. His left foot rests on a slab of rock shared with a crouching, much-impressed Promethean eagle. The "hero, martyr, and redeemer of mankind," as Professor Bouillon writes, following Wagner, is lost in thought and unaware of the feathered biped. The back of the

---

[1] *Gustav Klimt*: Drawings, by Serge Sabarsky. Mt. Kisco, New York, 1985.

throne, in bronze relief, juxtaposes a Birth of Venus and a Crucifixion, that confrontation of the classical and Christian worlds already explored by Klinger in his *Christ in Olympus.* The sculptor is said to have been inspired by Phidias' legendary chryselephantine statue of Zeus, but the result belongs in the Campo Santo in Genoa.

Without the statue, removed after the exhibition to the Gewandhaus in Leipzig, Klimt's frescoes lack a raison d'être, and without the printed program of the Secession, or other crib, any link between Beethoven's Ninth Symphony and the painter's symbolic pictorializations of it would never be remotely suspected. Even the two-dimensionality of the frescoes must be understood as a response to the spatial volume of Klinger's sculpture.

The exhibition program is still the best guide to interpreting the paintings:

> Longing for happiness. The sufferings of feeble humanity: their pleas to the well-armed strong man as the outer, compassion and ambition as the inner moving forces, persuading him to take up the struggle for happiness. The hostile powers. The Giant Typhoeus, whom even the gods could not overcome. His daughters, the three Gorgons, sickness, madness, death. Lust and wantonness, intemperance, nagging sorrow. The longings of men rise above it all. Longing for happiness finds satisfaction in poetry. The arts take us into the realms of the ideal where alone we can find pure joy, pure happiness, pure love. Chorus of the angels of paradise: "Joy, beautiful divine spirit. This kiss for the whole world!"

Professor Bouillon—of Art History at the University of Clermont-Ferrand—reveals that Vienna in 1902 was "a strategically placed city," that the moment was "crucial," and that these twin factors largely determined the significance of the *Frieze.* Professor Bouillon does not resist many of the opportunities for exegeses that the panels provide, but suffice to say that he follows Wagner's 1846 program notes for his revival of the Ninth Symphony and his 1870 commentary, which disregards Schiller's *Ode to Joy* and discovers the meaning in the music itself. According to Wagner, the Symphony represents a "struggle of the soul fighting for happiness against the oppression of the hostile powers." The Blake-like, Jan Toorop-like, figures that float above the frescoes can be understood as Klimt's translation of Wagner's phrase, "the tireless instinct which drives us with the energy of despair." In Wagner's view,

Beethoven's third movement represents love and hope, the last movement, "the cry of universal human love."

Is the *Frieze* Klimt's magnum opus? The work's most perceptive critic, Alessandra Comini, remarks that Klimt's pictorial response to the Symphony "was essentially one of fantasy," not philosophy, and that his imagination was excited above all by "the depiction of the Hostile Powers."[1] And in truth, we look longer at this part of the mural—the Gorgons, the Beardsley parody figure "Excess," and the Giant Tryphon (whose opal-glass right eye must have been intended as the *oculus mundi*), than at any other part of the epic. Unhappily, the conclusion of the narrative, the triumph of art and poetry, is pictorially its weakest episode. And it must also be said that most of the painting from this brilliant colorist is pallid—grisaille. The successful aspect of the *Frieze* is in its embodiment of musical principles, rhythm, movement, linearity, progression. But Klimt is at his greatest in landscapes, portraits of dressed-up Viennese women, and drawings of undressed ones.

The latest "Klimt book," Jane Kallir's *Gustav Klimt: 25 Masterworks*[2], indicates that a measure of critical balance may be entering the largely adulatory literature about the artist. Kallir describes Klimt's allegories for the University of Vienna as "ponderous" and "tame and dated," and goes on to compare their elaborateness unfavorably to the concise erotic paintings of a few years later. No less refreshingly, she discriminates among the famous portraits, calling the one of Margaret Stonborough-Wittgenstein a "wax doll . . . the wallpaper is more interesting than the woman." In short, Kallir provides an antidote to Jean Clair's attribution[3] of a parallel importance to Klimt's 1907 Adele Bloch-Bauer portrait ("one of the most beautiful pictures that Occidental art has ever produced") and Picasso's *Demoiselles d'Avignon*, which is to make the highest claim for the Viennese artist to date. According to Clair, the similarities between the pictures and their painters, though at first (and second and further) sight they hardly seem to come from the same planet, are the representation of women with erotic connotations essential to the meaning, and the appearance of both works at a time of crisis in the public careers and private lives of their creators—superficial connections at best. In Klimt's case, the reference is to the University of Vienna's

---

[1] *The Changing Image of Beethoven, a Study in Mythmaking*, by Alessandra Comini. New York, 1987.

[2] New York, 1989.

[3] *Le nu et la norme: Klimt et Picasso en 1907* by Jean Clair. Paris, 1988.

rejection of his allegories, his resignation from the Secession, and the resulting change in style to flat, two-dimensional pictures with abstract decorative motives inspired by the mosaics of Ravenna, and to accentuate the icon-like qualities of his portraits, an abundant use of gold.

What Clair does not say is that Adele was an end, the *Demoiselles* a beginning; that Klimt's art depends on style and abstraction, while Picasso's vehemently opposes both ("*Le style c'est quand on est mort*"), and that Klimt's women, unlike Picasso's, are sexually desirable in the here and now. The Adele consists entirely of abstract decoration—featuring the sexual symbol of cloven almond shapes enclosed in squares—which surrounds and covers a body petrified by gold and precious stones. Kallir quips that Adele is "not wearing the dress but the painting," adding that the decorative trappings are a "metaphorical chastity belt"—albeit one that Klimt himself seems to have had little trouble in unbuckling. *Pace* Clair, the more richly colored portrait of Adele as Salome, with its suggestion of dance movement and of cruelty in the face and clawing hands, is a far more powerful picture.

Kallir adds to our exiguous knowledge of Klimt the man, telling us that, childlike, he derived amusement by throwing hats from the window of the Flöge salon and seeing them "alight on the heads of unsuspecting strangers below"; that he spoke a heavy dialect which marked him as the son of a tradesman (a gold engraver, appropriately); and that he was shy and lonely (he remained a bachelor). He does not seem to have been very shy of women, however, though his erotica, compared with Schiele's, exposes him as the voyeur, Schiele as the participant. On one occasion, according to Kallir, Klimt declared that the glutaei of one of his models were "more beautiful and intelligent than most people's faces," and, I.Q.'s apart, his best nudes present a strong case for the first part of the assertion. What cannot be doubted is his potency and ability to refocillate. After his death, fourteen illegitimate children—a fifteenth had died—made claims on their omnifutuant father's estate! Priapus be praised!

Index